ROYAL HISTORICAL SOCIETY

STUDIES IN HISTORY

New Series

CULTURE, IDENTITY AND NATIONALISM

FRENCH FLANDERS IN THE NINETEENTH AND TWENTIETH CENTURIES

CULTURE, IDENTITY AND NATIONALISM

FRENCH FLANDERS IN THE NINETEENTH AND TWENTIETH CENTURIES

Timothy Baycroft

THE ROYAL HISTORICAL SOCIETY
THE BOYDELL PRESS

First published 2004

A Royal Historical Society publication
Published by The Boydell Press
an imprint of Boydell & Brewer Ltd
PO Box 9, Woodbridge, Suffolk IP12 3DF, UK
and of Boydell & Brewer Inc.
668 Mt Hope Avenue, Rochester, NY 14620, USA
website: www.boydellandbrewer.com

ISBN 0 86193 269 2

ISSN 0269–2244

A catalogue record for this book is available
from the British Library

Library of Congress Cataloging-in-Publication Data
Baycroft, Timothy.
    Culture, identity and nationalism : French Flanders in the
nineteenth and twentieth centuries / Timothy Baycroft.
        p. cm. – (Royal Historical Society studies in history. New series)
Includes bibliographical references and index.
    ISBN 0–86193–269–2 (hardback : alk. paper)
1. Flanders (France) – History – 19th century. 2. Flanders (France)
– Politics and government – 19th century. 3. Flanders (France) –
History – 20th century. 4. Flanders (France) – Politics and
government – 20th century. 5. Regionalism – France – Flanders.
6. Group identity – France – Flanders. 7. Flemings – France –
Ethnic identity. I. Title. II. Series.
    DC611.N823B27 2004
    944'.2806 – dc22   2004003559

This book is printed on acid-free paper

Printed in Great Britain by
Antony Rowe Ltd, Chippenham, Wiltshire

Contents

List of Maps

List of Tables

Publication of this volume was aided by a grant from the Scouloudi Foundation, in association with the Institute of Historical Research.

Acknowledgements

No work such as this is ever accomplished alone, and I have been fortunate to have received so much assistance over the years. I would like to acknowledge with thanks the financial support I received from the Arts and Humanities Research Board, the British Academy, the Cambridge Commonwealth Trust, Wolfson College, Cambridge, and the Department of History, University of Sheffield.

This research has also benefited from the helpful comments of numerous colleagues, teachers and students. I would like in particular to thank my supervisor Robert Tombs, who has provided me with helpful suggestions at every stage of the work, and patiently read through drafts. Various part of this research have been presented in seminars and at conferences, and I am grateful to many colleagues for thought-provoking comments and questions. In particular I am indebted to Máire Cross, Robert Gildea, Jonathan Steinberg, Daniel Power, Mark Greengrass, Colin Jones, and anonymous reviewers from the Royal Historical Society. Pertti Ahonen was generous with his time in reading through an entire draft of the manuscript, and I am grateful for the careful copy-editing of Christine Linehan.

During my stay in France, I was given helpful advice by Antoine Prost, Alain Corbin, Gérard Bodé and Jean-François Chanet in Paris, by Bernard Ménager, Philippe Marchand and Firmin Lentacker in Lille, and by Luc Verbeke in Kortrijk, Belgium. I also received much friendly guidance from the staff at the Archives départmental du Nord in Lille, from Madame Mortelette at the Bibliothèque du Comité Flamand de France in Hazebrouck, and from the staff at the Archief van de Franse Nederlanden in Kortrijk, Belgium.

I would also like to thank my parents, who provided me with a great deal of support, both throughout my studies and since. Finally I would like to thank my wife Christine, for encouragement and help of every kind. Any errors, omissions or limitations of this work are wholly my own.

Timothy Baycroft
2004

Abbreviations

ACFF	*Annales du Comité Flamand de France*
ADN	Archives départementales du Nord
AN	Archives nationales
BCFF	*Bulletin du Comité Flamand de France*
BN	Bibliothèque nationale
CFF	Comité Flamand de France
DFN/LPBF	*De Franse Nederlanden/Les Pays-Bas français*
HTN	*Hommes et terres du Nord*
JCH	*Journal of Contemporary History*
KFV	*Komitee voor Frans-Vlaanderen*
MSD	*Mémoires de la Société Dunkerquoise: pour l'encouragement des sciences, des lettres, et des arts*
RFB	*Revue franco-belge*
RHMC	*Revue d'histoire moderne et contemporaine*
RN	*Revue du Nord*
VVF	*Vlaamsch Verbond van Vrankrijk*

Introduction

In his letter to the Polish of 1772, Jean-Jacques Rousseau wished to advise the Polish how, although they could not prevent themselves from being 'swallowed' by their neighbours, they could prevent themselves from being 'digested' through the preservation of their separate linguistic and cultural traits.[1] The chief aim of this work is to investigate the process of nation-forming in modern France as it was experienced by the inhabitants of a boundary region during the nineteenth and twentieth centuries, a time when France succeeded in 'digesting' many of those provinces that had been 'swallowed' during the *ancien régime*. It will explore national identity as a dynamic concept, integrating yet interactive, and as one of a series of overlapping identities which both compete with and complement one another. It will also investigate the relationship between culture and identity, analyse the ways in which different cultural elements rival one another in a regional context as identities evolve and develop and question Rousseau's assertion that cultural difference is a successful barrier to national integration and cultural assimilation.

The various dimensions of the assimilation debate will be examined through an analysis of French Flanders, a region lying in the north of France along the Belgian border. Because of its position at a cross-roads between cultures and states, and the early impact of the industrial revolution on its socio-economic structure, French Flanders is a particularly useful region upon which to base a study of the interaction and evolution of identity and culture, and their relationship to local, national and international political movements. The remainder of this introduction will attempt to place this case study into its theoretical and historical contexts, first through a discussion of nationalism as a political and cultural force, and second by examining the complex theoretical relationship between nationalism, national culture and national identity. Finally, it will examine the classical historical interpretations of the growth and development of nationalism in post-revolutionary

---

[1] 'To prevent his people from melting into foreign peoples, he gave to it morals and customs incompatible with those of other nations, he overloaded it with special rites and ceremonies . . . to make each member always a stranger among other men, and all of the fraternal links he could forge between the members of his republic were as much barriers which kept them separate from their neighbours and prevented them from mingling with them': Jean-Jacques Rousseau, 'Considérations sur le gouvernement de Pologne et sa réformation projetée', in *Oeuvres complètes*, III: *Du Contrat social/écrits politiques* (manuscript dated 1772), Paris 1964, 956–60.

1

France and the spread of French national identity to the countryside, as well as some more recent interpretations derived from other regional case studies, against which the findings from French Flanders can be tested and compared.

Theories of nationalism

The rise of nations and nationalism in the two hundred years since the French Revolution is one of the most prominent and characteristic features of the nineteenth and twentieth centuries, and a key to understanding much of modern history. Before beginning this detailed study of French Flanders, it will be useful to provide an explanation of how these terms will be used and understood, as well as of the general European ideological context.

Nationalism is first and foremost a theory of political legitimacy, a principle which holds that 'the political unit and the national unit should be congruent', and that ethnic borders should not cut across political ones.[2] It has arisen and developed in opposition to various theories which derive political legitimacy from other principles. First, the absolutist claim to the divine right of kings, contested during the French Revolution and elsewhere by those who held that the nation was a more legitimate source of power than a monarch.[3] Second, nationalism can be seen in opposition to Marxist theories that aristocratic or bourgeois supremacy should or will be replaced by the unification of the proletarian lower classes around the world, where class is held to be legitimate, rather than a nation (giving economics precedence over culture).[4] Some Marxists, such as Renée Balibar and Dominique Laporte, argue that for nationalism to penetrate the lower classes, it must be unnaturally imposed by the ruling middle class, and is therefore merely a guise for bourgeois domination.[5] They seek to integrate the ideology of nationalism into a class-based understanding of the world by labelling it as a 'bourgeois' theory of legitimacy. Nationalism in the nineteenth and twentieth centuries can thus be understood as one theory of political legitimacy competing with others for acceptance; indeed it is commonly regarded as the most powerful and influential of the theories over this time span.[6]

2 Ernest Gellner, *Nations and nationalism*, Oxford 1983, 1.
3 See Timothy Baycroft, *Nationalism in Europe, 1789–1945*, Cambridge 1998, 3–9.
4 See ibid. 42–50, and Montserrat Guibernau, *Nationalisms: the nation-state and nationalism in the twentieth century*, Cambridge 1996, 13–21, both of which discuss the relationship between nationalist and Marxist theories of legitimacy and historical interpretation.
5 Renée Balibar and Dominique Laporte, *Le Français national: politiques et pratiques de la langue nationale sous la Révolution Française*, Paris 1974, 109. See also Roger Magraw, *France, 1814–1915: the bourgeois century*, Oxford 1983, 318–22.
6 See, for example, Zeev Sternhell, *La Droite révolutionnaire, 1885–1914: les origines française du fascisme*, Paris 1978, 401, who argues for the predominance of the nation over class as 'the motor of history' in the pre-First World War period. For an interesting critical evaluation of this view see Hudson Meadwell, 'Republics, nations and transitions to modernity', *Nations and nationalism* v (1999), 19–51.

But how is it that nations claim their political legitimacy? The idea of the nation as a principle of political legitimacy is derived from the theories of natural law developed during the Enlightenment. Political thinkers of that era held that sovereignty lay exclusively with the people,[7] and should be exercised through a social contract in which certain groups constitute nations and select their leaders from among themselves.[8] A people can be considered a nation when it shares any number of real or perceived characteristics, can identify the members of the group and express the desire or will to remain together in some form of (usually political) organisation.[9] Specific nations may stress ethnicity or race, language, culture, historical traditions, religion, a particular shared territory with natural or historic frontiers, specific institutions, or indeed an opposition to any of the above. The wide variety of possible common characteristics – some, but not all of which are essential to define and identify a nation – has meant that each historical combination has been different.

Some writers subdivide nations into two broad categories – civic and ethnic – depending upon the fundamental defining characteristic of that nation. Classic examples are the German nation, conceived as essentially ethnic, and the French, which stresses citizenship and the role of the land or territory itself.[10] An objective definition of the nation by its characteristics therefore becomes difficult, as exceptions can always be found.[11] This flexibility, however, has merely contributed to the wide diversity of possible applications of the concept, and added to the power of nationalism as a political force.

The two essential constituting elements in the preceding definition of the nation – shared characteristics and the desire to remain together – need further discussion. In his book *Nations and nationalism*, Ernest Gellner refers

[7] See, for example, E. J. Sieyès, *Qu'est-ce que le tiers état?*, first publ. 1789, 2nd edn, Paris 1989.
[8] See Baycroft, *Nationalism*, 5–6, and Jean-Jacques Rousseau, *Du Contrat social* I.v, first publ. 1762, Paris 1966, 50, where he defines the social contract as the act by which a people becomes a people, and which is the true foundation of society.
[9] Ibid. 3.
[10] See Jacques and Mona Ozouf, 'Le Thème du patriotisme dans les manuels primaires', *Le Mouvement social* xlix (Oct.-Dec. 1964), 7; Rogers Brubaker, *Citizenship and nationhood in France and Germany*, Cambridge, Mass. 1992; Anthony D. Smith, *National identity*, London 1991, 99–142. For a critical discussion of the strengths and weaknesses of the ethnic/civic framework of analysing nations see Dominique Schnapper, 'Beyond the opposition: "civic" nation versus "ethnic" nation', and Anthony D. Smith, 'Civic and ethnic nationalism revisited: analysis and ideology', both in *ASEN Bulletin* xii (Autumn/Winter 1996/7), 4–8, 9–11. For a gendered perspective on nationalist thought and this debate see Glenda Sluga, 'Identity, gender, and the history of European nations and nationalisms', *Nations and Nationalism* iv (1998), 87–111.
[11] See E. J. Hobsbawm, *Nations and nationalism since 1780: programme, myth, reality*, Cambridge 1990, 5–6.

to them as common will and culture.[12] Common will can be further separated into straightforward self-recognition or 'identity' by means of which the members identify and think of themselves and the others in the nation, and the deeper desire to remain as a group, which implies a readiness to act consciously as a group in order to secure and defend some level of group autonomy. It is important to note that identity must come first, and that even a common identity does not necessarily lead to the will to act upon it, and turn the group identity into a national one. In this way potential nations may not ever form because in spite of common characteristics, and possibly even recognition of them, a strong desire to join together and form a 'national' political entity never developed.[13]

While it may be required, however, common will alone is not sufficient to engender nations, without a unifying cultural base around which to crystal-lise. Culture is that shared element which binds and unites the group, such that it can be identified and called a group. The question of how certain cultural characteristics come to be identified as those defining a nation, as well as how they come to exist in the first place, has inspired a great deal of thought in recent decades. Two scholarly debates in particular are of interest here: first the question of invention or pre-existence of nations, and second whether nations and nationalism are linked to modernity.

The first position with regard to the origins of the common cultural base, that nations are invented or imagined rather than naturally existing, is outlined by Benedict Anderson, who defines nations as imagined political communities.[14] This imagination does not imply 'falsity', but only that the reality of national cultural characteristics lies in the perception of them by both the members and those outside of the nation, rather than in an under-lying 'fact' of their existence independent of any consciousness of them. Further to this idea is the notion that much of the culture defined as national is made up of what Eric Hobsbawm and Terence Ranger have so aptly described as 'invented' traditions: rituals or symbols 'which seek to inculcate certain values and norms of behaviour by repetition, [and] which automati-cally imply continuity with the past'.[15] According to this position, when examining questions about the nation it is more profitable to begin with nationalism and the nation than with the reality they represent.[16] It is the differing concepts of the nation which eventually, through time, inscribe themselves into the very society which they claim to portray. Ernest Gellner writes that the high culture which characterises nations is not something

---

12 Gellner, *Nations and nationalism*, 50–2.
13 Ibid. 49.
14 Benedict Anderson, *Imagined communities*, 2nd edn, London 1991, 6–7. He writes that they are imagined as both limited and sovereign.
15 Eric Hobsbawm, 'Introduction: inventing traditions', in Eric Hobsbawm and Terence Ranger (eds), *The invention of tradition*, Cambridge 1983, 1.
16 Hobsbawm, *Nations and nationalism*, 9.

which is natural, but which must be learned, and nationalism's roots must be found in the pervading social order rather than in human nature, instinct or the human psyche.[17] The defined national culture gradually infuses the rest of the population with the image(s) it has formed of itself: 'it is nationalism which engenders nations, and not the other way round'.[18] As evidence for such a position, Eugen Weber demonstrates that the France of the nineteenth century did not exhibit any of the characteristics commonly considered to indicate a nation (common language, traditions, sentiment, history . . .) and also concludes that nationalism or patriotism, 'far from instinctive, had to be learned'.[19] The case of invention has been made, not just for the more obviously transmittable cultural characteristics (such as language), but also for ethnicity as it has been used as the defining feature of nations.[20]

The opposite position is that national cultural characteristics exist, and are a natural result of humans living in society.[21] This is the position of the 'perennialists', who argue that nations, whether natural or not, have existed as long as humans have lived in 'society', as well as of many nationalists who seek to claim that their nations are 'natural', having existed for many centuries. To such writers, the history of nations and nationalism can be found by tracing the evolution of the cultural characteristics which define each nation and their inscription on the human landscape over time. Even where the characteristics are considered to be symbolic or mythical, they are held to pre-exist consciousness of them by members of the 'nation'.[22]

This debate is linked to, but not completely identical with, the question of the existence of nations in the pre-modern period. Some writers argue that even if they have not 'always' existed, nations have existed in Europe for several centuries, and their development is not directly linked to the arrival of modernity.[23] Their arguments are based upon the certain existence and consciousness of large ethnic groupings, as well as the use of the word nation by these groups to describe themselves during the Middle Ages.[24]

---

[17] Gellner, *Nations and nationalism*, 34, 49.
[18] Ibid. 55.
[19] Eugen Weber, *Peasants into Frenchmen: the modernisation of rural France, 1870–1914*, London 1979, 112–14.
[20] See Baycroft, *Nationalism*, 33–9, and Marcel Mauss, 'Nation, nationality, internationalism', (1920–1), trans. Iain Hamilton Grant, in Stuart Woolf (ed.), *Nationalism in Europe, 1815 to the present: a reader*, London–New York 1996, 85–101.
[21] See, for example, Miroslav Hroch, *Social preconditions of national revival in Europe*, trans. Ben Fowkes, Cambridge 1985, 3.
[22] See, for example, John A. Armstrong, *Nations before nationalism*, Chapel Hill 1982, esp. pp. 3–9.
[23] See ibid. and also Adrian Hastings, *The construction of nationhood: ethnicity, religion and nationalism*, Cambridge 1997.
[24] For a further discussion of the debates of modernity and inventedness of nations see Lesley Johnson, 'Imagining communities: medieval and modern', and Anthony D. Smith, 'National identities: modern and medieval?', both in Simon Forde, Lesley Johnson and Alan V. Murray (eds), *Concepts of national identity in the Middle Ages*, Leeds 1995, 1–19,

For the purposes of this analysis, nationalism has been defined in terms of a theory of political legitimacy and a popular political force, and falls therefore within the modernist interpretation, linked to the social, political and institutional changes which were initiated from roughly the end of the eighteenth century.[25] This does not mean that other definitions may not be appropriate for other analyses; however the definitions used to incorporate pre-modern 'nations' are not sufficiently precise to be of use in this case study. Nor do the arguments of the perennialists provide a sufficient explanation of the complex relationship between nationalism as a political force and the growth and diffusion of national identity and culture as it can be observed in the modern period to be used as a useful starting point. Therefore this analysis will also begin from the point of view that nations are invented, seeking, through this particular analysis of a region at a cultural and political cross-roads, to explore the ways in which the cultural base of 'common characteristics' comes to be identified (or selected) and in some cases even created. Before passing on to a description of the traditional explanations of the growth of the French nation, it will be useful to further examine the general mechanisms of the creation and development of national identities, as well as the spread and transfer of culture and national cultural characteristics, beginning with the use of myth and history, and going on to examine general cultural practices or traditions, language and institutional structures.

National identity and culture

The creation of a modern nation can be described as the pedagogical process of transmission of the high culture to society at large and its reappropriation by that society. In this process, particular aspects of history are commonly used to form 'a mythical story, serving necessarily both explicative and mobilising functions'.[26] To take one example, Raoul Girardet refers to the role of the myth of unity as a key element, 'the central core' in the formation and propagation of the French nationalist ideology, and through it 'inscribes the very principle of Unity most profoundly on social reality'.[27] Thus the idea of the nation as an historical, inevitable and even natural entity forms a part of

---

21–46; Ernest Gellner, *Encounters with nationalism*, Oxford 1994, 182–200, and especially Anthony D. Smith *Nationalism and modernism: a critical survey of recent theories of nations and nationalism*, London 1998, who provides a very thorough analysis of this debate.

[25] This particular brand of modernism has been articulated, for example, by Ronald Wardhaugh, who writes that 'The idea that ethnic groups are entitled to "nation" status, that nation states are more legitimate than states based on some other principle, and that there is something natural and right about "nationalism" as an organising principle for political entities is a relatively new one in the history of the world': *Languages in competition: dominance, diversity and decline*, Oxford 1987, 53.

[26] Raoul Girardet, *Mythes et mythologies politiques*, Paris 1986, 160.

[27] See ibid. 154–63.

the nationalist doctrine itself. This vision of the nation is taught and encouraged among the masses by stressing certain carefully selected elements from history combined with certain myths of national unity, and often supported by 'invented' traditions, which imply continuity with the nation's past even though they have not necessarily been drawn directly from that past.[28] These traditions should ideally be universal but not clearly defined: 'emotionally and symbolically charged signs of club membership, rather than the statutes and objects of the club'.[29] When inventing traditions in the France of the Third Republic, writes Hobsbawm, the republicans had to stick with general symbols, ambiguous in themselves, such as the tricolour and Marianne, which as much as possible 'kept away from history' in the strictest sense, since that history was either royalist or clerical.[30] Marianne was a success as a feminine symbol of the republic, writes Maurice Agulhon, for the very reason that she was polysemic.[31] The ambiguity of such symbols allows the diverse members of a nation to identify with the nation as whole, without necessarily becoming aware of possible varieties between regions or groups within society, each of which can appropriate the symbols for themselves according to their own needs.

While history is an important tool in the construction of a national identity, and all nationalisms claim deep roots in the past, only certain aspects of this history are remembered, and others need, on the contrary, to be forgotten. In his famous speech at the Sorbonne in 1882, Ernest Renan had already identified that key element of nation building: forgetting, or 'historical error'.[32] Thus the creation of a national history, or national mythology, charged with symbols and events, must be carefully crafted and developed by a selective reading of history, including some outright invention, and then spread to the members of the nation in order that they may identify with it. Thus far the actual selection process – who selects the events and symbols of the nation, and how they are accepted – has been presented as conscious, and in many instances it was a more or less conscious decision taken by national or would-be national leaders. It is also, however, a slow process involving less explicit selection and acceptance of the particular interpretation or symbol by the people, but also of potential symbols coming from the masses themselves, who are not completely passive in the process. One of the objectives of

---

28 Hobsbawm, 'Introduction', 1.
29 Ibid. 11.
30 Idem, 'Mass-producing traditions: Europe, 1870–1914', in Hobsbawm and Ranger, *Invention of tradition*, 272–3. On this subject see also Raoul Girardet, 'Les Trois Couleurs: ni blanc, ni rouge', in Pierre Nora (ed.), *Les Lieux de mémoire*, I: *La République*, Paris 1997, 49–66.
31 See Maurice Agulhon, *Marianne au pouvoir: l'imagerie et la symbolique républicaine de 1880 à 1914*, Paris 1989, 344.
32 Ernest Renan, 'Qu'est qu'une nation?', talk given at the Sorbonne, Paris, 11 March 1882, repr. in Ernest Renan, *Qu'est qu'une nation? Et autres essais politiques*, textes chosen and presented by Joël Roman, Paris 1992, 41–2.

this book is to examine in detail the process of identification with symbols and history as it occurred in one particular region, in order better to understand the general forces at work.

Similar to national histories or mythologies, national cultures, cultural practices and traditions, especially those which are elevated to the status of defining national identity, are also drawn from a selected reading of the cultural landscape of the 'nation', as well as 'invented'. Such cultural dimensions as religion, architecture, cuisine, holidays and festivals, dress and leisure activities such as sport can each be called upon (or not) to form a part of the national image, becoming labelled as national characteristics. Examples abound in the modern period, and involve the identification, selection or invention of a cultural practice as 'national', which will then be reproduced or encouraged throughout the nation.[33] Adoption may be extremely conscious and deliberate, as in the selection of a particular style for public buildings intended to be visible and identifiable throughout the national space, or somewhat more spontaneous, such as the increasing popularity of a particular festival or culinary dish which is merely helped along through nationalist publicity. Such cultural practices and traditions have more weight than the purely symbolic or historical, because they form a part of the behaviour and lifestyles of the people. They exemplify the significance of nationalism as a cultural force, through its encouragement of, if not an outright change in behaviour, a reinterpretation of current behaviour.

The difference between these 'national' cultural practices and national identity needs to be examined briefly. National identity is the identification with and the self-definition through mythical histories or cultural practices (which may or may not, at a given time, be used as the hallmarks of the same identity in other parts of the nation by other people). National culture is composed of those practices that are common throughout the nation, which may in fact not, at a given moment in time, constitute a part of its members' definition of self.[34] Part of nationalism as a cultural force involves identification with existing (sometimes regional or minority) cultural practices – religion and religious practices are typical examples – and their (re)definition as 'national'; but part also involves actual cultural change or the adoption of new cultural practices which were defined as national before they were adopted. Various examples of these two processes, which can be distinguished by the terms 'appropriation' and 'assimilation', and their relationship to one another will be explored further throughout this case study. One of the most significant dimensions of 'national' culture which is diffused throughout the nation is language, which merits a brief discussion of its own.

[33] See several articles in Hobsbawm and Ranger, *Invention of tradition*, and Nora, *Lieux de mémoire*, which refer to the nationalising of particular cultural practices or traditions.
[34] For an example of the distinction between culture and identity see David Hopkin, 'Identity in a divided province: the folklorists of Lorraine, 1860–1960', *French Historical Studies* xxiii (2000), 639–82.

The literary aspect of nationalism, and the need to have a popular written language associated with, or indeed central to the development of a national cultural movement, has also been treated by numerous writers.[35] The language identified with a national movement is always a 'high' language, and even in multi-lingual states such as Switzerland the different *patois* and dialects have had to give way to literate forms. This process has meant that in the case of modern European national identities, language has taken on a particular role in the formation and self-definition of societies.[36] Anthony R. Lodge describes the changes which have appeared in language perception:

> The emergence of the great European standard languages has left a profound imprint on European culture, most obviously in the way Europeans subconsciously view language and its role in society: it has come to be widely accepted, for instance, that the ideal state of language is one of homogeneity and uniformity (rather than diversity), that its ideal form is to be found in writing (rather than speech), and that the ideal distribution of languages is for there to be a separate language for every separate 'nation'.[37]

Another component of this new image of language is that language has come to be seen as something linear. Maps can be drawn showing the spatial limits of a given high language as a single uninterrupted line, which does not really represent the plurality, the reality of infinite small variations and nuances from one village to the next.[38] These maps have great pedagogic value in terms of spreading the idea of a linguistic territory in popular consciousness, and have become arguments in themselves to justify territorial claims. The nineteenth century saw linguistic differences, long considered to be indicative of class and socio-cultural distinctions, gradually become spatial distinctions: 'Not only does language inscribe itself on a territory, but it becomes more and more identified with a nation. Linguistic maps multiply and can become one of the means of expressing national claims.'[39] The novelty of linguistic maps was less in the relationship of language to the national sentiment, as in the uses of graphic technique to further nationalist causes.

Changing attitudes towards language led to new approaches to writing the history of these languages. The high language is considered superior, as the winner, and history is viewed as leading to this inevitable conclusion. In the

---

35 See, for example, Jaroslav Krejčí and Vítezslav Velímsky, *Ethnic and political nations in Europe*, London 1981, who argue that language is the central feature of any ethnic group, and Gellner, *Nations and nationalism*, 50–2, 95.

36 For the importance of language in the case of France see Pascal Ory, 'Le "Grand Dictionnaire" de Pierre Larousse: alphabet de la république', and Pierre Nora, 'Lavisse, instituteur national: le "Petit Lavisse", évangile de la république', both in Nora, *Lieux de mémoire*, i. 227–38, 239–75, and David C. Gordon, *The French language and national identity (1930–1975)*, The Hague 1978.

37 Anthony R. Lodge, *French: from dialect to standard*, London–New York, 1993, 2–3.

38 See Jacques Revel (ed.), *L'Espace français*, Paris 1989, 160–2.

39 Ibid. 161.

history of the French language, for example, French is commonly traced back to a single Paris dialect of the Middle Ages, which distorts the variety which has really led to the modern idiom. Often it is a national history of France which is given, rather than a history of French.[40]

Within modern societies, high language in some measure always contains political meaning, whether a part of an overtly nationalist state or not. Antonio Gramsci, in the last of his *Prison notebooks*, discusses what he calls normative grammar, which is roughly akin to what has here been referred to as high language. Gramsci distinguishes between two sorts of grammar: immanent, which is the unconscious structure which governs the way in which people speak 'grammatically' without knowing it; and normative, which is written and appears to an observer to be the only grammar which exists.[41] In its historical evolution, normative written grammar emerges out of an innumerable set of influences arising from contact with other languages, he argues, and always represents a choice, 'a cultural orientation, that is to say always a political act which is culturo-national'.[42] The best way in which to present this 'choice' in order that it may be widely accepted is debatable, but there can be no doubt that the choice is never neutral, but rather is directly associated with political goals. If this were not the case, there would be no need for the tremendous effort to 'scientifically' justify the existence of the high language, or to elaborate its history: 'the study of languages as cultural phenomena was born of political need (more or less conscious and consciously expressed)'.[43]

Since the growth and development of nations is linked to the participation of the masses in high culture, leading to a claim for political legitimacy, the question which Gramsci put aside is of particular concern to us here: how to get the 'choice' not only of a mythical history but also of a normative grammar or standardised high language, widely accepted. Put another way, what are the concrete mechanisms of the transfer of high, literate culture to the masses which has just been described?

The modern state is central in this endeavour both as a framework within which nationalist movements can operate, and also as just such a mechanism to encourage identification with the national history and its associated images, and the extension of the national high culture which is at the centre of the nation's identity. John Breuilly, in his book *Nationalism and the state*, stresses this role of the modern state and its institutions in the growth of nationalism, and argues indeed that the modern state is the most important

[40] See Lodge, *From dialect to standard*, 3–12. The work by Jacques Chaurand (ed.), *Nouvelle Histoire de la langue française*, Paris 1999, goes some way towards remedying this omission.
[41] Antonio Gramsci, *Cahiers de prison 29: notes pour une introduction à l'étude de la grammaire*, trans. Claude Perrus and Pierre Laroche, Paris 1991, 366–7. This was originally written in 1935.
[42] Ibid. 367–8.
[43] Ibid. 370–1.

feature of the political context within which a nationalist movement can arise.[44] This does not imply that nationalism is a direct product of the modern state, only that within the context of such a state nationalism has much greater potential as a political force. Nationalism, seen as a form of political opposition to absolutism within the newly emerging type of state, leads directly to a conflict over organisation and sovereignty. The resulting national ideology, its character and specific composition, will be determined by the structure of the state to which it is opposed and 'closely related to the institutional framework within which the conflict took place'.[45] The increasing significance of the state, its institutions and administrative structure, as well as its ability to control and manipulate images in the modern period also contributes to the extension of both national ideologies or traditions and the literate culture to the masses once one group of nationalists has gained control. It is interesting to note that it is not only traditional political parties that were able to profit from nationalism within modern states. Often others, such as a locally popular and politically aware Church, defending a culture as well as a religion oppressed by the state and defined as national, have been able to make gains and increase national identification among the population.

Contributions to the national mythology, and efforts to spread the high culture throughout the society, can come from all parts of the otherwise diverse political spectrum. Robert Tombs distinguishes nationalism – the ideology of subordinating all other loyalties or beliefs to the values and interests of the nation – from the sentiment of nationhood, of belonging to a national community, which is 'compatible with a wide range of social, political and intellectual positions, from royalist to socialist'.[46] Michel Winock has described the different types of nationalism and shown how in France the political 'Right' and 'Left' stress quite different aspects of national history and mythology, which are both equally national.[47] He also distinguishes between 'open' nationalism, filled with the civilising mission, self-praise for its own national virtue and solidarity with other would-be nations, and 'closed' nationalism which arises in times of crisis (especially economic) and focuses on internal purity and rivalry with the 'enemies' who are ostensibly responsible for the crisis.[48] In this way, even political opponents with differing visions of certain aspects of society and of how it ought to function, foster and develop a history which is 'national'. Both Right and Left favour and encourage the construction of what Raoul Girardet calls: 'the genesis of a *Patrie*, its territorial constitution [and] the formation of a "common heri-

44 John Breuilly, *Nationalism and the state*, Manchester 1982, p. x.
45 Ibid. 44, 61, 115. In some cases the opposition can be imaginary.
46 Robert Tombs, 'Introduction', in Robert Tombs (ed.), *Nationhood and nationalism in France from Boulangism to the Great War, 1889–1918*, London 1991, 3.
47 Michel Winock, *Nationalisme, antisémitisme et fascisme en France*, Paris 1990, 12.
48 Ibid. 37–8.

tage" '.[49] As we have seen, this common heritage has often been as much created as drawn from the literal past.

The driving force of nationalism, to generate a common heritage through national history and mythology, to teach a standard high language, to adopt or highlight common religion or cultural practices stems from the quest for unity which lies at the root of nationalist ideology.[50] The impetus to bring about cultural change is such that one can speak of nationalism as a cultural force, independently of nationalism as a political force. The pressures to bring about cultural change or homogenisation come not only from 'above' from the nationalists, but also from within society at large, which during the last two centuries underwent such changes as to render nations, national cultures and national identities attractive. The modern state often created situations in which nationalism was very attractive.[51] The pressure for unity augmented through the nineteenth century. As nationalism became the dominant political ideology and the nation state the primary political organisation in Europe, the definition of the nation came to be not only a sovereign people, but a unique sovereign people, distinguished from other peoples, not only from absolute monarchs.[52]

In summary, the pressure for unity comes both from above and below, and is a witness to the power of nationalism as both a political and a cultural force in the modern period. The political and cultural changes they engender occur alongside, and develop in relationship with, the growth of national identities and national consciousness. These forces are not inevitable and cannot always be predicted to evolve in exactly the same way, or to lead to the same results in different regions. This study will attempt to investigate the relationship between these forces through its analysis of the French Flemish. Before starting on that analysis, we will briefly examine the conclusions which have been drawn by other scholars who have attempted similar investigations in modern France.

The national question in France since the revolution

The historiography of the growth and development of the French nation is extensive and has taken many forms. Since the French Revolution, diverse interpretations of French national history have been put forward by rival political groups with a view to shaping French collective memories of a 'national' past in such a way as to support and legitimise their own particular

---

[49] Raoul Girardet, Le Nationalisme français: anthologie, 1871–1914, Paris 1983, 25.
[50] On the importance of unity in nationalist movements see idem, Nationalismes et nation, Paris 1996, 31–2.
[51] See also Breuilly, Nationalism and the state.
[52] See Liah Greenfeld, Nationalism: five roads to modernity, Cambridge, Mass. 1992, 6–8, and Baycroft, Nationalism, 51–8.

ideology and political position.[53] The best known example of such a conflict is that between royalist and republican histories of France, over the understanding and interpretation of the 1789 Revolution. Neither objective nor universally accepted, Robert Gildea describes all such rival histories as 'myth, not in the sense of fiction, but in the sense of a construction of the past elaborated by a political community for its own ends'.[54]

The acuteness and intensity of political rivalries has intensified the importance of historical interpretation in France, to a level unrivalled elsewhere, and examples of such 'mythical' histories abound. Even the earliest of the rigorous, scholarly, 'professional' historical works on modern France were written by a school of historians convinced of their mission on the political scene. From Michelet, Guizot and others in the mid-nineteenth century through the multitude of writings during the Third Republic (Lavisse, Monod, Aulard, Seignobos) to such school books as the infamous Malet-Isaac which was used in French schools until well into the Fifth Republic, there is a long-standing tradition of well-researched, well-written but undoubtedly mythical French national histories which not only represent the roots of contemporary French historiography, but which have also helped to shape popular French nationalistic feelings.[55]

Although it is never possible to separate the two groups entirely, one can attempt to make the distinction between those writing 'national' historical narratives and constructing the myths, and those describing or analysing them. As the writing of history became increasingly professionalised, individual work could indeed be further removed from its close association with a political ideology, and the latter type of historical work became increasingly possible. Methodological and interpretative debates between different historical schools, as well as the contributions made by foreign historians, also furthered this kind of writing. Gildea distinguishes five principal schools of

---

53 For a thorough analysis of the relationship between the articulation and development of French collective memories and their links to political culture see Robert Gildea, *The past in French history*, New Haven–London 1994. For a detailed analysis of numerous French writers on nationalism see Tzvetan Todorov, *On human diversity: nationalism, racism and exoticism in French thought*, trans. Catherine Porter, Cambridge, Mass. 1993, and Martin Thom, 'Tribes within nations: the ancient Germans and the history of modern France', in Homi K. Bhabha (ed.), *Nation and narration*, London 1990, 23–43. For a more specific example of history used for political ends see François Furet, 'French historians and the reconstruction of the republican tradition, 1800–1848', in Biancamaria Fontana (ed.), *The invention of the modern republic*, Cambridge 1994, 173–91, esp. p. 179.

54 Gildea, *The past*, 11–12.

55 For descriptions of this tradition in French historiography see Marcel Gauchet, 'Les "Lettres sur l'histoire de France" d'Augustin Thierry', and Pierre Nora, 'L'"Histoire de France" de Lavisse', both in Nora, *Lieux de mémoire*, i. 787–850, 851–902, and Furet, 'French historians'. See also Pim Den Boer, *History as profession: the study of history in France, 1818–1914*, trans. Arnold J. Pomerans, Princeton 1998. The work of Albert Malet and Jules Isaac was begun in 1902, and went through numerous editions: *L' Histoire*, Paris 1958–61.

historical writing in France: the positivist, Marxist, *Annales*, modernist and English empiricist or *pointillist*.[56] Each has made a contribution to the understanding of the process of nation-building in France. The remainder of this section will attempt to examine several conclusions drawn by historians from the more recent of these schools, in order to raise a series of questions about the relationships between French national identity and culture, and to situate the current study methodologically and historio-graphically.

Much of the early work on the history of the French nation and French nationalism briefly referred to above took the form of straightforward historical narratives describing the (usually) inevitable rise of France, the French language, people, or the republican system of government. The analysis and explanations behind the growth and development of the French nation as described remain essentially restricted to the political and presuppose the unity or uniformity of the French people behind their political leaders (social and economic explanations were given in Marxist analyses insofar as they are linked to the political class movement). In more recent times, this type of writing has not disappeared, and books such as Brian Jenkins's *Nationalism in France*, as well as many general textbooks, offer an essentially political perspective on the rise of the French nation.[57]

A monumental work which turned away from high politics and the centre to focus on the regions, launching in its wake a great deal of further research was Eugen Weber's *Peasants into Frenchmen*, which appeared in 1976.[58] An example of the modernist school of historiography, Weber argued that for the bulk of the French population down to the mid-nineteenth century, 'France' held little or no significant meaning. National awareness and identity came to the French comparatively recently, as modern society gradually replaced traditional society through the agents of the centre as well as the rise in standards of living brought about by increased trade and contact with other regions.[59] He dated this development to the early Third Republic (1870–1914) and provided an explanation of how national identity and culture came to the French countryside.

Weber's conclusion is essentially that the integration process can be seen as a top–down infiltration of elite values into the mass of the population through the schools, the penetration of roads and railways, military service and political propaganda. He describes how

---

[56] Gildea, *The past*, 2–9. See also Den Boer, *History as profession*.
[57] See Brian Jenkins, *Nationalism in France: class and nation since 1789*, London–New York 1990, and also Douglas Johnson, 'The making of the French nation', in Mikulás Teich and Roy Porter (eds), *The national question in Europe in historical context*, Cambridge 1993, 35–62.
[58] Weber, *Peasants into Frenchmen*.
[59] Ibid.

peasants in certain parts of nineteenth-century France, still largely indifferent to the national state, and to the urban led world around them, were gradually lured into that 'modern' orbit; they were, in other words, integrated into values and activities that had long remained, or appeared to them, irrelevant.[60]

The interpretation of the top–down process can be one of luring or coaxing on the part of the central authorities, but it can also be seen as a pressure to conform, to accept the national model. Certain Jacobin strains in French national political circles showed 'obsessive vigilance against potential dissidents' and lobbied very hard to get their republican national vision accepted by all.[61] In both cases the model is dualist and characterised by opposition: local culture and rural, backward, popular values are left behind and progressively replaced by national, urban, 'modern' ones; assimilation of the population is opposed to cultural diversity.[62]

Numerous other historians have followed Weber's lead in exploring questions of national identity and assimilation in the provinces and from the bottom. The acceptance of the basic ideas that the regions had not always been simply 'French' and that one can put a date on the penetration of national identity into the countryside has led to further investigation of the question of chronology, comparing the extent of assimilation and the time-frame for the integration of different regions, as well as the associated question of the mechanism of the diffusion.[63]

One variation on the theme of the integration of rural France into the national mould is the examination of the role of various local elites as intermediary agents. In his work on village notables in the nineteenth century, Barnett Singer attributes a more active role in the integration process to these local leaders, and stresses the 'in-betweeness of their function in rural society'.[64] They brought the national message to the rural areas and could aid or resist centralisation depending upon the situation; they were 'both agents of the retrograde, and agents of change'.[65] He does not entirely dispense with the dualist model of rural integration, but shows that the process of transmission of high culture to the regions is not completely one-way, but mediated by and dependent upon local elites, which explains variation from region to region.

60 Idem, 'Comment la politique vint au paysans: a second look at peasant politicisation', *American Historical Review* lxxxvii (Apr. 1982), 358.
61 See Jack Hayward, *The one and indivisible French republic*, London 1973, 17.
62 On the opposition of assimilation to diversity see Brian Jenkins, 'The one and indivisible republic: French identity and identities', in Tony Chafer (ed.), *Multicultural France*, Portsmouth, 1997, 1–6.
63 On the question of chronology see, for example, Johnson, 'Making of the French nation', who asks the question of when France was born. For regional studies see below.
64 Barnett Singer, *Village notables in nineteenth-century France: priests, mayors, schoolmasters*, Albany 1983, 1–2.
65 Ibid. 2.

Weber's general conclusions, based upon the whole of the French country-side, have also been tested by numerous detailed studies of individual regions. In her discussion of Brittany, Caroline Ford challenges his view of national identity as 'a curiously refined object', a complete package formed at the centre which was transfused out to the lower classes of rural France, where it was gradually accepted and assumed.[66] For Ford, 'the creation of national identity is a process continually in the making rather than the imposition of a fixed set of values and beliefs'.[67] Each region has its own contribution, and comes to understand national identity in a way which is coloured by the particular character of the region. She shows how the Catholic Church, which was traditionally held to be an opponent of national French republican identity, can be seen in Singer's model of brokers or mediators in the cultural conflicts between the centre and the region. In this role the Church was also creative as it attempted to forge an identity out of compromise between region and nation.[68]

Ford's work raises the question of the importance of local conditions not only on the speed of acceptance of national models, but also on the form that they took in different localities and regions. Joseph Fèvre and Henri Hauser write that: 'Of all the countries of Europe, France is one of those which presents the strongest unity. This unity, however, is not uniformity.'[69] The idea that each region took on attributes of the national culture in its own way, gave them a regional flavour, and in some ways fashioned its own version of national identity runs in conflict with the traditional dualist view that modernisation meant 'to "moralise" and "civilise" workers and peasants, . . . to integrate them into a national culture through the destruction of their own particularistic subcultures and the imposition of supposedly universal values'.[70] The national culture was in many ways built upon the different subcultures, which gradually evolved towards a more uniform conception of France. To suggest that national culture has only one form is to fail to recognise the diversity it truly represents from one part of France to another.

These findings have been reflected in other studies as well. Rebecca McCoy, in her work on an Alsatian village, describes how even within the context of one local community not everyone shared the same concept of what it meant to be French, but that alone does not deny that all could feel French.[71] Deborah Reed-Danahay's study of an Auvergnat village also stresses that the inhabitants had forged a multiple identity of which the national

---

[66] Caroline Ford, *Creating the nation in provincial France: religion and political identity in Brittany*, Princeton 1993, 5.
[67] Ibid. 5.
[68] Ibid. 5–7.
[69] Joseph Fèvre and Henri Hauser, *Régions et pays de France*, Paris 1909, 1.
[70] Roger Price, *A social history of nineteenth-century France*, London 1987, 258.
[71] Rebecca McCoy, 'Alsatians into Frenchmen: the construction of national identities at Sainte-Marie-aux-Mines, 1815–1851', *French History* xii (1998), 431.

'French' component was only a part, and adapted to local conditions and circumstances.[72] James R. Lehning, in his study of the department of the Loire, analyses the opposing category of 'peasant' and the relationship between French and rural cultures, concluding that the predominant image of rural dwellers as ignorant, backward and not 'French' was also constructed, or at least manipulated, by the educated urban centre.[73] His work is essentially a detailed social history of the peasantry in one department, in which he attempts to challenge the idea of the peasant as unchanging and passive in his acceptance of national identity.

Peter Sahlins has also reacted to the dualist model of a centre-imposed national culture and identity in his work on the Pyrenees.[74] He argues that in the particular border region of Cerdanya, the sense of nation and the adoption of national identities was grounded in local interests, and a local sense of place, opposing certain local communities against other ones.[75] In this way national identity was as much an extension of local identity as the reverse.

These several regional studies nuance and challenge the classic interpretation of the replacement of regional culture and identity with national ones. Maurice Agulhon confirms this for provincial France as a whole, pointing out that it is not evident that French consciousness killed 'a pre-existing regional consciousness'.[76] Regional identity had as much to be developed as national identity: 'The consciousness of belonging to any large space is necessarily abstract, hence something to be learned, and the historical provinces are no more natural than the State.'[77]

In this way regional and national communities can still be seen as rivals, but no longer in a transitional sense: it is not a passage from one to the other, but a question of choice or emphasis between alternative conceptions of group identity which present themselves to rural society as it modernises. The various choices are not necessarily seen as contradictory, for national identification is not completely incompatible with other identifications, and is in fact always combined to some degree with other identifications.[78] Ford also makes this point for Brittany, that to be French and Breton were not seen as mutually exclusive possibilities, as does McCoy for Alsace, where Frenchness did not contradict German cultural heritage.[79]

---

72 Deborah Reed-Danahay, *Education and identity in rural France: the politics of schooling*, Cambridge, 1996.
73 James R. Lehning, *Peasant and French: cultural contact in rural France during the nineteenth century*, Cambridge 1995.
74 Peter Sahlins, *Boundaries: the making of France and Spain in the Pyrenees*, Berkeley 1989.
75 Ibid. 164–5.
76 M. Agulhon, 'Conscience nationale et conscience régionale en France de 1815 à nos jours', in J. C. Boogman and G. N. van der Plaat (eds), *Federalism: history and current significance of a form of government*, The Hague 1980, 256.
77 Ibid.
78 See Hobsbawm, *Nations and nationalism*, 11.
79 Ford, *Creating the nation*, and McCoy, 'Alsatians into Frenchmen', 451.

The fact that identity could be formed without apparent contradictions did not mean that there was no political rivalry between regional and national interests. After all, a concerted programme was put in force and had been supported by the various regimes in Paris since 1789 to attempt to integrate the masses into the national culture and teach them the national language.[80] Nineteenth-century regionalism can in part be seen as an attempt by local notables to retard the incursion of the national culture in order to preserve their local hegemony, whereas access to education and the French language freed the peasantry from the domination of the local elite.[81] In this way, language was a means to preserve or establish social distinctions.[82] As Singer and others have demonstrated, however, this is only part of the picture, and was not universally true for the various local leaders. Regionalism can also be considered the political outlet for the regional aspect of identity, to defend both regional cultural variations and social positions. The implication is, however, that cultural change, particularly as it is manifested in politics as either regionalism or nationalism, is a good indicator that some important social changes are taking place, be they the formation or enlarging of a ruling class, or simply the reorganisation of cultural hegemony or the relationships between the leaders and the national-popular masses.[83]

The political motivations behind the pressure to integrate the population into the national culture, both coming from the centre and from certain elements of the regional elites, for all their importance, can only be considered to be a part of the process which led to the formation of French national identity. Each region or locality built up its own set of associations and identifications, which were often at least in part constructed around local characteristics, forming its own version of national identity coherent with the local situation, and evolving towards greater unity and similitude with other regions.

Sahlins proposes two theoretical models to describe the relationship between the different levels of identity: first, as a series of concentric circles (overlapping) from the local through the regional to the national, and second as a series of pairs, each identity opposed to another of the same level (one village versus another, one region or nation versus another).[84] All individuals see themselves through both models, sometimes thinking of their own iden-

[80] This is a prominent theme which has been well treated by historians, and will be discussed in further detail in ch. 4 below. A good discussion of the national politics of integration can be found in Ford, *Creating the nation*, 12–17.
[81] See Christophe Charle, 'Région et conscience régionale en France', *Actes de la recherche en sciences sociales*, XXXV: *L'Identité* (Nov. 1980), 37–43.
[82] See Michel De Certeau, Dominique Julia and Jacques Revel, *Une Politique de la langue: la Révolution Française et les patois: l'enquête de Grégoire*, Paris 1975, 9.
[83] See Gramsci, *Cahiers de prison 29*, 369.
[84] Sahlins, *Boundaries*, 110–13. For a further discussion see also Timothy Baycroft, 'Changing identities in the Franco-Belgian borderland in the nineteenth and twentieth centuries', *French History* xiii (1999), 417–38.

tity in opposition to another, and at other times seeing the two as complementary. In this way, one might be Flemish as opposed to Norman one moment, but at the same time Flemish and French, which includes Norman.

The results of the various *pointillist* regional studies of national identity and culture in the provinces demonstrate that national identity was not created at the centre and simply imposed via modernisation upon resistant peasants in backward regions. National identity was not incompatible with a variety of regional identities and interpretations, and national culture developed gradually through interaction between the centre and the regions. All sorts of identities are invented, and the provinces, far from mere receivers of or resistors to national ideas and images, were active participants in the construction of French national imagery and identity.

It is the purpose of this study to examine the case of the Flemish in the north of France, in order to test the findings of Weber and others through an analysis of this regional variation of the process of national integration, and the particular version of French national identity which was formed in this highly populated and economically developed border region. It will examine several interconnected questions dealing with the mechanism of assimilation, to see how, when and why the Flemish came to be absorbed into the national culture of France, while being careful to distinguish between nationalism, the formation of national identity and the spread of national cultural characteristics. It is hoped that this examination will lead to an understanding of the evolution and development of identity in terms of Sahlin's model, as well as of the dynamic relationships between culture, identity and nationalism, and their mutual influences upon one another.

After a brief introduction to the region and its history, chapter 1 will assess the cultural distinctiveness and the evolution of cultural practices in the Westhoek. It will examine both changing language use across the nineteenth and twentieth centuries, and the persistence of numerous other cultural characteristics from religion to festivals, in an attempt to establish a time-frame for national cultural integration (or non-integration).[85] Chapter 2 will turn from the cultural to the political characteristics of French Flanders, and identify both regional specificities and the relationship with national political agendas.

Having outlined Flemish cultural and political characteristics, the next few chapters will analyse influences upon identity formation in the Westhoek during the nineteenth and twentieth centuries. Both active and passive, numerous factors played a role in the gradual evolution of national and regional identities, cultural and political identities, and their relationships one with another (consciously and unconsciously) for the French Flemish.

---

[85] Some writers, using a variety of criteria to define 'national integration', have outlined other time-frames than the classic model: Ford, *Creating the nation*, 2–3; Weber, 'Peasant politicisation'; Fernand Braudel, *The identity of France*, I: *History and environment*, trans. Siân Reynolds, London 1988, 95–6.

Chapter 3 will explore the ways in which structural changes in the economy, the meaning and perceptions of the Franco-Belgian border and the nature of relations with the neighbouring Belgian Flemish altered conceptions of group identity across two centuries. As the French Flemish grew conscious of the border, and it became a more tangible division between the two Flemish peoples, the relationship between regional and national identity began to change, and the two identities were drawn more closely together. Chapters 4 to 7 will look at the numerous active agents seeking consciously to influence the course of identity formation in the Westhoek. Beginning with the French republican elites seeking integration and assimilation, through the Catholic Church and the labour movement to local interest groups such as the press, industrialists and Flemish cultural organisations, each chapter will detail the motivations, goals, objectives, means of influence and success of each group in seeking to encourage the French Flemish to take a particular stance with respect to their own collective identity. Chapter 7 will also incorporate a consideration of the development of a third level of identity, between French and Flemish, that of the newly created Nord–Pas-de-Calais region, which acquired a place in the collective consciousness during the second half of the twentieth century.

Chapter 8 will discuss in greater detail the Belgian situation and the historical process which gave rise to the Belgian Flemish movement. The much greater place accorded to Flemish ethnic and cultural identity in collective consciousness will provide a useful contrast to the situation in French Flanders and permit a more balanced judgement of the weight and impact of the diverse factors which influenced identity formation in French Flanders.

Through this analysis of the process of cultural integration and identity formation, it will be shown that while regional and national sentiment can be compatible on a cultural level, they lead to conflict on a political level. The absence of a regional political movement can ultimately undermine significant cultural differences between regions, notwithstanding the perpetuation of a handful of regional traits. Cultural practices may also remain unchanged themselves, but over time be reinterpreted in such a way as to alter their meaning and significance in terms of the identity which is derived from them. It will also be shown that the Second World War marked an important turning-point in the process of integration, at a variety of levels. Identity formation, like nationalism, is complex and closely linked to the social, political and economic circumstances of the region in question. It is hoped that this study will help to expose and clarify the nature of the evolving relationship between local, regional and national cultures, identities and political loyalties.

1

The Westhoek and Cultural Evolution

The Flemish-speaking population of the *département du Nord* in the nineteenth and twentieth centuries was concentrated largely in the *arrondissements* of Dunkerque and Hazebrouck, an area known in Flemish as the *Westhoek* (*see* map 1). The name means literally west 'hook', describing its curved shape, and the fact that it lies to the west of the greater Flemish-speaking population. Flemish is a regional variation or dialect of Dutch, and thus the Westhoek forms the westernmost or southernmost part of the Dutch-speaking region which includes the northern part of Belgium and the Netherlands.[1] Still within France, but outside of the Westhoek, a sizeable number of Flemish-speakers could also be found in the Lille–Roubaix–Tourcoing urban area, and some in the neighbouring department of Pas-de-Calais.

The Westhoek also forms one part of the region called the Nord–Pas-de-Calais, one of the few regions in the modern administrative reorganisation of France which is completely unhistoric (unlike neighbouring Picardy and Normandy, for example), created simply by regrouping two adjoining departments. In many ways, the integration of the Flemish into France has been paralleled by their integration into the Nord–Pas-de-Calais, involving the creation of a regional identity corresponding to the newly created region.[2] The term French Flanders will be used throughout this work to refer specifically to the Westhoek, or the formerly Flemish-speaking area, rather than to the whole of the region Nord–Pas-de-Calais with which it is occasionally confused in the latter half of the twentieth century.[3]

The exact number of Flemish-speakers in France at any given moment is difficult to ascertain, since language was deliberately excluded as a criterion in any French census, although estimates put the Flemish population during the nineteenth century at between 150,000 and 230,000.[4] One estimate has the Flemish-speakers still at 150,000 as late as 1940.[5]

---

1   The Westhoek is also sometimes referred to as 'Zuid Vlaanderen' (South Flanders) or French Flanders.
2   See chapter 7 below for further discussion of the Nord–Pas-de-Calais region.
3   In this way the English 'French Flanders' will be synonymous with the Flemish use of the equivalent 'Franse Vlaanderen'.
4   See Krejcí and Velímsky, *Ethnic and political nations*, 155, and Wardhaugh, *Languages in competition*, 99.
5   Jacques Julliard (ed.), *Les Conflits*, Paris 1990, 487.

Map 1. The Westhoek and surrounding area

Flanders was last independent as a political entity in the thirteenth century, and has since been attached to several different European empires. The border has shifted numerous times since the Middle Ages, reflecting the results of the most recent war and the balance of power between the states.[6] Following a long period of such wars and shifts of the dividing line between France and the Austrian Netherlands (previously Spanish), the first time that the border attained more or less its present position came with the Treaty of Utrecht in 1713. This divided the county of Flanders, leaving the Westhoek as a part of the France of Louis XIV. Throughout the eighteenth century the

---

6   See Philippe Despriet, *Geschiedenis van Frans-Vlaanderen: van de oudste tijden tot de oorlog van 1870–1871*, Kortrijk 1988.

border remained relatively stable, until the Revolutionary and Napoleonic periods when it was again shifted to the east in France's favour.[7]

The treaties of Paris of 1814 and 1815, which marked the end of the French empire, brought the border more or less back to its previous position. These were followed by the Treaty of Courtrai in 1820, considered the origin of the present Franco-Belgian border, which defined in precise terms its exact demarcation. In the five years which followed the Treaty of Courtrai, the exact local limits of the boundary were established by the prefects and governors, in collaboration with local authorities from both sides. This was the first time that any strict, linear local division had been laid down. Throughout the previous period, the lands of a given seigneur passed from one crown to another, but on the local level little changed or was noted exactly, and the boundary was anything but strict and rigid. The border as it was defined in 1820 is a more or less arbitrary line running through the countryside, often dividing individual farms in two. The only part which can be said to follow a 'natural' line is the section corresponding to a segment of the Lys river, which has ironically been the least stable part of the border. Since rivers are important strategically and commercially, control of both sides was often desired in order to maintain the operation of locks, or assert sovereignty, and it was this section which saw the most conflict and adjustment over the centuries.[8] Thus the line which has now become the Franco-Belgian border came almost arbitrarily to divide historic Flanders in two, and to leave a sizeable Flemish-speaking population under France's rule.[9]

French Flanders, covering approximately 1,400 km^2, is comprised of flat, low-lying plains, with some wooded areas to the south. For the nineteenth and most of the twentieth century it has been characterised by a high rural population density, with a large number of small and middle-sized population centres throughout.[10] The soil is not of the highest quality, but due to intensive labour has been made extremely productive, and a wide variety of crops has been produced. Although the principal activity is agriculture, small-scale domestic industry, such as linen, has figured significantly in the development of the region. In the late nineteenth and early twentieth centuries, as the

7   For a discussion of the origins of the boundary see Nelly Girard d'Albissin, *Genèse de la frontière franco-belge: les variations des limites septentrionales de la France de 1659 à 1789*, Paris 1970; Firmin Lentacker, *La Frontière franco-belge: étude géographique des effets d'une frontière internationale sur la vie des relations*, Lille 1974, 13–24; Marc Blancpain, *La Frontière du Nord, 843–1945: de la mer à la Meuse*, Paris 1990. For more on the theory of borders in the earlier periods, as well as information on French internal borders, see Daniel Power, 'French and Norman frontiers in the central Middle Ages', in Daniel Power and Naomi Standen (eds), *Frontiers in question: Eurasian borderlands, 700–1700*, Basingstoke 1999, 105–27, esp. pp. 106–12.
8   See Nelly Girard d'Albissin, 'À Propos sur la frontière', *Revue d'histoire de droit français et étranger* iii (1969).
9   See also Baycroft, 'Changing identities', 417–38.
10   Michel Tozzi, *Apprendre et vivre sa langue*, Paris 1984, 43–5.

neighbouring Lille conglomeration became one of the leading industrial regions in France, the Westhoek also benefited from the incursion of larger-scale industrialisation.[11] The Westhoek was therefore one of the most economically advanced regions in France and shared numerous cultural, social, geographic and religious traits with the Belgian Flemish living just across a border which lacked long-standing local historical tradition. One of the main purposes of this study is to examine how, why and to what extent this Flemish-speaking population of the Westhoek came to be culturally assimilated into France. The remainder of this chapter will describe the cultural characteristics of the French-Flemish inhabitants of the Westhoek in the early part of the period, in order to identify the extent of their cultural specificity, as well as to gain some sense of the cultural evolution which took place during the nineteenth and twentieth centuries. The first section will examine language, to gain an idea of the extent to which Flemish and French were in use in the Westhoek. The second section will go on to examine non-linguistic cultural characteristics of French Flanders.

Language

The nineteenth and twentieth centuries saw an alteration in language use in the Westhoek, and we will begin with an analysis of the time-frame of linguistic transition from Flemish to French, through an examination of who spoke which language in the various parts of French Flanders at what time. The demarcation of the linguistic border between the French and Flemish-speakers has been the object of numerous studies. Scholars since the early nineteenth century have sought to determine the extent to which each language was spoken, where the bilingual buffer zone was found, and to attempt to analyse the rate of advancement of French and predict what each author viewed as the possibility of Flemish survival. A comparison between several of these studies spanning the period discussed will present a reasonable picture of the rate of decline of Flemish as the everyday language of the inhabitants of the Westhoek.

For the purposes of this study, reference will be made to four different surveys of the region dating from 1806, 1856, 1906 and 1930.[12] The first was

---

[11] See R. Blanchard, *La Flandre: étude géographique de la plaine flamande en France, Belgique et Hollande*, Lille 1906; Els Witte, 'Une Flandre appauvrie', in Els Witte, Renée Doehaerd, Wim Blockmans, Hugo Soly and Jan Craeybeckx, *Histoire de Flandres des origines à nos jours*, Bruxelles 1983, 181–245; ADN, M 473 35–6.

[12] Charles Coquebert de Montbret, 'Limite de la langue française sous le premier empire', fonds Coquebert de Montbret, Bibliothèque de Rouen, nos 721, 191, and AN, F 17A 1209, summarised in Ferdinand Brunot, *Histoire de la langue française des origines à 1900*, IX: *La Révolution et l'empire*, i: *Le Français langue nationale*, Paris 1927, 525–99; E. de Coussemacker, 'Délimitation du flamand et du français dans le Nord de la France', *ACFF* iii (1856–7), 377–97; J. Dewachter, 'Le Flamand et le français dans le Nord de la France', in

Table 1
Languages in the Westhoek

Year	Exclusively Flemish	Exclusively French	Predominantly Flemish	Predominantly French
1806	103	14	2	4
1856*	74	11	17	19
1906	77	12	12	22
1930	68	12	12	31

Totals by language

Year	Flemish	French
1806	105	18
1856*	91	30
1906	89	34
1930	80	43

* The 1856 survey did not have entries for two of the communes.

Sources: Coquebert de Montbret, 'Limite de la langue française'; de Coussemacker, 'Délimitation du flamand', 377–97; Dewachter, 'Le Flamand et le français', 97–114, and 'Le Recul du flamand', 89–98.

carried out for the government of Napoléon I by Charles Coquebert de Montbret, and for the most part distinguished merely between the French- and Flemish-speaking communes, without reference to any bilingual zone. It was a part of a national survey with a view to identifying all the regions of France in which a *patois* or language other than French was spoken. The other three are independent studies by academics of the Nord who had a particular interest in Flemish and its position: the 1856 survey by Edmond de Coussemacker (of whom we will hear more later), and the two from 1906 and 1930 by J. Dewachter. In these works, careful attention was paid to identifying the language spoken in each commune, and in the cases where both were employed, which one was predominant.

Since the Revolution, many such surveys measuring the extent and change of the language border have been undertaken and published. These four have been selected because they are among the better scholarly works and are representative of the changes in linguistic use over the period.[13] De

Congrès International pour l'extension et la culture de la langue française, 2e session, Bruxelles 1908, 97–114, and 'Le Recul du flamand dans le Nord de la France depuis 1806', in *1er Congrès international de géographie historique*, II: *Mémoires*, Bruxelles 1931, 89–98.

[13] Several other works were limited to letters from only one 'notable' per commune, such as the mayor (who may have allowed politics to influence his answer), or merely described

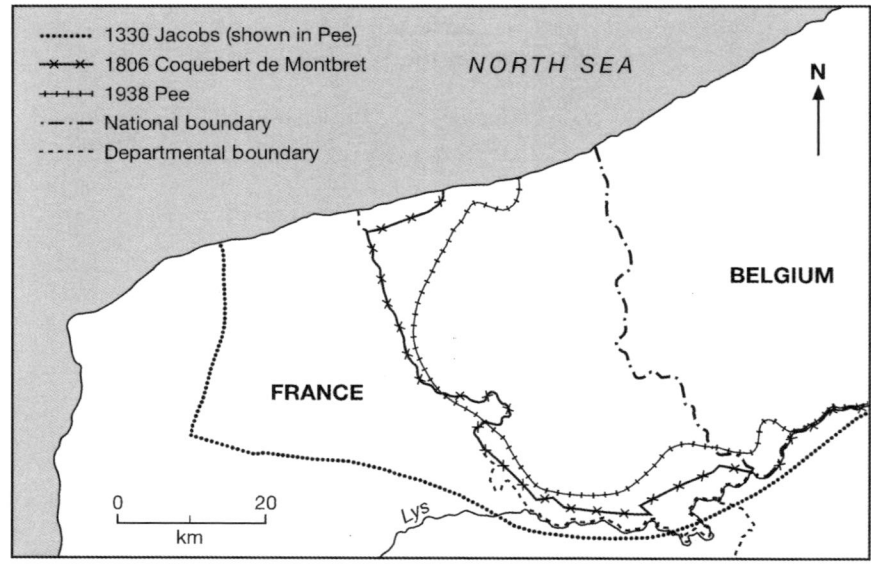

Map 2. The linguistic border, 1330–1938

Coussemacker's survey was based upon letters to several notables in each commune, requesting them to describe, in their view, which language either dominated or was used exclusively in their respective communes. Dewachter's work was based partly upon such letters, and partly upon trips to the various communes under consideration. Some of his linguistic research was undertaken in collaboration with one of the leading geographers of French Flanders, Raoul Blanchard, who also wrote about the language situation.[14]

The summary of the findings of these surveys can be seen in table 1 (*see also* appendix for greater detail). What is most striking is the relatively limited decline of Flemish between 1856 and 1906, a period which is traditionally considered to have witnessed great progress by the French language in the provinces.

The data from these surveys can be thought of in linear form through what is known as the 'language border'. Map 2 shows three versions of the language border as it was delineated by different scholars. For purposes of reference, a representation of the linguistic border in the Middle Ages is shown, drawn

changes in the linguistic border, rather than providing complete information for the entire region. For a brief description and analysis of other linguistic surveys of Flemish in France covering the period 1806–1956 see Willem Pee, 'La Situation linguistique en Flandre française et les fluctuations de la frontière linguistique de 1806 à 1956', BCFF xvi (1958), fasc. 1, 107–24.

[14] See Firmin Lentacker, 'La Flandre de Raoul Blanchard', DFN/LPBF iii (1978), 10–23.

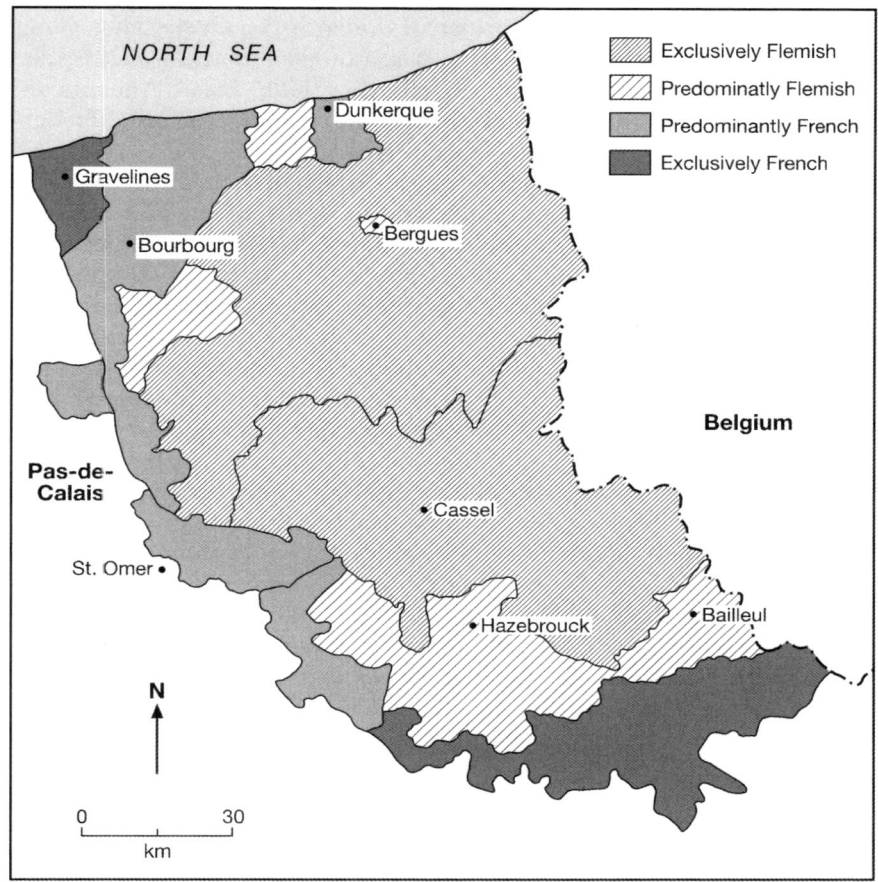

Map 3. Languages in the Westhoek, 1856

from the information provided by William Pee,[15] along with the line
described in Coquebert de Montbret's survey, and Pee's own work of 1938,
which closely approximates to the language border as it was described by
Dewachter's surveys in both 1908 and 1928. Map 3 goes beyond a simple line
border separating the French from the Flemish districts and illustrates clearly
the areas in which Flemish and French were spoken exclusively, as well as the
two varieties of bilingual zone. It is based on the cartographic work of
M. Bocave, whose work accompanied the survey undertaken by De Coussemacker, and showed his results by commune for 1856.

It can be seen from these two maps that the Flemish-speaking Westhoek
does not coincide exactly with the *arrondissements* of Dunkerque and

---

15 Pee, 'La Situation linguistique'. See also Maurits Gijsseling, 'Ontstaan en verschuiving
van de taalgrens in Noord-Frankrijk', *DFN/LPBF* i (1976), 70–85.

Hazebrouck. Two sections in particular are evidently French-speaking. Along the southern extremity of the *arrondissement* of Hazebrouck, which borders the Pas-de-Calais and the *arrondissement* of Lille (near Armentières) following the north shore of the Lys river, can be found a series of French-speaking communes. The other French-speaking area is the coastal plain beginning at Gravelines, and making progress along the coast up to the city of Dunkerque. It is perhaps worth noting that the community at Fort Mardyck, located along the coast about half-way between Gravelines and Dunkerque, was formed by the planting by Louis XIV of 'A colony of seamen from Boulogne' soon after his conquest of the region and its attachment to France.[16] Albert Dauzat writes that this small colony was never absorbed into the Flemish region which surrounded it, and eventually formed a part of the narrow French-speaking coastal strip as French advanced from Gravelines along the coast. It is interesting to note that in a major linguistic study just after the turn of the century by J. Gilléron and E. Edmont, which detailed the differences in language across France through the selection of representative communities and the analysis of their particular pronunciation and vocabulary, the community selected in the northern section of the *département du Nord* was Fort Mardyck: the one example that was untypical of the region.[17]

If we return to the data shown in table 1, careful, detailed analysis reveals several anomalies, particularly for the middle period. The number of 'exclusively Flemish' communes has increased from seventy-four to seventy-seven, while those in which Flemish dominates has declined from seventeen to twelve. A partial explanation may lie in the fact that the boundaries of the communes were altered between the two dates, and several new ones were created in the interval between 1856 and 1906. (A couple seem to have been re-established, since they had appeared in the survey of 1806.) In total, eight communes covered by Dewachter in 1906 do not appear in 1856. For six of them – Bray-Dunes, Malo-les-Bains, Fort Mardyck, St Pol-sur-Mer, Grand Fort Philippe and La Motte-au-Bois – the category to which they belonged is evident from the map which accompanied de Coussemacker's article, and they have been entered into the chart appropriately. Two others – Rosendaal and Nieurlet – lie on the dividing line between two sections, and it is impossible to tell where they belong from the map; as such they appear as 'no entry' in the table. Because of the change in boundaries, several of the communes may have had bits taken away which resulted in their being labelled 'Flemish dominating' in 1856, but 'exclusively Flemish' in 1906. This was certainly the case with Morbecque, 'Flemish dominating' in 1856 when it still contained La Motte-au-Bois, which after the separation was identified as 'French dominating' in the 1906 survey, leaving Morbecque 'exclusively Flemish'. It is also possible that the line between 'exclusively Flemish' and 'Flemish dominating'

16 See Albert Dauzat, 'Le Déplacement des frontières linguistiques du français de 1806 à nos jours', *La Nature*, 15 Dec. 1927, 532.
17 See J. Gilléron and E. Edmont, *Atlas linguistique de la France*, Paris 1908.

may have been minutely different for the two researchers or for those whose answers formed the bases of the results. If one examines the part of the table comparing the combined Flemish and French communes, this discrepancy disappears and we can observe a slow, regular change.

Between the surveys of Coquebert de Montbret and de Coussemacker, it seems unusual that the number of 'exclusively French' communes should decrease from fourteen to eleven. This is probably due to the extremely infrequent use of the category 'mixed' in Coquebert de Montbret's definition, and it is therefore probable that in several of the communes – Blaringhem, Boseghem, Mardyck and Loon Plage – Flemish was not unknown in 1806, yet insignificant enough for the communes to be considered by him as 'exclusively French'. These four all appear as 'French dominating' in 1856.

Table 1 contains information for the two *arrondissements* of Hazebrouck and Dunkerque, in which the vast majority of the Flemish-speaking population of France lived; however, important communities existed outside of the Westhoek which merit some attention. In the neighbouring department of Pas-de-Calais, lying to the west of the Westhoek, several communes contained Flemish-speakers. In the Middle Ages, Flemish was the main language of what is now the Pas-de-Calais, but by 1806 had been reduced to the area along the border with the Nord.[18] De Coussemacker writes that in 1845 Flemish was still spoken in the communes of Clairmarais, St Folquin, le Haut-Pont, Lyzel, St Omer-Cappelle, Oye, Ruminghem and Vieille-Église. He then goes on to add that at the time of his 1856 survey, it was in use only in Clairmarais, le Haut-Pont, Lyzel and Ruminghem.[19] In the tables to his article, Clairmarais and Lyzel were listed as 'Flemish dominating', and le Haut-Pont and Ruminghem as 'French dominating'. In Dewachter's surveys, Ruminghem no longer appears, but the other three are listed as 'French dominating' in both 1906 and 1930. It should also be mentioned that le Haut-Pont and Lyzel are not communes, but *faubourgs* of St Omer.[20] Thus the decline of Flemish in the Pas-de-Calais, where it had been widespread in the Middle Ages, can be for the most part attributed to the period preceding 1856, and indeed 1806, and the little which remained at mid-century suffered only a slight further decline by 1930.

For the *arrondissement* of Lille, unfortunately, neither Coquebert de Montbret nor de Coussemacker provide any information, and to measure the change leading up to the situation described by Dewachter, we are forced to rely upon the inferior work of V. Derode, who wrote about the situation in 1845.[21] Dewachter, in describing the changes which had occurred since

[18] See Pee, 'La Situation linguistique', maps 2 and 11, which show that in 1330 Flemish was spoken in most of Pas-de-Calais, and in 1806 (Coquebert de Montbret) the language border closely resembled the departmental one.

[19] De Coussemacker, 'Délimitation', 396.

[20] Dewachter 'Le Flamand et le français', 114.

[21] V. Derode, 'Sur la Carte de délimitation du français et du flamand dans le département

Derode's work, writes that 'in the *arrondissement* of Lille, without fear of refutation, we must speak of the regression and not the progress of the French language'.[22] Two communes – Halluin and Wervicq-Sud – were 'French dominating' in 1845, and by 1906 had become 'Flemish dominating'. The rest of the Flemish-speaking community consisted of four other communes – Bousbecque, Comines-France, Neuville-en-Ferrain and Roncq – which were bilingual with a preponderance of French. In the urban conglomerate of Lille, several Flemish-speaking communities were to be found, particularly in Roubaix, but also in Lille and Tourcoing.[23] The increase in the numbers of Flemish-speakers can be attributed to immigration from Belgium, which was important throughout the period, rather than to any simple progress of the language within France. There is no evidence that a greater sense of community developed between the Flemish-speakers of the Westhoek and those of the *arrondissement* of Lille than between the Westhoek and the larger Flemish-speaking community that included Belgium as well. The lack of greater French-Flemish identity could be attributed to the Belgian origin of those in the *arrondissement* of Lille, or just to distance and the tendency of Flemish communities to be locally focused.

In terms of their total numbers, Dewachter estimated that in the early 1930s the combined French and Belgian Flemish-speakers in the *arrondissement* of Lille formed a full eighth of the population. In the urban communities, the proportion had increased to a quarter of the population in Lille itself as well as the immediate suburbs of Lille, and a full third for Roubaix and Tourcoing.[24]

From these statistics it seems that the advance of French occurred principally in the half centuries before and after the period identified by Eugen Weber as the main period of linguistic assimilation of the French provinces as a whole, in which the French language supplanted the various regional dialects, *patois* and languages.[25] The explanation for the decline in French Flanders in the first half of the century could be that Weber's primary examples came from the less well-developed areas of southern France, and therefore those that modernised earlier would experience the transition first. While this may be partly true, the level of Flemish still evident in 1906, and indeed in 1930, would hardly indicate that the Flemish-speakers had all been linguistically assimilated and turned into 'Frenchmen' before 1856, if by Frenchmen we mean speakers of French or members of the French cultural

du Nord et dans celui du Pas-de-Calais', *Bulletin de la Commission historique du département du Nord*, Lille II (1844), 51–5, quoted in Pee, 'La Situation linguistique', 122.
22 Dewachter 'Le Flamand et le français', 100. Dewachter also wrote about the progress of Flemish in Belgium: 'Recul du français en Belgique à notre époque', Dunkerque 1908.
23 Idem, 'Le Flamand et le français', 100–1.
24 Idem, 'Sur le Front des langues', in N. Bourgeois and others, *Flandre notre mère: la Flandre française en douze tableaux*, first publ. Bailleul 1931, Steenvoorde 1994, 101.
25 See Weber, *Peasants into Frenchmen*.

community. The figure of 103 Flemish-only communes in 1806 may be a slight overestimate, because, as discussed above, Coquebert de Montbret's survey did not fully utilise the category of 'Flemish dominating'. Therefore the decline in the first half of the century would also be slightly less dramatic.

Further evidence can be found to testify to the presence of Flemish as the predominant spoken idiom in French Flanders during the inter-war period. Roger Taccoën states that:

> Everyone at that time in Flanders [the Westhoek] spoke Flemish... Flemish was the common tie between all of the inhabitants of this region in 1928. Certainly, it was not pure Dutch, since with time the locals had not had the chance to learn their language in school. . . . But Flemish was the language used by everyone in daily life, with a certain intonation, a particular music all its own.[26]

In another of his articles about the linguistic situation in French Flanders, Dewachter challenges a thesis put forward by two other writers, Achiel Kas and M. Allaeys, that Flemish was in fact progressing in France, particularly in the region between Lille and the valley of the Lys river.[27] Dewachter did not agree that Flemish was advancing; in fact he claimed that it had regressed slightly since the First World War, but that during the twenty years that he had studied the linguistic border, it had not changed or been pushed back.[28] He made it clear too that in spite of regression in the *arrondissement* of Lille, Flemish was still the predominant language in most of the Westhoek, although it was in slight decline there as well.

Thus it would appear that no great differences in the rate of change from Flemish-speakers into French-speakers occurred in the latter half of the nineteenth century or the beginning of the twentieth. With respect to French Flanders at least, the early Third Republic did not therefore achieve the cultural-linguistic assimilation for which it is often given sole credit. The slow, steady progress of French at the expense of Flemish had begun much earlier, and continued at more or less the same rate afterwards, leaving much of the Westhoek, as well as parts of the *arrondissement* of Lille and department of Pas-de-Calais, almost untouched by linguistic changes as late as the 1930s.

In the face of the four principal studies describing the evolution and gradual decline of the Flemish language in the Westhoek, it is interesting to note what each of the authors thought about the probability of the survival of Flemish in France. Coquebert de Montbret does not deal with the question, but de Coussemacker felt in 1856 that Flemish was already doomed, and predicted that French would soon supersede it in general usage by the popula-

---

[26] Roger Taccoën, *Une Certaine Joie de vivre*, Sartrouville 1993, 21–2.
[27] J. Dewachter, 'La Situation du français et du flamand dans le Nord de la France après la guerre mondiale', *RFB* viii (Jan. 1928), 27–33. He refers to the article by MM. Allaeys and Achiel Kas in *Ons volk ondwaart* (23 Jan. 1927), dealing with the linguistic border.
[28] Dewachter, 'La Situation du français et du flamand, 28.

tion of French Flanders. Dewachter, in 1906, predicted that Flemish would not die out, and that the trend was unmistakably towards bilingualism – note the fact that the number of 'exclusively French' communes had not increased at all since 1806.[29] His opinion had not changed in the inter-war period, and in his speculations on the future, he remained optimistic about the place of the Flemish language: 'Whatever may happen, we do not believe that Flemish will disappear from the north of France, and we think that the period of regression will soon cease.'[30]

This prediction was founded principally on his recognition of a rising movement in support of Flemish, and on his belief that the progress of French in the countryside indicated that French-Flemish society was moving in the direction of bilingualism, rather than towards the disappearance of minority languages.[31]

Maurice Agulhon points out the validity of such an opinion since, he writes, 'Those politicians and functionaries of the Third Republic who desired that all non-French dialects disappear were certainly not more numerous than those who had made bilingualism their goal.'[32] R. Anthony Lodge also describes the importance at the beginning of the twentieth century of bilingualism, which was gradually replaced by unilingualism as the century progressed.[33]

Writing at the same time as Dewachter, the geographer of Flanders, Raoul Blanchard, took the opposite view to his colleague, and believed that French was making great strides at the expense of Flemish, and would likely continue to do so in such a way as to bring about the complete disappearance of Flemish, at least as a daily mode of communication.[34] This, as was suggested by Ryckeboer, is also the opinion of many scholars and observers of the region today. In the words of Ronald Wardhaugh 'Extinction [of Flemish] seems imminent.'[35]

In the period since the 1930s, Flemish has indeed declined considerably, almost to the point of disappearance, particularly among the young. A survey was undertaken in the early 1970s by Piet Vandekerkhove of a small village called Pradelles, not far from Hazebrouck, and located in a commune listed as 'exclusively Flemish' by Dewachter in 1930.[36] He established that only 22 per cent of the population spoke Flemish regularly, and well over half were unable to understand more than a few words. A striking difference emerged

29 Idem, 'Le Flamand et le français', 98.
30 Idem, 'Sur le Front des langues', 102.
31 Idem, 'Le Recul du flamand', 90–1.
32 Agulhon, 'Conscience nationale', 243–66.
33 Lodge, *From dialect to standard*, 204–5.
34 See Blanchard, *La Flandre*, 480–5.
35 Wardhaugh, *Languages in competition*, 113.
36 Piet Vandekerkhove, 'Comportement langagier et le français parlé dans un village de la Flandre française: Pradelles', Brussels 1975, quoted in Hugo Ryckeboer, 'De Behoefte aan een taalsociologish onderzoek in Frans-Vlaanderen', *DFN/LPBF* i (1976), 159–60.

from his survey, between the over 60 age group, among whom the number speaking Flemish was 76 per cent, and the youth of Pradelles under 20, of whom 86.6 per cent could understand no Flemish whatsoever, while only 0.5 per cent could actually speak it.

The full breakdown of language by population for Pradelles can be seen in table 2, along with the statistics for the community of Merris for the same period. The results speak for themselves, demonstrating that the oldest generation can speak both Flemish and French, those of middle age can often understand Flemish, but can generally not converse fluently, and the youth are almost universally unilingual French-speaking. These findings were confirmed in 1976 in further studies which covered Vieux-Berquin, Sec-Bois, La Motte-au-Bois and Le Parc.[37] The conclusions for the other communities are similar to those of Vandekerkhove: that the use of Flemish has decreased dramatically since the Second World War and continues to decline, that a distinct division exists between generations and that the complete disappearance of Flemish from the Westhoek is a distinct possibility.[38]

A prediction of extinction is a common observation on the situation of Flemish in the Westhoek towards the end of the twentieth century. Pierre-Jean Thumerelle concluded in the late 1970s that no more than a vestige of Flemish could still be found in the farms and villages of the Westhoek.[39] So little remained that in 1979 no replacement could be found for the retiring professor of Dutch at the Catholic University of Lille, and the French had to turn to the Belgian government for help in order to fill the vacant chair, the oldest established chair of Dutch in France.[40] In 1985 Joseph Deschuytter concluded that one could no longer pretend that Flemish was not 'sick and dying as a means of expression, culture and communication'.[41] The abbé Depoers, a seventy-two-year-old priest from Hazebrouck, recalled that when he grew up in the 1920s he spoke Flemish all the time with his parents, and among his brothers Flemish for daily topics of conversation and French for elevated subjects such as politics. Later on, with his nephews, French was the only vehicle of communication; although they could understand some Flemish, they could not speak it. By the current generation, that of his great-nephews, Flemish had become completely

[37] Ryckeboer, 'De Behoefte aan een taalsociologish onderzoek', 156–68.
[38] Ibid. 156. For a further discussion of these results see H. Ryckeboer and F. Maeckelberghe, 'Dialect en standardtaal aan weersijden van de rijksgrens in de Westhoek', *DFN/LPBF* xii (1987), 129–52, and Roland Willemyns, 'Language shift through erosion: the case of the French-Flemish "Westhoek" ', *Journal of Multilingual and Multicultural Development* xviii (1997), 59–60.
[39] Pierre-Jean Thumerelle, *La Population de la région Nord–Pas-de-Calais: étude géographique*, thèse présentée devant l'université de Rennes II le 30 mars 1979, Lille 1982, 487.
[40] See Luc Ravier, '70 jaar Nederlands aan de Katholieke Universiteit van Rijsel/70 années de néerlandais à l'Université Catholique de Lille', *DFN/LPBF* xii (1997), 201.
[41] Joseph Deschuytter, 'Destin du parler flamand dans le département du Nord', *Plein-Nord La Gazette: revue historique et culturelle du Nord de la France* xi (mai–juin 1985), 35.

Table 2
Flemish-speakers in Pradelles (1974) and Merris (1969)

a – Speaks only French, may know some Flemish words, but cannot follow a Flemish conversation.

b – Speaks only French, but can passively understand Flemish when heard.

c – Speaks both languages indifferently.

Age		Pradelles (%)	Merris (%)
Under 20	a	86.6	92.7
	b	7.5	7.3
	c	0.5	0
20–40	a	70.4	73.5
	b	20.4	23.8
	c	9.2	2.7
40–60	a	31.7	48.5
	b	43.9	43.7
	c	24.4	7.8
60 and over	a	20.0	6.5
	b	4.0	50.4
	c	76.0	43.1

Source: Ryckeboer, 'De behoefte aan een taalsociologish onderzoek', 159–60; Anne Lauwers, 'Étude socio-culturelle du Westhoek français: l'étiolement du dialecte flamand', Hoger Rijksinstituut voor Vertalers en Tolken, Brussels 1970.

unknown.[42] He asserts too that the general situation currently was similar to that of his family, that some of the elderly can still speak Flemish, but rarely can any of their young or even middle-aged descendants speak it. One does not any longer, he adds, ever hear Flemish spoken in the street or market-place. This claim was in part not accepted by Madame Mortelette, the librarian of the *Centre de Documentation Flamande* (who does not herself speak Flemish). She agrees that Flemish has all but disappeared, and that it is only the elderly who still can speak it, but believed that enough remained to occasionally hear it spoken in the marketplace. She herself had never heard any, but she knew of people who had.[43] M. Staes, one of the administrators of the *Comité Flamand de France*, confirmed that the current situation in the Westhoek was that Flemish had all but disappeared, for the most part since the Second World War.[44] In the closing years of the twentieth century,

[42] Interview with the *abbé* Depoers, Hazebrouck, France, 20 Dec. 1993.
[43] Interviews with Mme Mortelette, Hazebrouck, France, 22–3 Dec. 1993.
[44] Interview with M. Michel Staes, Hazebrouck, France, 20 Dec. 1993.

Roland Willemyns observed several signs in the Westhoek of 'the final stages of language loss', and sees little future for Flemish or Dutch as a native language in French Flanders.[45]

Accurate estimates of Flemish-speakers in France towards the end of the twentieth century are few, and difficult to verify. The electronic journal *Ethnologue*, in its section devoted to minority languages of the world, puts the number of Flemish-speakers at 90,000, but gives as a reference a study from the mid-1970s, itself based on earlier work.[46] Another website devoted to the minority languages of Europe gives a total of 60,000, of whom two-thirds are only occasional speakers of the language.[47] They give statistics which show a significant difference of generation, classifying 99 per cent of the 'younger generation' in 1981 as French-only speakers.[48] In the late 1980s a survey concluded that Flemish was 'almost completely evicted' from the Westhoek as a regularly spoken language. Within the privacy of the home, 8 per cent of families used it occasionally and 4 per cent of the population listened to the Flemish radio, while at the same time its use was 'extremely rare' in the public sphere.[49] The strongest reference is in an encyclopaedia of European languages which concludes that only 'a few thousand' speakers of Dutch dialects remain in French Flanders at the end of the twentieth century.[50]

Thus the pattern of language usage in the Westhoek can be summarised as a trend in the latter part of the nineteenth and the early twentieth century towards bilingualism, with Flemish still the primary means of communication until the Second World War, followed by a rapid shift which saw the almost complete loss of the ability to speak or even to understand Flemish within two generations. Flemish cultural specificity went beyond language, however, and numerous other Flemish cultural characteristics can be identified as specific to the Westhoek.

---

45 Willemyns, 'Language shift', 54–66.
46 'France' Ethnologue, no. 16 (1996), http://www.sil.org/ethnologue/countries/Fran.html, consulted 14 March 2000. The reference is to Meic Stephens, *Linguistic minorities in western Europe*, 1976. His section on French Flanders (pp. 358–61) is primarily a summary of the Flemish movement, and is based upon three works dating from the 1940s and 1960s.
47 'Flemish in France', at the Euromosaic website http://www.uoc.es/euromosaic/web/document/neerlandes/an/i1/i1.html, consulted 14 March, 2000. Their numbers seem to come from the late 1980s but cannot be verified.
48 Ibid. It should be pointed out that they quote 'a study' without naming it, and that some of their percentages do not add up correctly.
49 Claude Wagnon, *Identités du Nord–Pas-de-Calais*, Lille 1988, 149–50.
50 Roel Vismans, 'Dutch', in Glanville Price (ed.), *Encyclopaedia of the languages of Europe*, Oxford 1998, 134. For further information see 'En France, une presse vivante, malgré tout', *Courrier International*, 24 Feb.–1 Mar. 2000, 39, where it is shown that unlike several other minority languages, no Flemish-language press existed in France in 2000.

Flemish local customs and culture

The existence of a distinctive regional culture should not be confined to its linguistic characteristics alone. It can also be seen in the everyday lifestyle, and even more so in the folkloric elements of local culture, its symbols and celebrations. These include local festivals and holidays, heroes and saints, forms of social interaction, cuisine and architecture, as well as traditional family and working patterns and techniques. Numerous examples characterise the French-Flemish culture, but before looking at them in detail, it is worth examining religion.

One of the most striking features of the culture of French Flanders was the overwhelming Catholicism of the region. The subprefect of Hazebrouck, in attempting to explain this phenomenon to the prefect in 1889, wrote that not only were all other forms of religion non-existent, but almost unanimously the inhabitants of the town, including the republicans, regularly observe the practices of the Catholic faith.[51] Earlier in the century, mass attendance attained a level so high that in a rural parish of 600, the local *curé* could not, on certain days, receive all the would-be penitents and communicants, so numerous were they.[52] In 1903 a police report described how in the village of Roncq, almost the entire population went to mass, regardless of their political views, or at the very least dared not attack the Church publicly:

> The liberal reactionary majority on the municipal council always attend church; the minority, made up of republicans calling themselves radicals, goes to mass as regularly as the majority; even the socialists do not dare to attack clericalism directly.[53]

Any attempt to struggle against the power of the Church, and what little there was of anticlericalism in the Westhoek, was founded purely upon resentment of the influential local position of the priests, and not upon any atheistic, or anti-religious feeling linked to some aspects of the lay-republican movement.

In terms of social impact, the mere opinions of the clergy often carried great weight locally, as the priests were able to exercise influence over language, education and indeed voting patterns through regular pastoral visits to their flock and in the confessional – not unimportant tools in a community as Catholic as the Westhoek. Their local political influence, in spite of the government's best efforts to constrain the clergy on this point, was often significant. In the lead-up to the elections of 1889, the subprefect of

---

51 Subprefect of Hazebrouck to prefect, 29 Oct. 1889, ADN, 2 V 56.
52 See Dominique Rosselle, 'Les Populations rurales du Nord de la France et la religion pendant la révolution: état de la question', in Alain Lottin (ed.), *Eglise, vie religieuse et révolution dans la France du Nord*, Villeneuve d'Ascq 1990, 68.
53 Report of police commissioner of Roncq, 31 Mar. 1903, ADN, 1 T 123 5. Titles of political parties were not capitalised in the original.

Hazebrouck stated that with respect to the weight of their political authority 'The Catholic clergy possesses a preponderant influence in the Flemish area.'[54] This Catholicism pertained particularly to the Flemish-speaking area, and isolated the Westhoek within the region of the Nord–Pas-de-Calais, much of which was not only less practising, but overtly 'red' and anti-Catholic. Indeed, in 1913 the diocese of Lille was created by subdividing the diocese of Cambrai into two along lines of religious practice: the more Catholic region from Lille through the Flemish-speaking area becoming the new diocese of Lille.[55]

The level of Catholic practice continued to distinguish the Westhoek from the surrounding area in the Nord–Pas-de-Calais region up to the end of the twentieth century. Just under half the French-Flemish population attended mass regularly in 1949, when the average for the diocese of Lille was 25 per cent.[56] While conforming to the general trend of religious decline in the post-war period, the rate of practice for the Westhoek remained approximately double that of the diocese as a whole until the 1970s, when the rates were just over a third and 17 per cent respectively.[57] While the rural areas also conformed to the general trends of higher practice than the urban areas, the cities of the Westhoek, with the exception of Dunkerque, also maintained considerably higher levels than the other urban areas of the greater region.[58] Yves-Maire Hilaire cites the Flemish influence as a significant factor in determining the higher rate of practice among workers in the Lys valley in the post-war period.[59] Down to the 1990s the decline, but also the relatively high rate of practice in the Westhoek continued, with almost all children being baptised, as opposed to well under half in greater Lille, and a considerably higher percentage attending catechism.[60] During the 1990s one student in five attended Catholic schools.[61] Thus throughout the nineteenth and twen-

---

54 Subprefect of Hazebrouck to prefect, 29 Oct. 1889, ADN, 2 V 56. He describes the subversive attitude of the clergy during the election period. See, for example, rector to minister of public instruction, 5 Jan. 1864, AN, F 17 2682 (this will be discussed further in chapter 5).

55 See André Legrand, 'La "Gauche" dans le département du Nord (1945–1962)', HTN (1964.2), 29–33.

56 Yves-Marie Hilaire, Fernand Boulard and others (eds), Matériaux pour l'histoire religieuse du peuple français, XIXe–XXe siècles, II: Bretagne, Basse Normandie, Nord–Pas-de-Calais, Picardie, Champagne, Lorraine, Alsace, Paris 1987, 94.

57 Ibid. See also Yves-Marie Hilaire and Robert Vandenbussche, 'Mutations idéologique et religieuses', in Yves-Marie Hilaire (ed.), Histoire du Nord/Pas de Calais de 1900 à nos jours, Toulouse 1982, 455–7.

58 See Jacques Verscheure, Gérard Deprost and Claude Traullé, Aspects sociologique de la pratique dominicale, diocèse de Lille, Lille 1961, 46. Their findings for the early 1960s confirm the rates of practice given (p. 45).

59 Yves-Marie Hilaire, 'Les Ouvriers du Nord devant l'église catholique (XIXe et XXe siècles)', Le Mouvement social lvii (Oct.–Dec. 1966), 189–91.

60 See Bruno Duriez, 'La Religion de la région du Nord: l'empreinte du Catholicisme', DFN/LPBF xxiii (1998), 16–19.

61 Ibid. 19.

tieth centuries, the Westhoek remained an area of consistently higher Catholic practice than the remainder of the Nord–Pas-de-Calais region.

Catholicism can also be associated with several of the other elements which distinguish Flemish culture from that of the remainder of France. Lucien Détrez and Joseph Crombé, in describing the nature of faith in French Flanders, depict it as characteristically ceremonial and festive.[62] Local processions and 'fêtes' were prominent features of village life. Many of the festivals were religious in nature, devoted to the recognition of saints with a special attachment to a given locality or a trade which was heavily practised in a specific community. The year was punctuated by the various church holidays and saint's days, which served to mark out the year for the Flemish.[63]

Although the Church was extremely important, not all the festivals were expressly religious in nature. One prominent example is the 'kermisse', a popular non-ideological local celebration, held on varying occasions throughout the year depending upon the particular commune, and involving much revelry, as well as games and competitions for the local populace. The word 'kermisse' derives its name from the Flemish words 'kerke', meaning church, and 'misse', meaning mass. Thus we can discover the religious origins of what are among the most popular and not strictly speaking religious of the local festivals. Charles Taverne de Tersud, describing these festivals at the end of the nineteenth century, writes that

> In all of the villages and communes of Flanders, the kermesse began on Sunday, continued on Monday, Tuesday, Wednesday and Thursday, everyone rested on Friday and Saturday, then began again and finished on the following Sunday.[64]

One aspect of Flemish festival which is representative of the region as a whole is the regularity with which one finds processions as a part of the festivities. It was usual during each festival to parade a figure or figures prominent in local legend through the streets, varying slightly in particulars depending upon the community in question. In one case of a *fête du travail*, it was only the women who had the right to organise the festivities on the day of the procession, and who were given the responsibility of parading the 'dressed-up mannequin' as well as inviting *les patrons*, all of the workers, their families and friends.[65]

In another such celebration, the 'mid-Lent festival' in Hazebrouck, the figure is referred to as the 'count' of mid-Lent. The origin of the myth is that a count of Flêtre in the Middle Ages had a nut tree, which he kept to himself

---

[62] L. Détrez and Joseph Crombé, *Le Régionalisme religieux: la foi de nos pères*, Lille 1926.
[63] See, for example, Catherine Carpentier-Bogaert, *Saints guérisseurs: rites et lieux sacrés* (Documents d'ethnographie régional du Nord–Pas-de-Calais vi), Béthune 1995.
[64] Charles Taverne de Tersud, *Hazebrouck depuis son origine jusqu'à nos jours: ses corporations, ses lois, ses moeurs et coutumes, sa fête du comte de la mi-carême, sa kermesse, ses gueux ses sorciers et sorcières, ses monuments*, Hazebrouck 1890, new edn, Hazebrouck 1987, 287.
[65] See Alexandre Desrousseaux, *Moeurs populaire de la Flandre française*, Lille 1889, 30–5.

except on the day of the festival, when nuts were distributed to the villagers. The festival originally saw the figure of the count paraded on a pedestal, while nuts were thrown to the crowd. During the Revolutionary period, the count became an object of derision and mockery; he was tied and jeered at while the nuts were distributed in spite of him. In the latter half of the nineteenth century, the two parts of the story were combined. In the first phase of the festival, the count is brought in on the back of a valet, and judged. In the procession which follows, accompanied by many floats and people in costume, the count is put back into his seat dressed as a sixteenth-century noble.[65]

In many cases, such ceremonies have evolved into the festivals of the 'giants'.[67] Many of the towns which had their own particular legendary figure made a large-scale model to be reused each year. The inhabitants of Hazebrouck, for example, continue to have processions with a giant called Tisje-Tasje (with the recent additions of his wife and a daughter), representing a seventeenth-century peddler who travelled the countryside and was reputed for his funny stories. In Cassel, it is the giant Reuze and his wife who tower over the procession.[68] The festivals of the giants constitute one element of regional culture which has flourished even more strongly in the twentieth century. The earliest festivals date back to before the Revolution, with several others developed during the nineteenth century. Many more have sprung up in the twentieth century, new ones being created well past the Second World War and into the 1980s and 1990s.[69] Various other small-scale processions or festivals honouring local legends, heroes or saints, sometimes associated with a particular trade or craft, can be added to the list of traditional cultural celebrations. Occasionally, the authorities attempted to reduce the power of the Church by banning religious processions, although they usually ran into staunch opposition from both clergy and people. In June 1895, for example, 80,000 citizens demonstrated in protest against laws banning religious processions for the *fête-dieu*.[70]

One of the chief characteristics of these festivals was their purely local, rather than regional, character. While the style of celebration, and particularly the feature of processing giant-sized models of characters drawn from popular mythology distinguished the region from neighbouring ones, no

---

66 Taverne de Tersud, *Hazebrouck*, 156–62. The original name was 'fête de la mi-carême'.
67 See Maurice Millon, *La Ballade des géants de la Flandre maritime française*. Dunkerque–Hazebrouck 1970, and Jean-Pierre Ducastelle and others, *Géants et dragons: mythes et traditions à Bruxelles, en Wallonie, dans le Nord de la France et en Europe*, Tournai 1996.
68 See Marie-France Gueusquin, *Fêtes, géants et carnavales du Nord–Pas-de-Calais: Cassel* (Documents d'ethnographie régional du Nord–Pas-de-Calais iii), Béthune 1993, 7, 15.
69 See Robert Chaussois, *Géants du Nord/Pas-de-Calais*, Lille 1998, 314–16; Monique Teneur Van Daële, *Découvrez le Nord: guide pratique des promenades et des loisirs*, Lille 1975, 144; Marie-France Gueusquin and Monique Mestayer, *Gayant: fêtes et géants de Douai* (Documents d'ethnographie régional du Nord–Pas-de-Calais v), Béthune 1994.
70 ADN, M 153 15.

single figure ever emerged as a cultural reference for the entire Flemish-speaking area. Each town or village, each different occupational group, had its own particular saint or hero. This meant that national symbols and festivals were unrivalled by any widespread, popular figures unifying the whole of the Westhoek.

Other particularly local events in cultural life existed, besides festivals. In his *Voyage en France*, Victor Eugène Ardouin-Dumazet describes a competition peculiar to French Flanders in which groups of people would bet to see which from among two bramblings (a kind of finch) would make the most sounds in an hour. They would crowd around the birds to take tally, which could be as high as 900 or a 1,000 calls per hour.[71]

The standard means for the Flemish to socialise on a day-to-day basis was also peculiar to the region. Every small community, neighbourhood, and often many rural areas had what is known as an *estaminet*, or a kind of local pub, in which the Flemish would come to drink, eat, sing, recite poetry, play games and to discuss with friends and neighbours. Each one served its immediate vicinity, and they were extremely numerous: in one small village, Boeschepe, in the 1930s there were thirty-five different *estaminets*, with a dozen in the main town, and the rest scattered throughout the surrounding countryside.[72] Maurice Houvenaghel described the *estaminet* as the only place of leisure and socialising for the inhabitants of the villages, especially in the period preceding 1920 when newspapers were rare, and news was sought each morning in the nearest *estaminet*.[73]

What differentiated the *estaminets* of French Flanders from pubs elsewhere in France was the fact that women and children were present and indeed welcome.[74] They were generally speaking clean and commendable, providing an atmosphere which was not 'mean or sordid' but genuinely pleasant and friendly.

Another characteristic feature of French-Flemish culture was a prominent long-standing literary tradition, extremely popular in French Flanders, centred around a loose organisation of local groups called the 'chambers of rhetoric'. Some tracing their origins as far back as the eleventh century, these chambers of rhetoric were small, localised groups which would get together to promote the literary and cultural life of their community, and 'even if the level remained modest, they bore witness to cultural activity in the smallest of parishes'.[75] At their meetings the members would read poetry, recite old

---

71 Victor Eugène, Ardouin-Dumazet, *Voyage en France*, 18e série: *Région du Nord*, I: *Flandre et littoral du Nord*, Paris 1899, 95–101. The French name for the birds is 'pinson'.
72 Maurice Houvenaghel, *Boeschepe: mon village*, Steenvoorde 1990, 57.
73 Ibid.
74 Patricia Hilden, *Working women and socialist politics in France, 1880–1914: a regional study*. Oxford 1986, 30–1.
75 Gérard Landry and Georges de Verrewaere, *Histoire secrète de la Flandre et de l'Artois*, Paris 1982, 286.

stories or perform plays, either written in Flemish, or often translations of the great classics from other languages, such as *Le Cid* by Corneille, which was one of the all-time most popular.[76] In addition to local performances and a substantial amount of translation by the members, they occasionally sponsored literary competitions for original composition in Flemish.[77] The chambers had their own names, often after local figures or saints, such as St Anne for Hazebrouck, 'Les Baptistes' in Bergues or 'Jone van herte', one of three chambers in Bailleul.[78]

The chambers of rhetoric were still quite active, numerous and widespread throughout French Flanders in the nineteenth century, but began to disappear gradually between 1850 and 1900.[79] Several survived the turn of the century however. The three chambers from Bailleul were reorganised in 1896 under the new name the 'Maetschappij der waere Vlamingen', the 'society of true Flemings', and survived until shortly before the First World War.[80] The longest lasting of the chambers of rhetoric was in the village of Eecke, founded officially in 1542, which remained active until 1939, only disbanding with the Second World War.[81]

Although much of what was performed in the chambers of rhetoric was in translation, it was performed in Flemish; and, particularly in the field of poetry, original work continued to come out of French Flanders. This can be seen from the results of the various composition competitions up to and including the inter-war period.[82] Flemish-language poetry from nearby West Flanders in Belgium also circulated freely in the Westhoek; indeed, the most famous of the nineteenth-century Flemish poets was Guido Gezelle (1830–99), a native of Kortrijk, who wrote profusely in the West-Flemish variation of the language which closely resembled the dialect used in the Westhoek.[83] Gezelle took an extremely active interest in French Flanders, corresponded with numerous intellectuals on the French side of the border, and wrote translations for them.[84] Through the activities of the chambers of rhetoric and poets and intellectuals such as Gezelle, specifically Flemish literary life was not completely absent from the Westhoek.

---

[76] See *L'Indicateur de l'arrondissement d'Hazebrouck*, 3 Jan. 1869, 2.

[77] D. Carnel, 'Les Sociétés de rhétorique et leurs représentations dramatique chez les flamands de France', ACFF v (1859–60), 29–88.

[78] R. Despicht, 'La Littérature flamande en Flandre française', in Bourgeois and others, *Flandre notre mère*, 108–9.

[79] See V. Celen, *Het Vlaamsch in Fransch-Vlaanderen*, Brussel 1925, 18, and Michel Loosen, *Hazebrouck: en histoire et en couleur*, Steenvoorde 1992, 128.

[80] Despicht, 'La Littérature flamande', 125.

[81] Landry and de Verrewaere, *Histoire secrète*, 268. See also C. Looten, 'La Flandre à travers les ages', in Bourgeois and others, *Flandre notre mère*, 59.

[82] See, for example, 'Rapport sur les concours de langues et littérature flamands 1929', *Le Lion de Flandre* vi (Nov.–Dec. 1929), 13–19.

[83] Émile Coornaert, *La Flandre française de langue flamande*. Paris 1970, 327.

[84] Ada Deprez, 'Over Gezelles briefwisseling met de Frans Vlamingen (1884–99)', *DFN/LPBF* x (1985), 228–45.

French Flanders can also be distinguished from the surrounding region by its cuisine and its architecture. Be it specific dishes such as the 'flamiche' or 'moules-frites', the consumption of beer or the preference for cooking with butter rather than oil, Flemish cuisine is clearly distinguishable from that of the rest of France.[85] Architecturally, one can identify a 'Flemish' urban architecture which extends into France well beyond the Westhoek, and features significantly in cities such as Arras or Cambrai.[86] Much of it dates from before the Revolution, but a characteristic Flemish urban style did continue into the twentieth century, most noticeably in the work of Louis Cordonnier, and is still very much in evidence.[87] In terms of rural architecture, it is possible to identify a style which also distinguishes the Westhoek from the other rural areas immediately adjacent. Traditionally, Flemish farm buildings were built in a style known as the *hofstede*, in which the courtyard was only enclosed on three sides, and in which the dwelling had one long corridor leading from the living room which immediately followed the main entrance to the kitchen which was built off the back of the house, and was called a 'kruiskeuken' (cross-kitchen).[88] This style was typical of the Westhoek through the nineteenth century, but in the twentieth century the *hofstede* has begun to disappear, as farm buildings are modernised inside and outside, meaning that architecturally, the Westhoek is on the verge of losing 'its specificity, its cachet of originality'.[89] Thus, although much of the 'Flemish' architecture extended to the urban areas beyond the Westhoek, it is nevertheless possible to describe and identify specifically Flemish dwellings which differentiated the Westhoek from the neighbouring areas within France.

Another consideration in this discussion of French-Flemish cultural characteristics is the attachment to the land and to long-standing agrarian traditions. This is a natural force which tends to resist and to check any tendency towards change. Pierre Bonnaud described the power of attachment to land and 'entrenchment' in cultural traditions related to agriculture: 'this link to the land is always at the root of things'.[90] He further described the strong link

85 For a description of Flemish cuisine and concrete examples see Claude Tchou (ed.), *La Cuisine du Nord par ses chefs*, Paris 1996, and André Gamblin, *Le Nord–Pas-de-Calais: 20 circuits touristique*, Colmar 1984, 6. A 'flamiche' resembles a pizza, and 'moules-frites' describes the traditional dish of mussels and chips.

86 See, for example, Gamblin, *Le Nord–Pas-de-Calais*, 4–6.

87 See pamphlets and clippings in ADN, 136 J 62, 63; Paul Parent, 'Les Caractères régionaux de l'architecture dans le Nord de la France', *RN* xiii (Feb. 1927), 5–43; Odile Lesaffre, 'Louis-Marie Cordonnier et l'architecture du Nord de la France', *DFN/LPBF* xxiii (1998), 45–64.

88 See Christiane Foutrien, 'Evolution récente de l'habitat agricole à Winnezeele (Flandre Intérieure)', and Henri Desplanques 'L'Évolution récente de la maison agricole en Flandre française: l'exemple de Steenbecque', *HTN* (1974.1), 27–33, 34–8. For a comparative description of neighbouring styles see Raymond Dion, 'L'Évolution de la "maison agricole" à la Flamengrie (Thiérache de l'Aisne)', *HTN* (1974.1), 39–47.

89 Foutrien, 'Evolution récente', 33.

90 Pierre Bonnaud, 'Terres et langages: peuples et régions', thèse de doctorat ès lettres, Clermont-Ferrand 1980, 406.

between the land and the region and its dialect or language, which is 'a cultural instrument defended against subversion' and which through its structure and stability allowed the Flemish to comprehend and remain faithful to their roots.[91] Thus traditional links to the land resist change as does the language itself, which plays a conservative role and 'resists the invasion of modern ideas'.[92] The *abbé* Détrez and Joseph Crombé, in their discussion of religion and regionalism, write that regional life is like family life: linked to respect for traditions. They claim that all sorts of regionalism (historic, economic, political, literary, artistic) have their roots in 'family' regionalism, based on a similarity of familial traditions.[93] Susan Cotts Watkins shows that these family traditions are reflected in the demographic structure of the populations on either side of the language border (which is true for both northern France and Belgium).[94]

The family structure referred to by Détrez and Crombé was inextricably linked to the traditional way of life of the Westhoek Flemish. Although primarily agriculturalists, small-scale industry was developed early in the Westhoek, and formed an integral part of the history of the Flemish. G. M. Triquet argues that because the Flemish had never known serfdom, 'to survive, this peasantry had to turn quite early to non-agricultural remunerated activities: the craft industry, and especially textiles', both for local use and for export.[95] This basic structure of agriculture, combined with domestic industry, led to the familial culture described by Détrez and Crombé, which remained more or less stable until the Second World War, when the traditional rural way of life was transformed beyond recognition. Damien Vanhyfte and Alain Wagret describe the transformation which took place in a typical Flemish village in the Westhoek in the thirty years which followed the Second World War, not only in farming techniques, but the 'artisanat' as well: until the war the village was home to specialist craftsmen and workers, who had all disappeared by the time they were writing in 1979.[96]

The final French-Flemish characteristic to be discussed here is a certain kind of political passivity. It is likely that the long history of the occupation of French Flanders by one power or another had left the population with an acceptance of whoever was ruling at the time, accompanied by a desire to be more or less left alone by them. Unlike other regions of France, the Flemish were always the least resistant to paying their taxes and the least likely to

---

91 Ibid. 279.

92 Gabriel, Le Bras, *Études de sociologie religieuse*, I: *Sociologie de la pratique religieuse dans les campagnes française*, Paris 1955, 370.

93 Détrez and Crombé, *Le Régionalisme religieux*,

94 Susan Cotts Watkins, *From provinces into nations: demographic integration in western Europe, 1870–1960*, Princeton 1991, 134–6.

95 G. M. Triquet, 'Réflexion sur l'évolution historique des Flandres', unpubl. pamphlet. See also chapter 3 below.

96 See Damien Vanhyfte and Alain Wagret, *Un Village flamand . . . Sainte-Marie-Cappel*, Sainte-Marie-Cappel 1979.

avoid doing their military service when conscripted. As well as being extremely loyal, wrote Henri Cochin in 1917, the foundation of the Flemish character is independence, individuality and a close guarding of, and respect for, tradition and language.[97]

It can therefore be concluded that within the context of France, French Flanders possessed a cultural particularity characterised both by a separate language and literary tradition, and numerous other cultural characteristics, including religious practice, typically regional festivals, culinary traditions, forms of sociability, and work and family patterns. Some, like the use of the Flemish language, had diminished and all but disappeared by the end of the twentieth century, while others remained. It is important to note that this distinctive regional culture was not limited to northern France, but was shared with the population immediately across the border with Belgium. The Westhoek can be seen as culturally a part of greater Flanders, with numerous cultural similarities spanning both sides of the Franco-Belgian border. Before turning to look specifically at the border and its role in patterns of culture and identity, it will be useful to examine voting patterns and electoral politics in the Westhoek, to see if the cultural specificity of French Flanders also entailed identifiable regional political attitudes and behaviour.

[97] Henri Cochin, *Les Deux Guerres, 1870–1871, 1914–1917: images et souvenirs*, Paris 1917, 259–60.

2

National and Regional Politics

William Brustein, in his book *The social origins of political regionalism*, attempts to offer an explanation for particular consistencies in regional voting patterns over several decades through an analysis of two particular agricultural communities (Argentré-du-Plessis in the Ille-et-Villaine and Bonnieux in the Vaucluse) which exhibited striking consistencies over a 130-year period.[1] He defines political regionalism as 'a pattern of political involvement that is strongly associated with a regional base',[2] and believes that the political map of France is indicative of underlying regional characteristics. It is worth looking to see if French Flanders also possessed what could be called a distinctive regional political culture, which could potentially have served as a basis for regional identity or a regionalist movement. Along with the analysis of election results will be a discussion of the local political scene and some prominent political figures.

To investigate whether or not the Westhoek exhibits political traits which distinguish it from the surrounding area, we will begin by placing it within the traditional bipolar framework which has characterised French national political life since 1789. Most often referred to as *La Gauche* (the Left),[3] and *La Droite* (the Right),[4] the two opposing ideologies have also been labelled *Le parti du Mouvement* and *Le parti de l'Ordre établi*,[5] or alternatively *Le Mouvement* and *La Conservation*.[6] This duality had its origin in the French Revolution, as François Goguel and Alfred Grosser write: 'French politics in the nineteenth century developed under the sign of a sort of manichaeism, of a permanent conflict between adversaries to and partisans of the principles of the French Revolution.'[7] During the Revolution, one was labelled either for it, or against it, particularly when it came to the question of the execution of

---

1   William Brustein, *The social origins of political regionalism: France, 1849–1981*, Berkeley 1988.
2   Ibid. 2.
3   For a general history of the Left in French politics see Jean Touchard, *La Gauche en France depuis 1900*, 2nd edn, Paris 1981, and G. Lefranc, *Les Gauches en France, 1789–1972*. Paris 1973.
4   For a general history of the Right in French politics see Jean-François Sirinelli (ed.), *Histoire des Droits en France*, Paris 1992, and René Rémond, *Les Droites en France*, Paris 1982.
5   François Goguel, *La Politique des partis sous la Troisième République*, 3rd edn, Paris 1958, 17.
6   Patrick Lagoueyte, *La Vie politique en France au XIXe siècle*, Paris 1989, 13.
7   François Goguel and Alfred Grosser, *La Politique en France*, Paris 1984, 23.

Louis XVI, leaving no middle ground on which to stand. This gave birth to a dualism which has remained present in French politics ever since: 'the division of French public spirit into two opposing, and most often irreconcilable families of political temperament'.[8] Goguel and Grosser go on to identify as the constant theme permeating French politics a special valorisation of *La Gauche* and its particular concept of progress, and describe French history as a series of failures of *La Droite*.[9] Individual movements began on the Left, moved to the centre as they acquired power, and finished up on the Right, from which they were eventually displaced.

Within this general bipolar division can be identified a multitude of political parties, factions and divisions, and a general instability leading to a succession of numerous short-lived administrations. In spite of the overwhelming complexity of parties, labels and movements, the generalisation of Right and Left still emerges clearly and is a necessary simplification for purposes of analysis. Elections tended to favour the removal of nuances and the restratification of the numerous factions into two blocs.[10] François Goguel writes that however unjustified the conviction may appear objectively, and in spite of the diversity within the two camps, the behaviour of the French electorate demonstrates that in their eyes, 'a fundamental link existed between the various Rights on the one hand, and the various Lefts on the other'. This created an illusion of unity on both sides, which, even if it was a myth, was a powerful, influential myth which had a concrete impact on political reality whenever the electorate was consulted.[11]

When examined in the light of this bipolar framework, several trends emerge which characterise the politics of the Westhoek and set it apart from the surrounding region. The Flemish tend to vote on the Right relative to the rest of the department, demonstrate a concern for economic over strictly political issues and often give their support to local individuals. The Church also remained an important political force in French Flanders, particularly through the development of the Christian Democratic movement from the end of the nineteenth century.

The Right

The tendency to support the Right, as well as the primacy of economic concerns over political ones, emerges in the Westhoek early in the nineteenth century. Alain Lottin demonstrates that from 1831 to 1839 the inhabitants of the Westhoek also voted conservatively, and points out for the

---

8 Goguel, *La Politique des partis*, 17.
9 See Goguel and Grosser, *La Politique en France*, 23–4.
10 Jean-Pierre Florin, 'Présentation des forces politiques dans le département du Nord en 1914', *RN* lvi (Apr.-June 1974), 176.
11 Goguel, *La Politique des partis*, 19.

Table 3
Local elections in the Nord, 1855, 1860

Arrondissement	1855			1860		
	success	failure	%	success	failure	%
Dunkerque	57	3	5	56	4	6.7
Hazebrouck	51	2	3.8	48	5	9.4
Lille	115	14	10.9	112	17	13.2
Douai	62	4	6.1	53	13	19.7
Valenciennes	77	4	4.9	72	9	11.1
Cambrai	109	9	7.6	99	19	16.1
Avesnes	144	9	5.9	107	46	30.1

Source: Adapted from Ménager, *La Vie politique*, ii. 537.

elections under the July Monarchy that 'In terms of this study one is easily convinced that the political significance of the elections is not primordial . . . but these elections have above all economic and social significance.'[12]

During the Second Empire, support for the Right can in part be measured by the results obtained by the 'official' candidates. Table 3 shows the percentage of success and failure of the official candidates, by *arrondissement*, in the local elections in 1855 and 1860. The two *arrondissements* of the Westhoek, Dunkerque and Hazebrouck, demonstrated a great deal of support for the regime in place, more than in the five other *arrondissements* of the Nord in 1860.

The tendency of the Westhoek to vote to the Right of the rest of the department can also be clearly seen in table 4, which shows the election results for the Third Republic from 1871 to 1936, giving the percentage of votes cast for candidates of the Right, Left, and for the later years also the centre. The centre is here defined as the 'moderate' parties, often formerly of the Left, who became moderate as they acquired power and shifted towards the Right. The centre was particularly present in the 1919 and 1924 elections, 'thanks to proportional voting by list', which lasted until 1926, after which time the return to the *scrutin d'arrondissement* once again favoured the Right–Left polemic.[13] The results for the two *arrondissements* of French Flanders indicate a distinct pattern of support for the Right, particularly when compared with figures across the entire department. When contrasted with the neighbouring department of Pas-de-Calais, or with France as a whole, the

---

[12] Alain Lottin, 'Les Elections législatives de 1831 à 1839 dans le département du Nord', mémoire principal, DES, faculté de lettres, université de Lille, November 1958, 211–12.
[13] See Florin, 'Présentation des forces politiques', 176.

Table 4
Legislative elections in the Nord, 1871–1936

Date	Gauche	Droite
8 Feb. 1871		
Dunkerque	14.1	85.9
Hazebrouck	6.8	93.2
Nord	22	78
2 July 1871		
Dunkerque	50.9	49.1
Hazebrouck	45.2	54.8
Nord	71	29
1876		
Dunkerque	29.4	70.6
Hazebrouck	34.9	65.1
Nord	55	45
1877		
Dunkerque	22.6	77.4
Hazebrouck	17.3	82.7
Nord	45.9	54.1
1881		
Dunkerque	46	54
Hazebrouck	39.4	60.6
Nord	68.4	31.6
1885		
Dunkerque	36.4	63.6
Hazebrouck	17.9	82.1
Nord	43.9	56.1
1889		
Dunkerque	33.6	66.4
Hazebrouck	21.6	78.4
Nord	46.6	53.4
1893		
Dunkerque	74.1	25.9
Hazebrouck	54.2	45.8
Nord	62.2	37.8

Date		Gauche	Centre	Droite
1902				
		67.8		32.2
		4		96
		68.9		31.1
1906				
		35.6	29.9	34.5
		13.7	86.3	
		55	21.7	23.3
1910				
		41.4		58.6
		21.8		78.2
		61.3	5.3	33.4
1914				
		36.7		63.3
		44.9		55.1
		73.6	7.2	19.2
1919				
	I	26.5	47.4	26.1
	II	9.6	43.4	47
		13.5	49.3	37.2
		33.4	48.6	18
1924				
	I	46.4	24.3	29.3
	II	17.4	28.7	53.9
		22	28.3	49.7
		50.8	25.2	24
1928				
	I	52.2		47.8
	II	10.2		89.8
	I	19.9	31	49.1
	II	29.3		70.7
		48.3	9.3	42.4
1932				
	I	46	4.2	49.8
	II	12.4		87.6
		14.9	40.1	45
		45.9	12.3	41.8

Date	Gauche	Droite	Date	Gauche	Centre	Droite
1898			1936			
Dunkerque	67.7	32.3	I	53.8	2.4	43.8
			II	21.9	16.1	62
Hazebrouck	3.9	96.1		24	22	54
Nord	68	32		53.2	12.6	34.2

Sources: ADN, M 30 28; M 35 1; M 35 7; 5 Z 49; Libert, 'Les Élections législatives'; Hilaire, Atlas électoral.

Westhoek also comes out as more strongly to the Right than the average.[14] Thus it can be said that throughout the nineteenth century and up to the end of the Third Republic, the Westhoek demonstrated the characteristics of regional political distinctiveness, corresponding quite closely with the limits of the Flemish-speaking area. Bernard Ménager writes that 'the most resistant monarchist bastion coincides with the map of Flemish'.[15]

The political distinctiveness of the Westhoek remained in place for several years following the Second World War and then began slowly to disappear. Up to the early 1960s, the Left had still not penetrated the Westhoek, which André Legrand explained as a combination of persistent Catholic sentiment and the importance of the textile industry in creating a Left-voting electorate.[16] His assessment of the situation in the early 1960s was that the link between the Flemish language and the anti-Left bastion was beginning to break down.[17] By the 1970s the socialists began to make inroads into French Flanders, which Bernard Toulemonde and André Legrand attribute partly to a shift of the Christian Democrat electorate towards the Socialist Party, and partly to increased industrialisation in the Westhoek, principally in Hazebrouck and the Lys river valley.[18] By the 1980s it is difficult to discern a distinct and regular voting pattern for the Westhoek with respect to the rest of the department and the Pas-de-Calais.[19] One explanation for this trend is

[14] For a comparison with Pas-de-Calais and France see Yves-Marie Hilaire, André Legrand, Bernard Ménager and Robert Vandenbussche, Atlas electoral Nord/Pas-de-Calais, 1876–1936: Troisième République, Villeneuve d'Ascq 1977, and François Goguel, Géographie des élections française sous la Troisième et Quatrième Républiques, Paris 1970.
[15] Bernard Ménager, La Vie politique dans le département du Nord de 1851 à 1877, III: Les Débuts de la IIIe République, thèse présentée devant l'université de Paris IV, Lille 1983, 1216.
[16] See Legrand, 'La "Gauche" ', 8–10, 34.
[17] Ibid. 33–4.
[18] See Bernard Toulemonde and André Legrand, 'Les Élections législatives des 4 et 11 mars 1973 dans la région du Nord', RN lvi (no. spéciale sur la vie politique dans le Nord et le Pas-de-Calais au XXe siècle) (Apr.–June 1974), 279. On the shift of the Christian Democrat electorate towards the socialists see also Christelle Gille, 'Quarante Ans d'Action Catholique ouvrière dans la diocèse de Lille (1950–1990)', RN lxxix (Jan.–Mar. 1997), 154.
[19] Bernard Ménager and Christian-Marie Wallon-Leducq (eds), Atlas electoral Nord/Pas-de-Calais (1973–1992), Lille, 1993. The actual statistics for each section of the departments are not given, but from examining the series of maps which are provided, the

the nature of the economic crises of the post-war period for the region as a whole, especially in the 1970s, which 'tended, relatively, to homogenise its behaviour with the impact and growth of the crisis'.[20] Another possibility is the decline of specifically French-Flemish culture and identity which may have been contributing to the distinctive behaviour.

Turning to the breakdown of voting patterns within the region, it can be seen that Dunkerque and Hazebrouck are not equally strong in their support of the Right, that of Dunkerque being somewhat less pronounced on several occasions. Indeed, in the period 1893–1902, Dunkerque supported the Left as much as the rest of the Nord, or more so. This is in part due to a distinction within the *arrondissement* of Dunkerque, which appears in table 4 for the period following the First World War, where the results have been divided according to the two electoral constituencies. It can be seen that the first constituency, comprising the coastal cantons of Dunkerque *est*, Dunkerque *ouest* and Gravelines, voted very much to the Left, while the second constituency, comprising the cantons of *La Flandre Intérieure* – Bergues, Bourbourg, Hondschoote and Wormhoudt – supported the Right as strongly as the *Houtland*, forming the *arrondissement* of Hazebrouck. Thus the earlier Left leanings of Dunkerque can be attributed primarily to the influence of the coastal region within the *arrondissement*. Referring to the Westhoek, Bernard Ménager outlines a total of three internal divisions which were clear from the early Third Republic onwards: in the north, a coastal band supporting the radical Left, which became socialist during the Fourth Republic; in the middle a bastion of the classic Right; in the south, a territory which was favourable to the rise of Christian Democracy.[21]

The coastal region demonstrated a different attitude from the rest of the Westhoek for several reasons. In part the presence of the port and consequent contact with other areas left it more open to external influences. The coastal plain was also a more French-speaking region than the interior,[22] which only serves to confirm the fundamental distinction between the Flemish-speaking area and its surroundings. The geographical difference was maintained through the inter-war period, as the subprefect of Dunkerque described in a letter to the prefect in 1924:

> the differences which separate the two constituencies of the arrondissement of Dunkerque, from the economic point of view, also exist from a political point of view. The majority of the electorate in the first constituency is republican,

---

Westhoek only stands apart in the earliest years of the period covered in this atlas, and by the 1980s no systematic distinction can be made. See, for example, pp. 111, 131, 133, 135, 145, 152, 166. A similar lack of pattern can be seen, for example, in the results of the 1998 cantonal elections: *Régionales et cantonales 1998 (15 et 22 mars): résultats*, Paris 1998.

[20] P. Bruyelle, 'De La Région pilote à la région déprimée, 1952–1980', in Hilaire, *Histoire du Nord/Pas-de Calais*, 451.

[21] Ménager, *La Vie politique*, iii. 1219–20.

[22] See chapter 1.

and supports the elements of the Left, while the second only elects representatives who profess very moderate ideas. The war did not bring about any significant changes to this situation.[23]

In this letter, he discusses the possibility of re-establishing single-member constituencies (since the war the French had voted for departmental lists), and believes that were Dunkerque to be separated into the two original constituencies, the coastal one would remain republican, and the interior conservative. He ascribes a republican leaning to the canton of Bourbourg, which is a part of the interior, and was previously referred to as being conservative along with the other cantons of the second constituency. In discussing the possibility of redrawing the lines, and including Gravelines in the second constituency, the subprefect did not think that the republican influence of Gravelines, together with that of Bourbourg, would be enough to swing the constituency away from its predominantly Rightist, conservative leanings in favour of the republicans.[24]

Thus, in spite of local distinctions, French Flanders is a region which for the most part politically supported *La Droite*, but which part or strain within *La Droite*? René Rémond has traced three strands within the French Right, according to which of the royal (or imperial) houses the members supported during the nineteenth century: the Legitimists, Orléanists and Bonapartists.[25] Even after a restoration ceased to be a real possibility or goal, Rémond argues that each tendency nevertheless carried on into the twentieth century, the Legitimists in Christian Democracy, the Orléanists in the economic liberalism of the centre-Right, and the Bonapartists in Gaullism. In the Westhoek, it was a combination of the two monarchist strains, Legitimist and Orléanist, which dominated.[26] Even more characteristic, it was a particularly moderate version of the Right, primarily in search of stability. One only needs to look at the efforts made by all the candidates to appear as calm, debonair and interested above all else in peace and stability to see the importance of moderation.[27] Elections were primarily fought between moderate monarchists and moderate republicans.

Economy over politics

This moderation and desire for stability stemmed from the particular importance of economic questions in the politics of the Nord as a whole. Unusual among Legitimist areas of France, aristocratic influence was very little felt:

[23] Subprefect of Dunkerque to prefect, 6 June 1924, ADN, 5 Z 50.
[24] Ibid.
[25] See Rémond, *Les Droites.*
[26] Bernard Ménager, 'La Droite dans le Nord: 1902–1914', *RN* lvi (Apr.–June 1974), 147–9.
[27] Louis Libert, 'Les Élections législatives de 1871 à 1875 dans le département du Nord', mémoire principal, DES, faculté de lettres, université de Lille 1959, 170–1.

'the aristocracy and the liberal professions play very little role, the Flemish are represented – with the occasional exception of a worker – by men who share their economic preoccupations'.[28] The nature of the economic prosperity of the Nord was one in which peace and stability were essential, and in which government intervention played a crucial part – principally by protecting their industries through tariffs and trade policy, but also through public works such as the improvement of the canal structure or the port facilities in Dunkerque. Voters tended to support those whom they felt were best able to guarantee the stability which was necessary for their prosperity, most usually represented by the conservatives of La Droite, and those who did not wish to implement any radical changes, of politics or regime. The Flemish manifest 'an aversion to extremism, be it of the Right or the Left, and an instinctive confidence in those who hold power'.[29] Thus it was that in the mid 1880s, the conservatives were supported for their programme of protectionism, but after they began to talk seriously about a restoration of the monarchy, their support in the following by-elections waned considerably.[30] It was a similar sentiment which inspired the prefect, Jules Cambon, when writing about the reactions of several factory-owners to government intervention during a large strike at Fourmies, to say that 'it is only that, in the Nord, when it comes to a question of interest, politics no longer plays any role whatsoever'.[31] Bernard Ménager echoes the viewpoint that, in the early Third Republic, in spite of the fact that the principal preoccupation of the politicians and their electoral campaigns was the future of the institutional structure, the people themselves were much more concerned with the solutions to the problems of the times: new taxes, reform of military service or the future of primary education.[32]

In this atmosphere, both major parties attempted to show that they were the best guarantors of the economic policies favourable to the Nord: the conservatives by claiming that they were the only true protectionists; while the republicans, in the period after 1881 and the republican national victory, claimed that the best way to protect economic interests was to avoid electing anyone who was hostile to the regime, and who therefore could not hope to get their proposals through the Chamber of Deputies, where political considerations were often the deciding factor.[33] La Droite seemed to represent the greatest stability and least menace to the region's economic security, because

---

[28] Jacques Néré, 'Les Elections Boulanger dans le département du Nord', thèse complémentaire pour le doctorat-ès-lettres, université de Paris n.d., 32.

[29] Les Flamands de France: Qui sont-ils? Que veulent-ils? Le manifest des flamands de France adopté à la IVe Université Populaire Flamande par les associations: Cercle Michel de Swaen, Menschen Lijk Wijder, CFF, Het Reusekoor, Tegaere Toegaen, Lille-en-Flandre 1982, 3.

[30] See ibid. 95.

[31] Report, Jules Cambon to minister of commerce, 3 June 1886, AN, 12 4661, quoted ibid. 18.

[32] Ménager, La Vie politique, iii. 1051–2.

[33] See Néré, 'Les Elections Boulanger', 11–12.

it was not seeking change which was unknown and therefore menacing. In their support of *La Droite*, particularly the moderate wing, the voters of the Westhoek were therefore showing more concern for the protection of their economic interests than for any purely political ideology.

Local political elites

The primacy of economic over strictly political questions meant that voters were occasionally able to demonstrate proof of independence with respect to the usually conservative local political authorities.[34] This was the case in the partial elections of 2 July 1871, which sent two republicans to the legislature (General Faidherbe and Armand-Achile Testelin, a medical doctor and former *préfet du Nord*), and in which 'so many of the Flemish voted for Testelin, a friend of Gambetta'.[35]

The prestige of local individuals and their social position was often a more decisive factor than political stripe in the elections of the Westhoek.[36] If we look at the latter decade of the Second Empire, we find substantial evidence of the local character of the elections. Table 5 shows the 1863 legislative election results, which are somewhat surprising. In a conservative region whose economic interests were best ensured by the maintenance of stability and the *status quo*, one would expect support for the ministry to be strong, and yet it is the constituency of Dunkerque/Hazebrouck which sees the official candidate defeated most resoundingly. This is because the winning candidate was Ignace Plichon, an Orléanist lawyer from the region who was popular and well respected locally. Bernard Ménager explains Plichon's election as demonstrating three characteristics of the voting patterns of the region – religious, local and political. Plichon was supported by the clergy and his local generosity gave him extremely strong local roots which led to a coalition of support of Legitimists from Bergues, Hoondschoote and Wormhoudt with Orléanists, republicans and voters who remained loyal to the Empire.[37]

Loyalty and fidelity to the regime did not prevent the French Flemish from supporting a local candidate who was very well viewed by his peers, particularly because of his views on the protectionist controversy, and who was also backed by local church authorities. The second decade of the Second Empire saw the liberalisation of politics, and a weakening of the personal power of Napoléon III to the benefit of the traditional regional elites, the industrialists

[34] Libert, 'Les Élections législatives', 111.
[35] Ibid.
[36] The division of electoral constituencies by *arrondissement* also favoured the election of local individuals: Frédéric Bon, *Les Élections en France: histoire et sociologie*, Paris 1978, 41.
[37] Ménager, *La Vie politique*, ii. 588–9.

Table 5
Legislative elections in the Nord, 1863

Constituency	Official candidate	Independent	Democrat
Dunkerque/ Hazebrouck	39	61	–
Hazebrouck/ Lille	–	55	45
Lille	59	–	41
Lille/Roubaix /Tourcoing	100	–	–
Douai	47.7	52.3	–
Valenciennes	52.1	47.9	–
Cambrai	48	42.2	9.8
Cambrai-Le Cateau	100	–	–
Avesnes	100	–	–

Source: Adapted from Ménager, La Vie politique, ii. 587.

and the clergy in the case of the Nord.[38] Several notables of the Westhoek were able to retain a great deal of political support in opposing the economic liberalisation of the Second Empire in the 1860s. In the second constituency of Hazebrouck/Lille, no official candidature was even presented to oppose Charles Kolb Bernard, a Catholic with Legitimist tendencies, and another influential man locally, who was elected 'by the rural vote'.[39] These two then teamed forces with another member from the Nord, Jules Brame, (the unopposed official candidate for Lille/Roubaix/Tourcoing), each devoting his time and efforts to dealing with a particular aspect of government policy. Brame dealt with defence of protectionism and the interests of manufacturers, Plichon with economic and financial policy, as well as internal questions, and Kolb Bernard with external affairs, each defending strongly the position of the Nord as a whole in the house and before the government, and receiving the support of the others in return.[40] Both Plichon and Kolb Bernard were re-elected in the final legislative elections of the Second Empire in 1869, unopposed by official candidates who recognised their solid establishment in their seats.[41]

---

[38] For a discussion of the liberalisation of the empire see Henri Hauser, Jean Maurain and Pierre Benaerts, Du Libéralisme à l'impérialisme (1860–1878), Paris 1939, 19–20.
[39] See Ménager, La Vie politique, ii. 592–3.
[40] See ibid. 501.
[41] ADN, M 30 28.

Another striking example of the local character of elections is the staunch republican Léon Claeys, a *brasseur* in Bergues, who became mayor of Bergues, *conseiller général* and senator for the Nord, in spite of the overwhelming Legitimist leanings of his area. In 1888, describing the election of Claeys as mayor of Bergues, it was reported simply that 'the election of M. Claeys has no political character; it is entirely due to his personal influence'.[42]

The lack of political significance and the importance of local individuals is even stronger in local elections. Table 6 shows the political opinions of the mayors of the communes of Dunkerque and Hazebrouck in 1870, immediately following the removal of a number among them who were particular Bonapartists left over from the empire. Once again, the marked trend for candidates of the Right stands out, as does the total of seventeen in the *arrondissement* of Hazebrouck who considered themselves to be apolitical, a full 32 per cent of the whole. Politics, strictly speaking, was obviously not a particularly high priority with a great number of the inhabitants, particularly for local elections. This angered the rector during one election campaign, who wrote to the prefect that 'What is the most striking in this whole battle is that it has no political character whatsoever, and that it is impossible to find in it anything other than personal animosity and bitterness.'[43]

A typical platform can be illustrated by the following letter, published in the *Indicateur de l'arrondissement d'Hazebrouck* in 1865, from Charles Plancke, a tile manufacturer in Hazebrouck. Addressed simply to his fellow citizens it stated that

> The electoral committee, composed of the industrial and commercial notables of this city, after your lively insistence, has pushed me to accept a place on the business list [*la liste de commerce*] as a candidate for the municipal council. I have accepted this candidature without condition and without any political opinion; I have sought only to use my limited strength for the interests of my locality. Child of the people, it was through work alone that I attained my present position in this city, I have come to present myself for your votes. . . . Liberal, although friend of order and public peace, without personal ambition, seeking nothing besides the well being of the working class, to which for many years I have been entirely devoted through my commercial relations, my efforts will be geared to augment the industry to which I belong, this industry which no one denies is one of the great riches of the area.[44]

Plancke was eighteenth on the *liste de commerce*, and with this simple plea was elected to the *conseil municipal* of Hazebrouck on the 23 July 1865 with 1,154 votes.[45] Describing the results of the elections around the region in

---

42 Comment under 'renseignements généraux' in a table showing the results of the municipal elections of 20 May 1888: ADN, M 89 43.
43 Rector to prefect, 5 Jan. 1864, AN, F 17 2682.
44 Letter dated 14 July 1865, *L'Indicateur de l'arrondissement d'Hazebrouck*, 16 July 1865, 1.
45 *L'Indicateur de l'arrondissement d'Hazebrouck*, 27 July 1865, 1.

Table 6
Political opinions of mayors, Dunkerque and Hazebrouck, 1870

	Conservative hommes d'ordre	Conservative/Liberal esprit gouvernmental	Liberal
Dunkerque	–	33	3
Hazebrouck	6	10	8

	Legitimist	Republican	Apolitical	NA
Dunkerque	2	1	1	20
Hazebrouck	4	2	17	5

Source: Ménager, La Vie politique, iii. 1025.

L'Indicateur de l'arrondissement d'Hazebrouck, it was said that 'The conflict seems to have had a political character only in very few places.'[46]

By 1888, as can be seen in table 7, quite a number of mayors and assistant mayors were elected from *La Gauche*, although still nothing like a majority, particularly in Hazebrouck. In the *arrondissement* of Dunkerque, the assistant mayors of the Left are almost equal in numbers to those coming from the Right. This can be attributed, at least in part, to the coastal cantons, which, as we have seen above, formed a region politically to the Left of the rest of the Westhoek. Although it does not show up in table 7, in quite a large number of cases, the mayor was of one political inclination, while one or more of his assistant mayors was of the other.[47] It was also periodically the case that the mayor was in opposition politically to the majority of his municipal council,[48] which is particularly striking since at the time mayors were elected by their councils.[49] Neither of these local oppositions seems to have caused much worry or debate among the departmental authorities who declined to comment upon it in their election reports, or found it sufficient to say that good relations existed between the said parties, and their political counterparts of opposing views.

A similar situation existed at the turn of the century with the *conseillers d'arrondissement*. One of the councillors, a reactionary politically, was described in a report as a militant clerical, who nevertheless maintained exemplary relations with the republican prefect.[50] This was a typical case;

[46] Ibid.
[47] ADN, M 89 43.
[48] Ibid.
[49] See Robert Vandenbussche, 'La Fonction municipale sous la Troisième République: l'exemple du département du Nord', *RN* lxxvi (Apr.–June 1994), 320–5, for a discussion of the procedure for electing mayors.
[50] Report on *conseillers d'arrondissement* in 1901, ADN, M 59 163. See also report on the *conseillers généraux* and *conseillers d'arrondissement*, ADN, 6 Z 1861.

Table 7
Political opinions of mayors and assistant mayors,
Dunkerque and Hazebrouck, 1888

	Gauche	Droite	Doubtful/Indifferent/NA
Dunkerque: mayors	27	35	3
assistant mayors	34	36	8
Total	61	71	11
Hazebrouck: mayors	13	39	1
assistant mayors	5	58	3
Total	18	97	4
Total for both arrondissements	79	168	15

Source: ADN, M 89 43.

most political opponents posed no particular problems to the administration and had good working relationships with the prefects and the government. In terms of political analysis, in 1901 Dunkerque was represented by six *conseillers d'arrondissement* from the Left, and three from the Right. In Hazebrouck the numbers were reversed, three from the Left and six from the Right.[51] In Hazebrouck in 1910, the next general elections saw one of the reactionaries defeated by a republican, leaving the totals at five and six respectively from Left and Right.[52]

In the elections to the *conseil général*, between 1919 and 1925 both Hazebrouck and Dunkerque voted more to the Left than to the Right, electing a total of sixteen councillors representing the Left, to only five representing the Right.[53] Considering that votes in the legislative elections were particularly strong in favour of the Right at the same time, this cannot be considered a fundamental change of orientation, but as further evidence that it was possible for popular or influential individuals to be elected, regardless of their political opinions. Roger Taccoën described the situation in the late 1920s: 'In any case, in municipal elections it was not a question of precise political views, but more a question of a man one liked or did not like.'[54] He related the story of a man seeking to become mayor by promising to slaughter one of his cows and divide it between the villagers if he were to be elected. In spite of displaying the cow prominently on election day in the village square

[51] ADN, M 59 163.
[52] ADN, 6 Z 1861.
[53] See ADN, 6 Z 1860, 1861, 1862; 5 Z 71.
[54] Taccoën, *Une Certaine Joie*, 25.

next to the slaughterhouse, he was unsuccessful in his bid, and returned sadly home with his cow.[55]

The prominent role of individual personalities as compared to party politics in the Westhoek continued beyond the Second World War through the Fourth and Fifth Republics. True both for the Left and the Right, and for the urban as well as the rural areas of French Flanders, the role of strong individuals, as well as long-standing roots in the community, continued to be important assets to electoral victory, as did the support of mayors for candidates for the legislature.[56] An example was Claude Prouvoyeur, the long-standing Right-wing mayor of Left-dominated Dunkerque, who commanded wide local support and tended to present himself to the electorate 'under the cover of apoliticism'.[57]

To get a better idea of the kind of profile held by a representative of the Westhoek, table 8 shows the socio-professional background of the mayors of Dunkerque and Hazebrouck in 1888. They come mostly from the category of farmer or worker, the vast majority being listed as *cultivateur* (144 of the 159).[58] Although mostly 'fermiers' (tenant farmers), this did not mean that they were essentially from what could be called the lower class. Landowners were often absent, and 'the "fermiers" were often gentlemen farmers, almost "Messieurs" '.[59] This indicates merely that they were all local, and that their notability came not from nobility or pure wealth, but from being the most successful and influential of the residents. Among the other local representatives, the *conseillers généraux*, *conseillers d'arrondissement* and the *conseillers municipaux*, a similar profile was reproduced in the sense that few landowners and *rentiers* were represented, although fewer farmers were to be found, and a greater number of merchants, tradesmen and manufacturers.[60] In his discussion of the *conseillers généraux* during the final decades of the Third Republic, Jean-Pierre Florin describes them as, independent of their political viewpoint, almost always elected in the canton of their birth, at a reasonably advanced age, coming from a middle-class family background linked already to politics, and having already served as a *conseiller municipal*, which was the 'source of a local political base which explains their guaranteed election the first time they stand for office'.[61]

55 Ibid. 25–6.
56 See Toulemonde and Legrand, 'Les Élections', 279, and Patrick Oddone, *Battailes autour des beffrois ou la vie politique de l'agglomération dunkerquoise de 1945 à 1978*, Dunkerque 1979, 16.
57 Oddone, *Battailes*, 221, 284.
58 ADN, M 89 43.
59 Néré, 'Les Elections Boulanger', 23.
60 See ADN, M 85 17; M 59 163; 6 Z 1861.
61 Jean-Pierre Florin, 'Contribution à une histoire des chemins du pouvoir sous la IIIe République: les conseillers généraux du Nord, du début du siècle à la veille de la Seconde Guerre Mondiale', *RN* lxxv (July–Sept. 1993), 631.

Table 8
Socio-professional background of mayors and assistant mayors,
Dunkerque and Hazebrouck, 1888

	paysan/ ouvrier/ employé	commerçant	professions libérales	industriel/ rentier/ propriétaire
Dunkerque:				
mayors*	42	5	4	13
assistant mayors**	52	7	6	6
Hazebrouck:				
mayors	25	7	1	20
assistant mayors**	40	7	4	14
Total	159	26	15	53

* Alphonse Bergerot, the reactionnary mayor of Esquelbecq, was listed as being a legislative deputy.
** In each *arrondissement* the profession of one assistant mayor was illegible.

Source: ADN, M 89 43.

The deputies who represented the Westhoek in the legislature had several characteristics in common with municipal and departmental representatives. They too were recruited locally, 'enfants du pays' most often born in one of the cities or large towns of the region from which they obtained the majority of their votes (infrequently rural). They had post-secondary education, possessed 'a solid legal or scientific education' and belonged to 'the qualified bourgeoisie, but were rarely civil servants'.[62]

They were almost all inter-connected in some way through marriage or family with the wealthy industrialists of the region. 'Son of a local notable . . . in the majority of cases the father-in-law belonged to the group of wealthy landowners or industrialists.'[63] One example is Charles Kolb Bernard, whose father-in-law was the head of a large sugar refinery near Lille, and whose sister was the grandmother of Charles de Gaulle.[64]

These political families were extremely common, with son following father or father-in-law into politics, and often 'inheriting' his seat. Political family connections were continually cultivated and reinforced, which led to

[62] Francis Przybyla, 'Les Députés du Nord au début de la Troisième République (1871–1885)', ibid. 567–8, 593.
[63] Ibid. 593.
[64] See Pierre Pierrard, 'Un Grand Bourgeois de Lille: Charles Kolb Bernard (1798–1888)', *RN* xlviii (July–Sept. 1966), 382.

the development of a veritable network.[65] Another good example is Ignace Plichon (deputy during both the Second Empire and Third Republic), whose son Jean Plichon, a civil engineer born in Bailleul, followed his father to become both a long-standing deputy and a *conseiller général*.[66] The elder Plichon was considered by some to be the *porte-parole* of a group of four land-holding dynasties of the region – the Cleenwerck, Vandewalle, Bieswal and de Coussemacker – who were all linked through marriage, and referred to as 'la grande famille'.[67] A chief characteristic of these families is that, unlike the rest of Legitimist or Right-wing France in the latter half of the nineteenth century, very few of the deputies were noble: indeed only four of twenty elected members of the Right in 1885 had a title.[68]

Although they may not have been noble, the deputies representing the Nord were very wealthy. In his recent work on the northern deputies, Francis Przybyla has shown that 'the extent of the wealth of the deputies . . . is much greater than one would suppose'.[69] Thus the representatives of the Westhoek during the nineteenth and early twentieth centuries were drawn from similar backgrounds, educated members of a narrow economic elite, which, whether of the Right or among the republicans, maintained family links with one another through intermarriage for several generations.[70]

In addition to their homogeneity, the deputies of the Nord, once elected, were likely to hold their seats for a number of years, and to combine several mandates at the same time. In the elections of 1902 seventeen of nineteen incumbents were re-elected, demonstrating a significant tendency of the departmental electorate: fidelity to their elected notables.[71] This was further demonstrated in the 1914 elections, when seventeen incumbents were again returned to serve a further term.[72] The average mandate for the deputies of the Nord as a whole was just under three legislatures.[73] Several in the Westhoek lasted well beyond the average, for example the *abbé* Jules Lemire, who represented Hazebrouck continually from 1893 until his death in 1928.

As well as serving long periods, it was also extremely common for deputies to hold departmental or municipal office, and for mayors to represent their commune at the level of the *arrondissement* or the *département*. As seen in table 8, one of the mayors in the *arrondissement* of Dunkerque was a deputy

65 This political network was also connected to the economic elite network. See chapter 7 and Pierre Pouchain, *Les Maîtres du Nord du XIXe siècle à nos jours*, Paris 1998.
66 See ADN, 6 Z 2072, and *Dictionnaire biographique illustré: Nord*, 2nd edn, Paris 1909, 884–5.
67 See Ménager, *La Vie politique*, iii. 1215.
68 Néré, 'Les Elections Boulanger', 5–7.
69 Przybyla, 'Les Députés du Nord', 575–80, 593.
70 Ibid. 593–4.
71 Robert Vandenbussche, 'Une Élection de combat dans le Nord: 27 avril et 11 mai 1902', *RN* lvi (Apr.–June 1974), 139.
72 Florin, 'Présentation des forces politiques', 173.
73 Przybyla, 'Les Députés du Nord', 584–5.

throughout the 1880s: Alphonse Bergerot, conservative mayor of Esquel-becque. In the first fifteen years of the Third Republic, only 13.7 per cent of the deputies of the Nord (eight out of fifty-eight) served no other mandate at the same time.[74] Among the eighteen *conseillers d'arrondissement* representing Hazebrouck and Dunkerque in 1901, twelve held municipal office as well: ten were mayors, one an assistant mayor, and one a *Délégué cantonal*.[75] Thus between the homogeneity of the representatives and their long periods in office, politics in the Westhoek were characterised by tremendous political stability and a tendency for individuals to have several political mandates at once at different levels of the political structure.[76]

Among those seeking political office in the Nord, competence in Flemish could be considered a trump card in their campaigns. Lemire could speak in either language to the local inhabitants and had campaign posters in Flemish as well as French, which he addressed directly to the Flemish people: 'Stemmers van Vlaender' ('Voters of Flanders').[77] In his French version the call was merely to 'electeurs'.[78] General Boulanger, in his campaign in the Nord, also had posters printed in Flemish to help win the support of the local people during the legislative election on 19 August 1888. For the most part, they were direct translations of the French version, and the two appeared side by side in a supplement to the *L'Indicateur de l'arrondissement d'Hazebrouck*. The striking exception was the final two lines preceding the signature, appearing in large, bold type, which in French read 'VIVE LA FRANCE! VIVE LA REPUBLIQUE!' and in Flemish 'LEVE VRANKRYCK! LEVE HET VADERLAND!'[79] In spite of his republicanism, General Boulanger was not at all unwilling, it seems, to use another language when he thought it necessary.

As has already been demonstrated in the previous chapter, the Westhoek can be distinguished from the surrounding area by the high level of Catholic practice among the French Flemish. This Catholicism is linked to the other political characteristics described in this chapter. The stance on the political Right was a moderate version of Legitimism, which can be understood as a defence of the Church, rather than a rigorous monarchism (the region responded to the pope's call to 'rally to the republic' in the 1890s with little

---

[74] Ibid. 587.

[75] ADN, M 59 163. The situation was similar in 1910: ADN, 6 Z 1861.

[76] For more on multiple mandates see Christophe Charle, *Histoire sociale de la France au XIXe siècle*, Paris 1991, 155, and Vandenbussche, 'La Fonction municipale', 331.

[77] 'Stemmers van Vlaender', election poster, 1893, ADN, M 37 33, no. 300, on display at a special exhibition celebrating the one hundreth anniversary of Lemire's election, Musée d'Hazebrouck, December 1993.

[78] 'Electeurs', election poster 1893, ibid. 1993.

[79] 'Long live France! Long live the Republic!' (French); 'Long live France! Long live the Fatherland!'(Flemish): *L'Indicateur de l'arrondissement d'Hazebrouck*, 14 Aug. 1888, supplément. At that time, the fatherland in such a context referred to Flanders, rather than France.

hesitation).[80] The priority of economic issues for the region can also be seen in the light of a patriarchal or paternalist tendency within the moderate Right which was closely linked to their Catholicism, the leaders seeking to represent the poorer citizens and workers of their region for whom they felt a sense of responsibility. Loyalty to whichever regime was in power and the tendency to support local notables can also partly be explained by a Catholic respect for hierarchy and order. The moderate conservative members of the economic elite who represented the region were also key members of local parishes, with the support of the Catholic Church and the local clergy. Describing the representatives in 1898, Yves-Marie Hilaire writes that they were almost all practising Catholics, republicans or rallied to the republic, and, with only one exception, represented the most socially-minded views among the local economic elite.[81] The attitudes of the Church itself towards politics in the Westhoek will be discussed in chapter 5.

Although the vast majority of the elected representatives of the Westhoek emerged from this relatively homogeneous local elite, several important national political figures also came into direct contact with the voters of French Flanders. During the July Monarchy Lamartine represented Bergues,[82] during the Third Republic General Boulanger was twice elected in the Nord, having been particularly well received and supported by the Flemish *arrondissements*, and Paul Reynaud represented Dunkerque during the Fourth and Fifth Republics.[83] Little evidence can be found which suggests that they significantly altered the general pattern of politics in the region described above, which returned to 'normal' after their departure, except to heighten local awareness of the French nation and national political agendas, and to demonstrate ways for the French Flemish to be more comfortable with the idea of the republic. Boulanger in particular, through his emphatic assurance that the republic did not have to be anticlerical, but could include Catholics, foreshadowed the success of the Christian Democrats in French Flanders.[84]

From the preceding analysis, it can be stated that a characteristic conservative regional voting pattern existed in the Westhoek, for both legislative and municipal elections, which can be used to differentiate the Flemish-speakers of the Westhoek from the inhabitants of the surrounding 'red' Nord–Pas-de-Calais region by their political views.[85] When the pattern for French Flanders is set against William Brustein's general conclusions about the effect

---

[80] Pope Leo XIII instructed French Catholics to cease fighting for the monarchy and to accept the republic. This led to a movement called the 'ralliement' (rallying) which had a mixed reception in Catholic France, and was not received with equal enthusiasm throughout the country. See Robert Tombs, *France, 1814–1914*, London 1996, 456–7, for further information, and also chapter 5 below.

[81] Hilaire and others, *Atlas electoral*, 104.

[82] See Lottin, 'Les Élections législatives'.

[83] See Oddone, *Battailes*.

[84] Néré, 'Les Elections Boulanger', 262.

[85] Jacques Néré considers that that these political differences date from the *ancien régime*,

of the mode of production on widespread political opinion, several small variations emerge. Brustein believes that a region characterised principally by small landholding (as is the Westhoek) would normally be politically on the Left.[86] In this category he identifies the north-east of France, along with the south. While his conclusions may be valid for much of the north-east, the Westhoek definitely does not fit the general model. One possible explanation is that intensive agriculture and the large numbers of agricultural labourers in the region left many of the rural inhabitants without land of their own. In this respect, the Westhoek resembles more closely the west of France, with a high rural population not owning land, and voting more consistently on the Right.[87] A second explanation is the Catholicism of the region, which as a conservative force may have been a greater determining factor in the long run than the pattern of landholding. The Church's support was, if not essential, at least a significant plus in seeking elected office in the Westhoek, as it continued to have some influence in the politics of French Flanders well into the twentieth century.[88]

In spite of boasting different characteristics from those he identified for the north-east, in Brustein's expression a form of political regionalism was clearly present in the Westhoek, since the pattern of political involvement was regionally based.[89] The unusual blend of Catholicism and traditionalism with economic opportunism meant that the local political culture did not fit the national political pattern,[90] and in general the relative independence of the region from national political questions and preoccupation with the local can be interpreted as a kind of passive rupture with French national political problems. Thus a regional political culture and tradition can be added to the other regional cultural characteristics identified in the previous chapter as typifying the Westhoek, and distinguishing it not only from the rest of France, but from the remainder of the Nord–Pas-de-Calais as well.

The next step is to examine the relationship between this distinctive and identifiable regional culture and the formation of identity during the nineteenth and twentieth centuries. As discussed in the introduction, no necessary relationship exists between culture and identity, and groups and individuals at all times have different levels of identity, which can be understood as both overlapping and competing with one another.[91] The extent to which Flemish cultural and political life led to the formation of a 'Flemish'

---

when feudalism had already been more or less dismantled in the Westhoek, but in the surrounding areas was still thriving: ibid. 21–2.

[86] See Brustein, *Social origins*.

[87] See Néré, 'Les Elections Boulanger', 37, who points out that in French Flanders the farm workers were merely exploited by the *fermiers*, rather then by land-owners.

[88] Further discussion of the Church's involvement in the politics of the Westhoek is to be found in chapter 5 below.

[89] See Brustein, *Social origins*, and page 45 above.

[90] Neither Legitimist nor Orléanist, strictly speaking.

[91] See introduction, in particular the passage discussing Sahlins, *Boundaries*.

regional consciousness and identity (which may indeed have outlasted those very cultural practices) will be considered alongside the ways it was integrated into a 'French' regional and national identity through reinterpretation and change. The relationship with the rest of the Flemish community, and the extent to which the French Flemish were aware of, and identified themselves with, their cultural compatriots across the border also had a significant impact upon identity formation. Before turning to a systematic examination of the numerous active agents seeking to influence identity formation in the Westhoek, the next chapter will focus specifically upon the impact of structural changes in the economy and society.

3

Structural Change and Identity

The nineteenth and twentieth centuries brought wide-reaching changes to the economy of France and of Europe, changes which ultimately transformed the nature of work and the structures of society.[1] In the first phase, through the nineteenth century and up to the end of the Second World War, as new, more efficient and reliable transportation networks grew, population patterns began to shift from rural to urban, subsistence farming was replaced by commercial agriculture and industrial activity increased in magnitude. Even the most isolated and cut-off regions of France experienced some modification, and traditional ways of life began to change and adapt through integration into national economies. The latter half of the twentieth century saw the development and extension of the welfare state, the depopulation of the countryside and significant increases in standards of living throughout Europe. At this stage traditional ways of life were metamorphosed by the extent of economic progress. The principal objective of this chapter is to analyse the influence of the major structural changes on perceptions of identity in French Flanders, beginning with the industrialisation of the economy in the nineteenth and early twentieth centuries. It will go on to a consideration of the legal demarcation and regulation of the border separating the Westhoek from the Belgian province of West Flanders, not only as an economic and territorial limit, but also a psychological one, with particular reference to French-Flemish perceptions of it over time, and conclude with reflections upon the impact of economic changes in the second half of the twentieth century.

Early industrialisation

As mentioned briefly in chapter 1, the economy of Flanders was one of the most developed in France. The principal urban centre was the Lille industrial basin, which lay not far from, but outside, the Westhoek and saw tremendous growth during the first phase of economic development through the nineteenth and early twentieth centuries, attracting numerous workers from all directions to its factories. The most important urban area within the

---

[1]   See, for example, Jean-Charles Asselain, *Histoire économique de la France du XVIIIe siècle à nos jours*, Paris 1984; François Caron, *An economic history of modern France*, London 1979; Colin Heywood, *The development of the French economy, 1750–1914*, London 1992.

Westhoek was the port of Dunkerque, with Hazebrouck, Bergues, Wormhoudt, Steenvoorde, Cassel, Bailleul and Bourbourg-ville the major secondary centres.

The largest sector of the economy remained intensive agriculture, partly industrialised, in which some drying out of land permitted the full development of the soil; as Henri See observed in the early 1940s, 'Flemish agriculture, already advanced in the nineteenth century has conserved all of its superiority.'[2] The Flemish produced a great diversity of crops including a variety of grains (particularly wheat), legumes, roots, tubers and animal fodder, as well as increasing quantities of industrial plants such as flax, rapeseed, poppyseed, chicory, tobacco, hops and especially sugar beets. Small-scale domestic industry such as linen remained important, and brick-making, industrial food production, factory textiles and manufacturing, notably metallurgy, expanded significantly as the nineteenth century wore on.[3]

Notwithstanding its position as one of the foremost centres of production and trade in France outside Paris, natural conditions vary in quality. The Westhoek is flat, and has mediocre, sandy soil susceptible to erosion. Although large quantities of coal are nearby, no important minerals are immediately available for extraction and development.[4] The major resource of the Westhoek in the nineteenth century was its population, which combined with its strategic location put it into a favourable position for agricultural and industrial development.

Like the rest of Flanders, the Westhoek was densely populated, with 494 inhabitants per square kilometre at the turn of the twentieth century, versus 325 per square kilometre for the whole of the department.[5] With the exception of the coastal plain around Dunkerque, the Flemish-speaking *arrondissements* had actually declined in population over the course of the nineteenth century, while in the department as a whole the population was increasing, most noticeably in the *arrondissement* of Lille.[6] The Westhoek was nevertheless left with an extremely high population, which it retained throughout the first phase of economic transformation.

The land-holding pattern was dominated by small farms well into the twentieth century, which contributed to the intensity and productivity of the agriculture. In his *Voyage en France*, Ardouin-Dumazet described what he considered to be a characteristic of French Flanders:

2   Henri See, *Histoire économique de la France: les temps modernes (1789–1914)*, Paris 1942, 319.
3   See, for example, Felix-Paul Codaccioni, 'De la Prospérité impériale à la belle époque (1851–1914)', in Louis Trénard (ed.), *Histoire des Pays-Bas français: Flandre, Artois, Hainault, Boulonnais, Cambrésis*, Toulouse 1972, 424–6.
4   Ibid. 428–9; Blanchard. *La Flandre.*
5   Blanchard, *La Flandre*, 474; Fèvre and Hauser, *Régions et pays*, 34.
6   Raoul Blanchard, *La Densité de population du département du Nord au XIXe siècle: étude de dix recencements de population*, thèse présenté à la faculté des lettres, université de Lille, Lille 1906.

It is true that the property, is heavily divided up, but the owners benefit intelligently either through animal rearing or cultivation. The peasant is extremely attached to the soil, and has a level of material well-being superior to that of other areas of France, which he owes as much to his domestic virtue as to the fertility of the soil. In general the holdings do not surpass twenty hectares.[7]

High population was therefore a leading factor in the development of sophisticated, intensive agriculture, and contributed as well to industrialisation. Raoul Blanchard writes that although at one level French Flanders appears over-populated, yet it is that very excess of population which led to the development of advanced agriculture and prosperous industry in a region which is not naturally rich in terms of the soil or of the primary resources necessary for industry.[8] G. M. Triquet adds that the Flemish, in addition to their sheer numbers, had the advantage that they picked up early on new developments in domestic industry, and the possibilities of supplementing their low agricultural income through home production. Since this became an established pattern in local working culture, these Flemish were later found to be adaptable, and a good source of factory labour in larger-scale manufacturing.[9] Thus high population had preceded and helped to foster industrialisation, and was not a product of it.

In addition to its high population, the location of French Flanders was extremely favourable to industrial development. Elsewhere in the immediate vicinity coal and steel were both readily available: the larger region's mining and metallurgy sectors representing respectively 14 per cent and 17.5 per cent of the total French production at mid-century during the Second Empire.[10] The local coal also made the Nord France's leading region for the production of steam power.[11] Power consumed by the machines in the chemical and heavy industries alone in the Nord grew from 47,355 horse power in 1869 to 392,000 in 1904, well ahead of the department of the Seine which was in second position.[12]

The port of Dunkerque and the Westhoek's location on the route to Belgium, Holland and parts of northern Germany made it a strategic trading centre as well. While it is not a natural port of the first rank, Dunkerque provided access to the North Sea, and traded extensively with England, Russia, the United States, the Argentine Republic, the British East and West Indies, Australia, Spain, Algeria and Tunisia. Total cargo passing through the port grew from 133,000 tons in 1846 to 3,408,000 tons in 1908, with the principal exports in 1909 being tools and metal goods, and the principal imports

[7] Ardouin-Dumazet, *Voyage en France*, 179–180.
[8] Blanchard, *La Flandre*, 474–5.
[9] Triquet. 'Réflexion'.
[10] Codaccioni, 'De la Prospérité impériale', 431.
[11] Price, *Economic history*, 119–20.
[12] E. Levasseur, *Questions ouvrières et industrielles en France sous la Troisième République*, Paris 1907, 162.

wool, oil-yielding fruits and grains, salt, flax, cotton, cereal grains, jute and zinc.[13] Imports, with a total value of 824 million francs in 1909, significantly exceeded exports, at 156 million francs.[14] In terms of national ranking for production, the Nord was the most important producer in France of sugar, tiles, crystal and glass, beets, wheat and linen. In each of these areas, the production of the Westhoek formed an important and integral part of the departmental totals.[15]

The Westhoek was strategically located from the point of view of internal trade and traffic as well. A network of rail, roads, canals and natural waterways linked it with the interior of France and across the border to Belgium and to the Netherlands and Germany. The development of the transportation infrastructure of the region was begun early in the century, and then greatly enhanced and developed as a result of the Freycinet Plan of 1879, which improved the roads, rail and port facilities as a part of the 500 million francs-worth of projects across France.[16] Ardouin-Dumazet described the particular advantages of improved transportation links for the commune of Bailleul, the local administration of which was able to secure the paving of more than fifty kilometres of local roads before the end of the nineteenth century.[17]

In particular, the penetration of railways has often been credited with strengthening national identity and creating national cultural unity to the detriment of *patois* and other regional distinctions by integrating the regions into the national economy.[18] Road construction went hand-in-hand with the advancement of railways, since rail facilitated the transportation of higher quality road-bed material such as paving stones directly to the locality. In the context of the nineteenth century, industrialisation came more quickly to regions with a developed transportation network. According to Roger Price, 'The improvement of communications created societies more open to external influences than ever before. This was the vital factor in stimulating change.'[19] The provision of easier access to markets by road, rail and canal encouraged a conscientious shift away from subsistence towards market-oriented agriculture. Production increased beyond the levels of local demand, and productivity became relevant to individual producers. This transition took time, but was more rapid and complete in the north of France not only because of its transportation network, but also, writes Price, because it was

---

13 Idem, *Histoire du commerce de la France*, II: *De 1789 à nos jours*, Paris 1912, 695–6.
14 Ibid. 696.
15 Przybyla 'Les Députés du Nord', *RN* lxxv (July-Sept. 1993), 262.
16 See, *Histoire économique*, 290.
17 Ardouin-Dumazet, *Voyage en France*, 180.
18 See, for example, H. A. C. Collingham with R. S. Alexander, *The July Monarchy: a political history of France, 1830–1848*, London–New York 1988, 331, and Alain Plessis, *The rise and fall of the Second Empire, 1852–1871*, trans. Jonathan Mandelbaum, Cambridge 1985, 112.
19 Price, *Economic history*, 81.

already characterised by an intensive polyculture.[20] In summary, roads and rail were crucial in encouraging the trend towards centralisation, cultural as well as economic. As Weber writes, 'There could be no national unity before there was national circulation', and Flanders was one of the regions which, before the onslaught of changes in the latter half of the nineteenth century, 'were either self-contained or part of entities to which the larger entity of France was largely irrelevant'.[21]

It is not immediately obvious why an enhanced development of transportation networks would increase national consciousness, however, and promote the national integration of the Westhoek, since numerous links were also created and developed across the border into Belgium. The chief result of improved transportation was to open the economy to the outside and integrate it into market forces (both national and international in the case of the Westhoek) and to encourage the population to think of itself more clearly in relation to others.

With reference to the chronology of economic change, many of the economic necessities to industrial take-off in the Westhoek were already present or developed in the first half of the nineteenth century. In 1830, seven navigable waterways linked the Nord to Belgium, four of which were in the Westhoek with the fifth running along its boundary with the *arrondissement* of Lille.[22] There was also a well-developed interior canal and river system, by means of which it was possible to navigate from French Flanders all the way to the Seine. The railway linking Dunkerque to Paris via Hazebrouck and Lille was inaugurated on 3 September 1848, which meant that a decisive step had been taken towards breaking the isolation of the countryside.[23] The new railway made local stations into the main enterprises of the towns or villages and, according to Émile Coornaert, 'breathed new air through the area'.[24] By 1865, three rail lines crossed the border from the Westhoek into Belgium: from Dunkerque to Furnes, and from Hazebrouck direct to Ypres and via Armentières to Comines and Menin.[25] With the main lines in place by mid-century, the latter half could be devoted to constructing smaller lines providing access to the main routes for otherwise marginalised towns and villages. J. Fèvre and H. Hauser wrote that what distinguished the Nord from the rest of France was its development of small railways of local interest.[26] They also considered that the region had a head-start in industrialisation

[20] Ibid.
[21] Weber, *Peasants into Frenchmen*, 218.
[22] Roger Price, *The modernisation of rural France: communications networks and agricultural market structures in nineteenth-century France*, London 1983, 14.
[23] Coornaert, *La Flandre française*, 301.
[24] Ibid. 300.
[25] *Carte des chemins de fer de la Belgique et des pays limitrophes*, prepared by A. Vuillemin, Paris 1865.
[26] Fèvre and Hauser, *Régions et pays*, 32.

because of the development there of weaving, dating back as far the Middle Ages.

To underline the early advance of industry in the north, the editor of the *Annuaire du département du Nord* wrote in 1829 of the extent to which the industrial and commercial resources of the region had been developed, especially in the area of cotton spinning.[27] The early opening up of the economy and the debut of industrial activity meant that the effects of industrialisation on rural societies in the latter half of the nineteenth century were that much stronger.

Many of the economic changes in the preceding paragraphs describe the Nord as a whole, of which French Flanders formed only a part, but are nevertheless accurate descriptions of the Westhoek. The effects of a high population density spawning agricultural innovation and the need to supplement farm activity with domestic production of goods such as linen were especially strong. The larger industrial activity, mining and heavy industry centred for the most part around the Lille–Roubaix–Tourcoing agglomeration, and was less significant in the rural regions of the *arrondissements* of Hazebrouck and Dunkerque.

Industrial growth and activity was not completely unknown in the Westhoek itself. Dunkerque developed rapidly, as did some other cities and towns, particularly those on the main rail line. Hazebrouck, although connected by rail from 1848, first experienced major changes in 1876 when mechanised spinning and weaving mills were opened in the city.[28] In numerous smaller centres scattered throughout the Westhoek industries such as mechanical spinning and weaving mills, lace-makers, distilleries, breweries, flour mills, marble workers, and tile-, brick-, glass- and drain-makers had already taken hold in the early Third Republic, and employed hundreds of workers.[29] Ten years later in many of the centres the number of workers in industry had increased substantially.[30] Changes were also marked in the production of industrial crops such as sugar beets, and the coming of the railway and increased reliance on trade outside of the region.

In spite of the flexibility of the Flemish rural economy, in the latter half of the nineteenth century population pressure in Flanders grew at a rate such that many were forced to quit the land and migrate in search of work.[31]

[27] *Annuaire du département du Nord* (1829), 334–6, repr. in Louis Trénard (ed.), *Histoire des Pays-Bas français: documents: Flandre, Artois, Hainault, Boulonnais, Cambrésis*, Toulouse 1974, 305–7.

[28] Coornaert, *La Flandre française*, 433.

[29] 'Etat des industries 1873, arrondissement d'Hazebrouck', by commune, ADN, M 653 41.

[30] See ibid. and Néré, 'Les Elections Boulanger', who gives the numbers of workers per commune in 1885 at pp. 23–30. The number of industrial workers in Bailleul, for example, increased by more than 50% between 1873 and 1885.

[31] Note that the rural population and average population density did not decline over the nineteenth and early twentieth centuries; it was the surplus population that was migrating.

Describing the nature of the urbanisation process in Flanders, Els Witte writes that at the end of the nineteenth century French Flanders was still among the least urbanised regions of Europe, and that the decreasing number of small villages did not lead to expansion in the larger agglomerations, but went to profit the medium-sized centres within the Westhoek.[32] In this way the countryside was able to preserve its dominant position. Hazebrouck is a typical example, having increased in population from 6,600 in 1801 to 11,332 in 1886.[33] While on the one hand this indicates growth of more than 70 per cent, while the *arrondissement* as a whole only increased by 11 per cent over the same period,[34] in terms of numbers it is evident that Witte's description is accurate. Urbanisation in the Westhoek took the form of the limited growth of medium-sized towns such as Hazebrouck and Dunkerque, and slightly smaller ones such as Bergues, Wormhoudt, Steenvoorde, Cassel, Bailleul and Hondschoote.

Although it is outside the Westhoek, the shift of population to Lille needs to be treated as a separate case. This movement can essentially be regarded as out-migration, leaving the Westhoek more or less intact, and not affecting its internal make-up and patterns. Lille itself cannot be considered solely a 'French-Flemish' urban area, since its population was drawn from all sides, including the other *arrondissements* of the Nord, Pas-de-Calais, Belgian Flanders, Wallonia and Picardy, resulting in a culturally mixed population speaking a variety of languages and *patois*.[35] This meant that French became the language of use, and linguistic assimilation was much more common in the urban setting. Exclusively Flemish neighbourhoods did, however, exist, particularly in Roubaix, but these were most often expatriate mixes of Flemish-speakers from various parts of Belgium as well as from French Flanders. Thus, although not uniquely 'French-Flemish', the possibility of the formation of a culturally-oriented Flemish community spirit, consciousness or identity existed within the urban setting in Lille during the growth phase of the nineteenth and early twentieth century.

The Westhoek, albeit transformed by progress towards market-oriented agriculture and the increase in magnitude of small industries, was a particularly marked example of the longest possible survival of a traditional society based on intensive agriculture. The symbolic role of the land in the life of the Flemish remained important, and they sought to remain on the land as long as possible, often supplementing earnings from a very small holding with the home labour that had been going on for centuries, or with part-time or

---

32 Witte, 'Une Flandre appauvrie', 181–2.
33 E. Levasseur, *La Population française: histoire de la population avant 1789 et démographie de la France comparée à celles des autres nations au XIXe siècle*, Paris 1889, i. 413.
34 Ibid. i. 449n.
35 There are no statistics for the migration of Flemish-speakers from French Flanders to Lille, nor of their total possible numbers. The only figures available are those based on nationality, which indicate the numbers of Belgians, rather than Flemish-speakers.

seasonal work in the nearest factories in the 'medium sized local centres'. The advanced state of agriculture and the proximity of medium-sized centres with access to markets through railway and other links were of course crucial in permitting so many people to remain attached to their land, and to resist urbanisation for as long as possible. The highly developed state of this type of semi-industrial rural economy in the Westhoek, relative to other parts of the country, accounts for the lengthy survival there of more traditional economic patterns.

A supporter of the traditional economic integration model, Pierre Bonnaud describes the links between these types of agrarian societies and the tenacity of their regional culture, arguing that cultural geography is fundamentally a question of the ways in which different groups attach themselves to the soil via agriculture.[36] In other words, it is ultimately divergent agricultural traditions which lead to regional cultural differences. In this way, in spite of the profound economic changes of the nineteenth and early twentieth centuries, conditions for the survival in the Westhoek of Flemish language and culture remained favourable, because of the particularity of the region's agrarian traditions.

Thus while the entire structure of the economy was transformed, the basic cultural lifestyle in French Flanders was not. The bulk of the French Flemish were able to remain on the land by adapting their agriculture to commercial and industrial crops and supplementing their farm income with other sources as much as possible, rather than by migrating permanently to the cities. An economic structure which permitted the persistence of traditional Flemish culture comes as no surprise, given the findings of chapter 1 which showed that although bilingualism increased, cultural practices in daily life remained relatively unaltered.

For the first phase of the transition at least, economic progress on both the group and individual levels was not linked to cultural change or assimilation. To argue that without French the Westhoek would remain backward, and the Flemish would not have any jobs was, as the archbishop of Cambrai wrote to the rector of the Academy of Douai, not to know anything about French Flanders, which as has been shown was prosperous and advanced when compared with most other regions of France.[37] Few purely economic changes in this period increased the motivation to learn French for reasons of perceived social mobility. For those who remained in the Westhoek, with its high rural population and relatively stable way of life, social mobility could be in part linked to French, in part to education in general (by no means a new phenomenon), but principally to adaptability in production, wages and opportunities for work.

[36] Bonnaud, 'Terres et langages', 16.
[37] Archbishop of Cambrai to rector, 22 Oct. 1866, AN, F 19 5798.

Thus the industrial revolution of the nineteenth and early twentieth centuries had profound effects on the nature of economic activity, and the structure and orientation of work and trade for the Flemish-speaking population of France, but in terms of both culture and the development of identity, the French Flemish remained largely unaffected by the changes.[38] While contact and ease of communication with other regions increased, trade and economic contacts were as much international as national, and brought the French Flemish as much into contact with the Belgian Flemish as with other areas of France. The economic changes, however, increased the importance of the Franco-Belgian border as a legal and psychological limit. This merits specific consideration.

The Franco-Belgian border

Changing perceptions of the Franco-Belgian border through the nineteenth and twentieth centuries were significant for the formation of identity in French Flanders. Communication and relations between the two population groups spanning the boundary, cross-border movement and contacts, as well as the economic role of the border as a tariff barrier all influenced group definitions. The strength of feeling with respect to the border's practical and psychological importance is a good gauge of the strength of national identity in the region.

One hypothetical answer to the question why the French Flemish were assimilated into France, while at the same time in Belgium (also a would-be francophone state at this time) the Belgian Flemish rose to new heights of regional 'Flemish' consciousness, concerns the isolation of the French Flemish within France. A small minority with little contact with other Flemish-speakers, did they figuratively turn their backs on the border? On the contrary, the long-standing attitude of the local inhabitants was that borders, if not arbitrary, were not natural either, having been established by convention between states, with the potential for change as new conventions were established.[39] The bottom line was that such borders were of little interest to local inhabitants, and could simply be ignored from the point of view of daily activities; unhindered crossing was viewed as a right, since it had always been so.[40] A. Lorbert, writing in 1918, claimed that if a border is too often a 'Great Wall of China jealously guarded and difficult to cross', then the border

---

38 See also Vanhyfte and Wagret, Un Village flamand.

39 See Sébastien Dubois, Les Bornes immuables de l'etat: la rationalisation du tracé des frontières au siècle des lumières (France, Pays-Bas autrichiens et principauté de Liège), Heule 1999, 412.

40 See Girard D'Albissin, Genèse de la frontière, 365–6; Judith Martin-Desmidt, 'Souverainetés et sociétés: la vie de la frontière du Nord au XVIIIe siècle', DFN/LPBF xxiv (1999), 162; Dubois, Les Bornes immuables, 420.

between French and Belgian Flanders did not fit the description at all, since it was breached by numerous road, rail and water links and separated neither economic interests nor the populations.[41] Lorbert goes on to say that deep feelings of warmth and friendship existed between the people of French Flanders and their brothers across the border, founded upon 'ethnic characteristics, morals, mentalities and a similar way of life'.[42] A series of 'Friendship books' were written which contained articles by several authors concerning France and Belgium, and 'expressing the secular friendship which exists between the two countries'.[43] In many cases tolerance permitted even the local representatives of national authorities only loosely to respect the border; police and *gendarmes* from both countries made arrests on the other side, and were occasionally even thanked for having done so.[44]

Ease of crossing, familiarity, friendliness and identification between the two groups of Flemish on either side of the border did not, however, empty the border entirely of meaning for the French Flemish. Development of a specifically 'French' identity can be linked to the extent to which the Franco-Belgian border entered into the consciousness of the French Flemish, and was perceived by them as a real indication of a differentiation between them and the inhabitants of West Flanders on the other side.[45]

As mentioned briefly in chapter 1, the current border took its form from the Treaty of Courtrai (Kortrijk) in 1820, which defined in precise terms the exact demarcation of the division. It was arbitrary in character and occasionally split individual farms, and it was not an effective barrier to the movement of people.

Throughout the nineteenth and the early part of the twentieth centuries social contact remained close between the Flemish-speaking populations, almost as though the border did not exist. The frequency of cross-border marriages is a good indicator of the extent of social interaction between the two communities. Frank Logie, in comparing intermarriage rates with the rates of immigration from Belgium to France, shows that between 1881–5 and 1926–30 the rate of mixed marriages, already high in the 1880s, increased while immigration decreased. In the inter-war period, from the point of view of social relations, he concludes that the border played only a symbolic role.[46] By the 1970s, however, the level of cross-border marriages had declined sharply, which indicated that by that time the border had begun to act as a brake on social interaction. In another paper discussing cross-border social

---

[41] A. Lorbert, *La France au travail: la région du Nord (Nord–Pas-de-Calais–Somme–Aisne)*, Paris 1927, 93.

[42] Ibid.

[43] Prefect to minister of the interior, 5 Jan. 1921 (describing regionalist activities in the Nord), ADN, M 154 318.

[44] Lentacker, *La Frontière franco-belge*, 33.

[45] See Baycroft, 'Changing identities', 417–38.

[46] Frank Logie, 'Grens en sociale relaties: huwelijkskringen als voorbeeld van de sociale invloed van staats grenzen', *DFN/LPBF* xi (1986), 46–58.

contact, it was shown that the 'rate of nuptiality' in several border communities declined from 22.4 per cent in 1900–5 to 12.3 per cent in 1967–77.[47] With reference to the present, the authors write that the political border has begun to act as a brake upon social relations with respect not only to marriages, but also to cross-border visits to friends and family.[48] These findings have been confirmed by Susan Cotts Watkins, whose comparative regional study of demographic patterns across Europe has shown that indicators of demographic behaviour such as age of marriage, marital fertility and rates of illegitimacy became increasingly 'national' between 1870 and 1960, those within the same boundaries behaving increasingly alike, differing from those in neighbouring nations.[49] In summary it can be said that up until the time of the Second World War a great deal of cross-border contact was preserved between the two Flemish communities, and that it declined sharply thereafter.

In addition to pure social contact, relations were also maintained through organised movements and societies which had membership and a following on both sides of the border. There were links, for example, between the socialist parties of Belgium and France, which exchanged pamphlets and speakers to further promote their movement.[50] There were also the Flemish learned societies, some of which later developed into *flamingant* groups, with branches on both sides of the border.[51]

It can be concluded that social interaction across the Flemish-speaking part of the Franco-Belgian border was extremely common throughout the nineteenth century, continuing into the twentieth century, but then declined sharply by the 1970s. This continued contact up to the Second World War meant that the Flemish of the Westhoek did not lose touch with their linguistic compatriots across the Belgian border, and that any strengthening of a purely French identity occurred in spite of these ties, and not for a lack of them.

At the level of professional contact between the two groups of Flemish, the permanent, seasonal, weekly and daily migration of workers was substantial and has been the subject of numerous studies. In spite of the desire to remain on their land, the significant over-population of Flanders forced many of the Belgian Flemish to seek work elsewhere, particularly around Lille and other areas of northern France. They went to France seeking factory work or general labour as it was available. The first wave began after the crisis of 1845, when the domestic linen industry in Belgium began to suffer from increased

---

47 Yola Verhasselt, Frank Logie and Bernadette Mergaerts, 'Espace géographique et formes sociabilité: quatre exemples de régions frontalières', *RN* lxiv (Apr.–June 1982), 594.
48 Ibid. 595.
49 Watkins, *From provinces into nations*, 168. See also pp. 134–6 for more on Flanders.
50 See Hilden, *Working women*; ADN, M 154 317–18. More will be said about co-operation between trade unionists and socialists in chapter 6 below.
51 For more on the *flamingant* groups and cross-border contacts see chapter 7 below.

competition because of mechanisation. At this stage it was mostly permanent immigration, with seasonal workers remaining at low or medium levels.[52]

Seasonal migration increased dramatically after the war of 1870–1. Belgian workers, often in work gangs, came principally to the north of France as agricultural labourers and brick-makers.[53] The intensive nature of the cultivation of sugar beets in particular required seasonal labourers and the Belgian Flemish were pleased to have work. They were referred to as 'Franschmans', which ironically is Flemish for 'Frenchmen', and often went repeatedly, year after year, to the same place in France, occasionally even passing the tradition on from father to son. Their destinations were principally in the north of France, but some made it further south.[54] Occasionally newspapers would devote articles to events back in Belgium to keep them informed, and a small French–Flemish lexicon was distributed to many of the *Franschmans* in 1900 in order to ease their passage in France.[55] It was even the case that Flemish-speaking priests would undertake the journey into France, in order to guarantee the *Franschmans* at least an occasional mass in Flemish.[56]

Edmond Ronse included among their reasons for coming, higher wages,[57] the industrialisation of agriculture in France which required more agricultural workers (particularly the labour intensive harvesting of sugar beets), the absence of natural borders or impediments and the consequent ease of the route, migration as a symbolic rite of passage, the opportunity for younger men to escape parental surveillance, and the underlying desire to acquire property of their own back home eventually.[58] Seasonal migration was the best route available in view of this final goal because they maintained contact with the home region while at the same time earning the necessary money which was not available in Belgium. Many returned year after year to the same location in France, since the conditions of work and remuneration were familiar to both workers and *patrons*, usually spelled out in seasonal contracts detailing the work to be done as well as the method of payment. Ronse estimated the total numbers of seasonal migrants each year to have varied between 40,000 and 60,000 in the period preceding 1913, although accurate measurement is difficult due to a lack of control and monitoring at the time.[59]

---

[52] Edmond Ronse, *L'Emigration saisonnière belge*, Gand 1913, 36.
[53] Luc Schepens, 'Émigration saisonnière et émigration définitive en Flandre occidentale au XIXe siècle', *RN* lvi (July–Sept. 1974), 429.
[54] Ronse, *Emigration saisonnaire belge*, 35.
[55] 'Voor de "Franschmans" ', *Het Vlaamsch Kruis: voor de Flamingen van Frankrijk*, 30 May 1900, 2.
[56] 'De Franschmans', ibid. 8 Mar. 1898, 1.
[57] Wages were three times higher before the First World War, declining subsequently: Bert Woestenborghs, 'Vlaamse seizoenarbeiders in Nord-Frankrijk, 1880–1970', *DFN/LPBF* xxiv (1999), 112.
[58] Ronse, *L'Emigration saisonnaire belge*, 36.
[59] Ibid. 70. He was supported in this view by Blanchard, who estimated that 57,000 Belgian workers came to France in 1898: *La Flandre*, 515.

The numbers of seasonal migrants varied little between 1870 and 1920,[60] reached a peak in 1950 at 80,000, and declined rapidly thereafter to several thousand in the mid-1970s, and 1,046 in 1997.[61]

With improvements in transportation, the length of stay in France could be more easily reduced, and by 1900 weekly or even daily commuting to factories and workshops was commonplace.[62] Several border communities grew substantially, permitting even easier daily access. Some factory-owners even organised their own buses to aid in the transportation of workers across the border,[63] and the Belgian government offered special train fares at reduced rates to the border.[64] Others came by bicycle, 'mixing in with those coming from the French villages'.[65] The crossing of the border from Belgium into France was unrestricted until the introduction of the *carte du travail* in 1929, accounting in part for the facility of this movement. In 1893 a law was passed requiring the registration of foreigners at the local town or city hall, but for many years this law was not properly observed.[66] That and other regulations such as the Franco-Belgian Convention of 1910 seem to have been designed more to monitor, than to restrict the crossing of the border.[67] Even the free transfer of livestock by a farmer from his fields on one side to his fields on the other side was not restricted until 1908, and in 1912 a farmer was still quite easily able to obtain permission to continue doing so 'after completing the necessary formalities'.[68] Furthermore, any farmer with land on both sides within five kilometres from the border was allowed to move his materials and produce back and forth without restriction.[69]

---

60 Schepens, 'Émigration saisonnière', 429.
61 Verhasselt, Logie and Mergaerts, 'Espace géographique', 598; P. Flatres, 'L'Évolution de l'agriculture dans la région du Nord', *HTN* (1964.1), 12; Woestenborghs, 'Vlaamse seizoenarbeiders', 110; Nele Depestel and Tanja Termote, 'Grensarbeid tussen West-Vlaanderen en Frankrijk', *DFN/LPBF* xxiv (1999), 117. During the 1990s the general trend reversed, and the numbers living in France and working in Belgium increased from several hundred in the 1970s and 1980s to more than 2,000 through the 1990s. The number of seasonal workers given varies between the study of Verhasselt, Logie and Mergaerts on the one hand, and that of Woestenborghs and Depestel-Termote on the other, especially in the period immediately following the Second World War. Verhasselt's figure of 80,000 has been employed, rather than those given by the others which are a great deal lower, since the latter studies seem to restrict the geographical area of provenance and work destination, and therefore do not include all the workers crossing the border.
62 See J. Theys, 'De evolutie van de grensarbeid tussen West Vlaanderen en Noord-Frankrijk in de 20ste eeuw', *DFN/LPBF* xiii (1988), 89–104.
63 F. Lentacker, 'Les Frontaliers belges travaillant en France: caractères et fluctuations d'un courant de main d'oeuvre', *RN* xxxii (1950), 133.
64 Blanchard, *La Flandre*, 515.
65 Lorbert, *La France au travail*, 93.
66 Georges Eeckhout, 'Les Ouvriers belges dans le Nord', *Revue sociale catholique* iv (1 June 1900), 268–9.
67 See ADN, 1 W 1094.
68 'Le Bétail belge en France', *Le Patriote des Flandres: journal de Steenvoorde et de l'arrondissement d'Hazebrouck*, 14 Apr. 1912.
69 Lentacker, *La Frontière franco-belge*, 34–5.

While many Belgian workers were travelling to the Nord, including to the Westhoek, a handful from the Westhoek were also engaged in daily commuting into the Pas-de-Calais. Raoul Blanchard wrote that in 1906 fifty workers per day left the village of Steenbecque for the coal mines, and fifty more for the steel mills, while 300 made the journey from Hazebrouck to Berquette and Béthune.[70] Some travelled by train, others by tram, while those in the southern section of the Lys valley could walk. The incentive for such French-Flemish miners was the superior salary paid by the mines, almost double that of weavers remaining in the Westhoek. Blanchard writes that these commuters were very content with the situation 'and feared nothing so much as strikes'.[71]

As commuting became more and more commonplace towards the end of the nineteenth century, permanent immigration declined. By 1906 Blanchard noted that it had significantly decreased, given the possibility of seasonal or daily migration which was much preferable to the Flemish, allowing them to remain relatively close to their home villages and preserving hopes of being able to return permanently.[72]

In spite of the decline of permanent immigration, Belgian residents in the Nord still formed a notable presence, living and working in industry, on the land and as domestic servants.[73] At the turn of the century almost 200,000 foreigners resided in the *département du Nord*, the vast majority Belgians.[74] J. Dewachter concluded that the arrival of so many French and Belgian Flemish in all the industrial areas of Dunkerque and Hazebrouck would certainly have had the effect of retarding the progress of the French language in the area.[75]

French immigration into Belgium was considerably less common during the nineteenth and twentieth centuries, although it did occur. In some cases political refuge was the goal. Numerous religious congregations moved across the border after the separation of the Church and State in France in 1905, and others went merely because the cost of living was lower. Some temporary migration of workers did occur, but not in anything like the numbers of Belgians working in France.[76]

It can be concluded, therefore, that 'intense' social relations were maintained across the Flemish-speaking part of the Franco-Belgian border throughout the nineteenth century which continued into the mid-twentieth, after which they then declined sharply. This decline occurred at the same time as the decline in cross-border commuting – after the Second World War.

If the border was no impediment to the movement of people, it did have a

---

[70] Blanchard, *La Flandre*, 10.
[71] Ibid.
[72] Ibid. 518.
[73] See Eeckhout, 'Les Ouvriers belges'.
[74] Fèvre and Hauser, *Régions et pays*, 36.
[75] Dewachter, 'Le Flamand et le français', 107.
[76] See Lentacker, *La Frontière franco-belge*, 256–61, 290–1.

role as a tariff barrier. When Belgium was founded in 1830, some question arose of setting up a free trading zone with France, which in the end was effectively blocked by other European powers who feared too much French domination in the new country, and by some manufacturers on both sides who feared competition.[77] This meant that, in the extremely protectionist nineteenth century, the industries of the north of France benefited from cheap, plentiful labour and were not subjected to Belgian competition for French markets. Although trade was liberated for the final decade of the Second Empire, and many in France became free-traders as the century wore on due to the possibility of American markets, the human landscape of industries in France with dormitory towns across the border in Belgium had already been firmly established.[78] In spite of a call from some quarters for lower tariffs, yet more were implemented in 1892 as a response to an agricultural depression, which led to incredible growth in the northern region. The effects of renewed protectionism saw 'the Belgians hordes arrive, and factories and workers' dwellings spring up out of the ground'.[79]

The tariffs, designed for the protection of agriculture and certain industries, did not, however, prevent a great deal of trade or investment between the two countries: the French figures for imports and exports with Belgium rose from 101.5 and 48.5 million francs, respectively, in 1846, to 315.5 and 295 million in 1869 and to 439 and 903 million in 1909.[80] Although it is difficult to measure the exact level of cross-border investment in the region, a business network developed 'for whom the border made little sense'.[81] The existence of tariffs influenced the location of industry within the larger Franco-Belgian zone, however, as the manufacturers and industrialists, ever adjusting their prices and concerned with competition and international circulation, sought to place their factories in the optimum location.

The extremely protectionist tariff policy meant that industries in the north of France benefited from cheap, plentiful labour and were not subjected to Belgian competition for French markets. This was the first instance of a difference coinciding with the border which could be felt and understood directly by the inhabitants of the region on either side of the border. Wages were higher in France, as was the cost of living in general, factors which contributed to the migrational structure of the workforce.[82] While not particularly sensitive to the presence of a tariff, the farmers and workers of Flanders were very well aware of the resulting discrepancy in wages and prices. The difference could also be evidenced in certain outward signs such as the kind of

---

[77] Levasseur, *Histoire du commerce de la France*, 785.
[78] For a discussion of the impact of tariffs on the industry and people of the north of France and Belgium see Blanchard, *La Flandre*, 399–401.
[79] Ibid. 401.
[80] Levasseur, *Histoire du commerce de la France*, 787. For a discussion of the importance of trade between France and Belgium see pp. 785–8.
[81] Lentacker, *La Frontière franco-belge*, 188.
[82] See Roger Dion, *Les Frontières de la France*, Paris 1947, 104.

bread regularly consumed in the two regions. Chris Vandenbroeke describes rye bread, or whole grain wheat or mixed grain bread as the standard fare of the Belgian Flemish: 'Only in the Westhoek and in the households of the rich dykeland farmers was white or half-white bread regularly served.'[83]

Although the border acquired a real meaning for the first time through its representation of a change in wage and price levels, this did not mean that the Flemish began to think of themselves as different from their brothers and sisters on the other side of the border. As we have seen, social contact remained close, and migration for work contributed, if anything, to the high rate of cross-border marriage. It meant that the inhabitants of the north began to identify with the French state, the state that was responsible for setting the tariffs, and 'protecting' them.

The role of the border as a barrier to the passage of goods, rather than alienating the people on either side, actually served to bring them into even closer contact through illegal smuggling, which created a 'mentality of solidarity and cohesion' in the border zone, acting as a 'veritable link between the populations officially separated by an international border'.[84]

Smuggling reached a peak in the inter-war period.[85] Quantities varied from the very small-time to large-scale operations, and included among the merchandise grocery goods, coffee, sugar, eggs, salt, beans, matches, tobacco, bread and even livestock – chickens, cows, horses and sheep.[86] There were naturally customs authorities and patrols, but the border was so open and frequently crossed that it was difficult to properly supervise and regulate in order to prevent the smuggling. Maurice Houvenaghel writes that although some of the customs officials were given to accepting drinks at the local *estaminet* in exchange for turning a blind eye in some directions, they had developed an elaborate system to try to catch the smugglers. Customs men were often locals who knew the region well, and were aware of the possible routes and various tricks employed by the smugglers. They would hide in a field along the border at night, taking turns sleeping on a portable cot, while the other watched and listened with his dog for the slightest sound or movement which might betray the smuggler.[87]

The smugglers usually had a base associated with one of the many *estaminets* of the border region, and used all manner of means to transport goods across the divide. They developed special packs with straps over each shoulder, the goods distributed in front and behind in small compartments. These packs had special catches which could be released in a second if the

---

83 Chris Vandenbroeke, *Sociale geschiedenis van het Vlaamse Volk*, Leuven 1984, 153.
84 Verhasselt, Logie and Mergaerts, 'Espace géographique', 598.
85 See Albert Deveyer, *La Flandre d'autrefois*, Dunkerque 1985, 127–37. For investigations into the smuggling of bread see ADN, M 149/36, which contains several reports about the difficulties of controlling such activity during the inter-war period.
86 Ibid; Ardouin-Dumazet, *Voyage en France*, 39.
87 Houvenaghel, *Boeschepe*, 59–60, 127–34.

chase got too close and the smuggler wished to avoid being caught with the goods on him. Albert Deveyer describes the techniques of the tobacco 'blauwers' as having to run and jump hedges, often stopping in a farm to hide his goods in the hay or feed of one of the barns, sleeping nearby. In this way, if he were caught, he could claim to be merely looking for work. When he departed, he would always leave a small sack of tobacco as a recompense, although the farmers as a rule would never reveal what they knew, since in these small communities it always leaked out who had been squealing.[88] Smugglers often had dogs with them, trained from an early age to hate anyone who wore a uniform. Some of the smugglers actually trained their dogs to wear packs and make the run themselves without involving any humans at all. In one case the smugglers used one of two cars with identical registration numbers, which gave them a perfect alibi when the car was apprehended at one border point, and the owner could therefore not be traced.

The motive for smuggling was pure gain, rather than any thrill of outwitting the authorities. In the tobacco trade, on one run carrying fifteen kilograms (the average was between twelve and eighteen) the smuggler could make a profit of 375 French francs. By way of comparison, the average farm labourer earned 370 francs per month (in addition to full room and board) which made smuggling an obvious temptation.[89] The exchange rate helped to contribute to the discrepancy in prices after World War One, especially during the 1930s. The depression hit Belgium particularly hard, and the rate of exchange went as high as 193 Belgian francs for 100 French francs.[90]

In summary, smuggling did two things in terms of the border: on the one hand it increased contact and cooperation between the Flemish living on either side, but on the other it reinforced the existence of the border in local consciousness. This *prise de conscience* of the border as a meaningful dividing line was slow in coming, and in spite of the continued social interaction between them, awareness of at least a nominal difference between the two populations became increasingly apparent in the early twentieth century. Perhaps some rivalry did exist on the level of competition for jobs between the two groups, but relations between the seasonal workers known as the *Franschmans* and the farmers who hired them were excellent. The fact that they had a label meant that at some level they were aware of a difference between the two groups, small though it may have been. The same can be said for the word *Belge*, which came to have negative connotations in French in later years. The French living in the border region also made the distinction between 'Belgian' and 'foreigner', the latter coming to signify southern Europeans and north Africans.[91] The Belgians were at the same time familiar

---

88 Deveyer, *La Flandre d'autrefois*, 132.
89 Ibid. 128.
90 See ibid.
91 For more on the perception of foreigners see Paul Lawrence, Timothy Baycroft and

as well as foreign. Sometimes to refer to Belgians, the French merely used the words 'them' as opposed to 'us'.[92] In one case this kind of thinking led a group of French villagers to accuse the inhabitants of a Belgian community across the border of stealing wood and chopping down trees, lacking any evidence which could justify their suspicion.[93] Rivalry on the job front did also occasionally manifest itself in a direct confrontation between the 'French' and the 'Belgian' workers, but not with extremely serious results.[94]

The perception of the difference, and the slight economic advantage of the French-Flemish region, led them to be proud of the difference between themselves and their Belgian Flemish neighbours. Thus all the while remaining on the best of terms socially, the French Flemish began to look down somewhat on their Belgian neighbours (hence the origin of Belgian jokes). It became derogatory to say to one of the French Flemish 'you are a Belgian, a Fleming from Belgium − back across the border'.[95] This perceived difference, marked by the border, served to reduce the possibility of a Flemish movement catching on, specifically a movement designed to demonstrate and cultivate the common aspects of their culture, and stress the unity of the two groups.[96]

Living next to a border across which invasion forces periodically swept, especially during the wars of the twentieth century, helped to accentuate a sense of Frenchness among the French Flemish.[97] Memories of foreign enemies and feelings of dependency upon the rest of France for defence from aggression were an encouragement to stress belonging to the nation, which represented greater safety. Since the enemy was not immediately across the border, feelings of risk did not increase the local sense of the border and divide them from the Belgian Flemish, however, since the two groups were equally subject to the misery of invasion.

The role of reconstruction and the manner in which it was carried out after the end of the First and Second World Wars also contributed to a sense of French identity in French Flanders. The damage which the wars inflicted was extensive, and it was clear relatively early on that funding for the recon-

Carolyn Grohmann, ' "Degrees of foreignness" and the construction of identity in French border regions during the inter-war period', *Contemporary European History* x (2001), 51–71.

92 See Verhasselt, Logie and Mergaerts, 'Espace géographique', 593.

93 Lentacker, *La Frontière franco-belge*, 33–4.

94 See ADN, M 624 6, which provides the example of a minor conflict among port workers in Dunkerque.

95 See Em. Lobbeday, *vicaire générale* of Cambrai, to the director of the *Direction général des cultes*, 24 July 1902, AN, F 19 5502, where Mgr Lobbeday tries to explain why the Flemish language is not a threat to French national unity.

96 Some of the Flemish leaders had hoped that this would happen through the pan-Netherlands movement. See chapter 7 below.

97 See Marc Blancpain, *La Vie quotidienne dans la France du Nord sous les occupations (1814–1944)*, Paris 1983

struction was coming from Paris.[98] Local politicians devoted time and energy to lobbying the central government for further financial support in rebuilding their region, and it was extremely clear to the French Flemish that the rebuilding was being carried out and paid for by France, just as the war had been about defending France. The need to lobby the national government drew the inhabitants of the region closer to national politics, and the dependency upon national institutions for regional reconstruction had the effect of reinforcing the 'French' aspect of their identity.[99]

Thus it was less the economic modernisation which came with industrialisation during the nineteenth and early twentieth centuries *per se* that influenced identity formation in French Flanders, but rather the way the economic changes altered perceptions of the Franco-Belgian border. Through its role as a tariff barrier, the border created spatial differences in wages and prices to which the residents of the region were sensitive, and came slowly to represent a dividing line, separating two identifiable groups. Little differentiated the two societies socially and culturally, however, and they continued to speak the same language, engage in the same form of traditional agriculture, attend the same Church and interact with one another on a social level. From the middle of the twentieth century, additional structural changes to the economy further strengthened the nascent identity of difference, and also had an impact upon cultural practices.

Economic progress in the twentieth century

The end of the Second World War marked the beginning of the second phase of the modernisation of the economy. Beginning with what became known in France as the 'thirty glorious years', followed by twenty-five years of economic crises alternating with further years of growth, this phase entailed more substantial population shifts, significant increases in standard of living, the creation of the welfare state and the development of new economic conditions no longer as compatible with traditional lifestyles described above.[100]

The rural population of the Westhoek remained extremely high throughout the nineteenth and early twentieth centuries, but during the second half

---

[98] For a description of damage see Jean Lestocquoy, *Histoire de la Flandre et de l'Artois*, Paris 1966, 113–14, and Jean-Marie Perret, *L'Usinor-Dunkerque ou l'espoir déçu des flammands*, Dunkerque 1978, 7.

[99] See Lawrence, Baycroft and Grohmann, ' "Degrees of foreignness" ', for more about the strengthening of national identity through dependency upon the central government during the inter-war period. See also chapter 7 below.

[100] For more on the French economy in the twentieth century see Asselain, *Histoire économique de la France*, ii; R. F. Kuisel, *Capitalism and the state in modern France: renovation and economic management in the twentieth century*, Cambridge 1981; and M. Lévy-Leboyer and J-C. Casanova (eds), *Entre l'Etat et le marché: l'économie française des années 1880 à nos jours*, Paris 1991.

of the twentieth century similar population levels were no longer sustainable on the land, and population density declined significantly. With well over 400 inhabitants per square kilometre in the early twentieth century, the Westhoek declined to just over 100 by the 1975,[101] at the same time as population density for the *départment* of the Nord as a whole continued to rise.[102] The distribution pattern within the Westhoek remained relatively similar to what has already been described – semi-urbanised – with a large number of medium-sized centres.[103]

The flight from the land in the second half of the twentieth century can be attributed to the genuine modernisation of agriculture and changes in agricultural techniques, a trend common to other regions of France as well.[104] Roger Price, in his book on modernisation demonstrates that in spite of substantial change, French agriculture as a whole remained labour-intensive until well into the twentieth century, and that it was only after the Second World War that 'the advantages of mechanisation and fertilisation became sufficiently clear, and the exodus from the countryside sufficiently great to overcome finally the economic and subjective "cost-advantages" of labour-intensive agriculture'.[105] Innovations such as the tractor, as well as more capital-intensive new techniques of farming were vital to the large-scale transformation of the Flemish countryside.[106]

Accompanying the modernisation of agriculture in this period were two other major structural changes in the economy: the active participation of the state through economic planning and the development of the welfare state, and significantly increased levels of prosperity and material well-being. State economic planning and the dependency of the economy upon state spending accentuated the reliance of the regions upon the centre which had begun earlier with respect to the tariff question.[107] Increased state involvement, especially through the expansion of the welfare state, also brought each

101 Thumerelle, *La Population*, ii. 432–3, 454–9. See also Roland Nistri and Claude Prêcheur, *La Région du Nord et du Nord-Est*, Paris 1965, 10–11, for a map and more detail on the population density of the region.
102 Thumerelle, *La Population*, i. 100.
103 Ibid. ii. 433.
104 See idem, 'La Population rurale de la région du Nord d'après le recensement de 1968', *HTN* (1973.2), 15, and Kenneth Mouré, 'The French economy since 1930', in Martin S. Alexander (ed.), *French history since Napoleon*, London 1999, 373, who provides statistics for employment in agriculture for the whole of France.
105 Price, *Modernisation of rural France*, 394–5. See also Christiane Foutrien, 'L'Élevage et les constructions subventionnés en Flandre intérieure', *HTN* (1975.1), 79–90, and 'Flandre intérieur: région en voie de spécialisation?', *HTN* (1975.2), 41–59.
106 See Jacky Landriu, 'La Vie paysanne dans la région Nord–Pas-de-Calais de 1945 à nos jours', in Marcel Gillet (ed.), *La Qualité de vie dans la région Nord–Pas-de-Calais au 20e siècle*, Lille 1975, 180–8.
107 See Mouré, 'The French economy', 375, for an indication of the increasing scale of government involvement in the economy after 1945, and Pierre Guillaume, *Histoire sociale de la France au XXe siècle*, Paris 1992.

individual into much closer contact with the national state and state institutions on a regular basis. Concern over income tax levels, national medical care, retirement schemes, to say nothing of the infinite variety of forms to fill in and regulations to comply with all reinforced links with the nation.

This subtle reinforcement of national affiliation through a variety of routine daily activities and reminders of the nation is what Michael Billig has called banal nationalism.[108] Banal only in the sense that each small reminder of the nation is unconsciously accepted. Billig claims that national identity has at its root 'the embodied habits of social life', in which the national element has become ever present.[109] In this way, from the 'national' forms mentioned above, to the shape and colour of post boxes, lettering on car number plates and vocabulary developed to describe diplomas, jobs, laws or customs, everywhere there are subtle and subconscious reminders of the nation.

Such national reminders have their origin not only in the national states themselves, but also in the expanding material culture of the twentieth century and in the media. Radio, television, the cinema and newspapers subtly reinforce the nation, as do national sports leagues. Watching French television rather than crossing the border to a Flemish *estaminet* became an increasing occupation for the inhabitants of the Westhoek.[110] For the French Flemish to see a 'national' weather report meant that they would hear what the weather was like in Corsica, but not in Brussels. In the years since the Second World War, the bureaucratisation of daily life and the economy, the 'nationalness' of many job qualifications, minor but identifiable differences in institutional structures, all meant that culture became increasingly national. Accompanying this trend was a tendency to focus on and think about the rest of the French nation, and less and less about greater Flanders, contributing to the development of French identity.

By the time of the economic recessions of the latter twentieth century which hit the north of France particularly hard at the end of the *trente glorieuses*, the patterns of identity arising from economic structures had been set. Common to both sides of the border, the crises of industry and the difficulties of the post-industrial transition did not have the effect of strengthening regional Flemish identity at the expense of French, but if anything reinforced dependency upon the national state.[111] The opening up of trade links which resulted from the European Economic Community and the European Union also had a limited impact on identity formation in the Westhoek, given the presence of the national state at all levels of the economy through

---

108 Michael Billig, *Banal nationalism*, London 1995.
109 Ibid. 8.
110 See Landriu, 'La Vie paysanne', 194. See also Jacques Monfrin, 'Les Parlers en France', in Michel François (ed.), *La France et les français*, Paris 1972, 770, for more about the influence of changing lifestyle in the twentieth century.
111 For a description of the crisis of the 1960s and 1970s see Perret, *L'Usinor-Dunkerque*.

regulations and modernisation which had taken hold during the post-war period.[112] A study of the border area in the 1980s showed that while individuals crossed the border to take advantage of lower prices, differences in administrative structure and concepts of the role of the communes meant that little or no official contact was taking place between municipalities and their institutions, and cross-border relations were 'more symbolic than concrete'.[113] The cumulative effects of modernisation and banal nationalism had the result that by the 1980s a striking reciprocal ignorance among the inhabitants of the border region about their cross-border neighbours revealed the extent to which the two communities had become divided.[114]

Profound as were the implications of participation of the national state in the economy and the changes in lifestyle brought about by increased material well-being in the latter half of the twentieth century, these structural changes were only one element influencing the development of identity in French Flanders. Several groups and individuals from both within and outside of the Westhoek sought actively to influence the development of identity in the region; the first of these to be examined is the republican elite.

112 See also Baycroft 'Changing identities', 438.
113 See Michèle Breuillard-Pollet and others, La Frontière et les communes: le cas des communes françaises et belges frontalières de la région Nord–Pas-de-Calais, Lille 1987, 13–20, 59, and Michel Langrand and Christophe Masse, 'La Frontière franco-belge: mythe et réalité', Cahiers du CRAPS iv (Feb. 1988), 31. It should be mentioned that the latter study also concludes that such contact is also limited within the Nord–Pas-de-Calais.
114 See Michèle Breuillard-Pollet, 'Existe-t-il un espace transfrontalier franco-belge?', Cahiers du CRAPS iv (Feb. 1988), 63–4.

4

Republican Politics of National Integration in the Westhoek

On the part of the central authorities, especially during the various republics, a national project existed which had the express goal of integrating the population of the French provinces into 'the nation'.[1] This meant fostering a strong sense of national identity and loyalty to the nation and the dissemination of French language and culture. For the republicans it also included developing a sense of republicanism. A variety of means was used throughout the nineteenth and twentieth centuries to achieve this goal, including the creation of national celebrations, the teaching of the French language, French history, French geography and secular civic morals, compulsory military service and the strategic use of the political and administrative structures of the state. In situations where it was not possible to assimilate the population, the French elite attempted to appropriate elements of regional culture and give them a 'French' significance so that they became a part of French identity.

Festivals

The first significant dimension of the republican national project to be examined is the attempt to replace local popular culture, mythology and traditions with national ones. Immediately after achieving power during the Third Republic, republicans actively sought to replace local festivals and their corresponding symbolism with new republican and national ones, with a view to increasing loyalty through familiarity. In particular 14 July, the commemoration of the taking of the Bastille, was used to fulfil this role. A revolutionary incident relatively free of strong emotional undercurrents (compared with, say, the execution of Louis XVI), which occurred on an insignificant day in the religious calendar (they wished to supersede in form the religious holidays, but dared not replace one literally), the national holiday was heavily promoted in the closing two decades of the nineteenth century.[2]

---

[1] For a balanced general discussion of the republican project see Tombs, *France, 1814–1914.*
[2] See Rosemonde Sanson, *Les 14 Juillet (1789–1975): fête et conscience nationale,* Paris 1976, 49.

The goal of such festivals was to encourage the people to forget their hardships for a day, and to associate the good times with the state. Bread was passed out without charge, and balls, games, drink and such exotic events as fireworks made the day 'the (historic) past and the future in a present which is less like everyday'.[3] A description of one typical 14 July celebration in the Westhoek in the early Third Republic went as follows:

> The national holiday on the 14th of July is inaugurated by a distribution of bread and meat to the locals the night before. On the day itself, the trumpets sound and the cannons thunder from early in the morning; at noon a concert is given by local musicians in the kiosque of the Main Square; in the afternoon the fire brigade sponsor an archery contest for its honorary members, games of 'boules' are organised in different neighbourhoods of the city and the happy winners are given prizes of silver. A torch-lit procession and a ball at the Town Hall conclude the public festivities.[4]

It was hoped that 14 July would solidify loyalty, but some, such as Charles Rearick, asserted that 'by 1900, republican fêtes, like the republic itself, had clearly not lived up to early hopes and expectations'.[5] The celebrations lacked the spontaneity of events such as funerals, and came to be characterised by an 'ignoble baseness' associated with drunken revelry. The people were certainly willing to celebrate and profit from the festive occasion, but this did not make them more proactive towards the republic then they were beforehand.

While they may not have strongly developed the republican loyalty desired, this did not make the celebrations completely unsuccessful, however, in terms of the national cause. One of the reactions of the Church was, in 1894, to institute the 'Fête de Jeanne d'Arc' as a rival to 14th July.[6] This was of course an equally national commemoration, and superseded local celebrations as effectively. Socialists, syndicalists and anarchists attempted to categorise the national holiday as a purely bourgeois day, and criticised it as such, the socialists attempting to encourage the celebration of 1 May as a rival festivity. Their challenge to the national day was uniquely from a class, and never a regional stand-point. Both of these reactions served to increase simple participation in what were national agendas.

The limited political impact of festivals over the short run of can be seen in the lack of variation between the level of popular enthusiasm for one celebration over another of differing political character. In the Nord, state visits, such as that of the Emperor Napoléon III and Eugénie in 1867, or of presidents of the republic, or indeed of the Tsar of Russia in 1901 were all received in

3   Ibid. 81.
4   Taverne de Tersud, *Hazebrouck*, 297.
5   Charles Rearick, 'Festivals in modern France: the experience of the Third Republic', JCH xii (1977), 455.
6   Sanson, *Les 14 Juillet*, 55.

more or less the same way.[7] As with the national holidays, the Flemish were keen to come out and cheer, but it mattered little to them whom it was they were cheering, whether their distant head of state was an emperor or a president. The republican festivals did not really alter the political culture of the region described in chapter 3, but did contribute to an awareness of the nation and made a contribution to the development of national identity.

Along the same lines as the 'fêtes', the republican government sought to promote the nation through symbols such as Marianne, the female incarnation of the spirit of the republic, or the tricolour flag. Even in this domain they had to be careful to put the statues in places such as the town hall, which were new, and already represented the civil, democratic power. The marketplace, with its established associations and values was often not appropriate, and busts of Marianne were not always welcomed there.[8] Although the republican authorities had to be careful about the specific location of such national symbols as Marianne and the tricolour flag, they did gradually create a place for them in each Flemish village, such that they did slowly become familiar to the inhabitants, and a part of their world.

While the celebration of national festivals and the encroachment of national symbols did not turn the French Flemish into republicans, they did in the long term contribute to the development of national identity in the Westhoek through their gradual acceptance and the familiarity they acquired in the local landscape and the calendar. By the mid-twentieth century, the same figures had been visible and the same festivals celebrated for several generations, and they had therefore had time to permeate the subconscious of the population. Local and religious festivals were not directly supplanted, and did not disappear, but were merely complemented by specifically national ones.[9]

Education

Many writers have identified the 'école publique' as the principal agent and key to the disappearance of the regional languages and *patois* of France and the solidification of national identity.[10] It was at school that the children

---

[7] See Pierre Dassau, *Le Nord vu par la presse 1860/1910*, Dijon 1981; Taverne de Tersud, *Hazebrouck*, 295–7.

[8] Agulhon, *Marianne au pouvoir*, 343.

[9] In some cases they were also 'appropriated' or 'nationalised': see the final section of this chapter.

[10] See, for example, Mona Ozouf, *L'École, L'église et la république, 1871–1914*, Paris 1982, 222. For a general introduction to the history of education in France see, for example, Donald N. Baker and Patrick J. Harrigan (eds), *The making of Frenchmen: current directions in the history of education in France, 1679–1979*, Waterloo, Ont. 1980; Antoine Prost, *Histoire de l'enseignement en France, 1800–1967*, Paris 1968; Joseph N. Moody, *French education since Napoleon*, Syracuse 1978.

learned the French language and studied French history, two effective means of engendering national pride and patriotism, and received training (under the republic) in the republican morals and values thought to be central to the republican national project. Through the primary schools, future citizens were made to feel a part of France, and (in theory at least) given the linguistic tools which permitted them to be full participants in the national culture.

It was the revolutionaries of 1789 who first set the goal of free, obligatory and public education for the masses.[11] These schools would, they hoped, unify the country and its people by inculcating 'revolutionary' republican values. This republican ideology was rooted in the rationalist philosophy of the Enlightenment, opposed to the institution of the monarchy and the privileges of aristocracy, and deeply anti-Catholic. Against the Catholic use of Latin and in parallel with the development of the 'rational' metric system, the revolutionaries were strong defenders of the patriotic use of a standardised French language. It was viewed as a necessity to the survival and the completion of the mission of the republic itself to spread the ideals of the Revolution to the masses. This could only be achieved, they felt, through French, the language of the republic and rational philosophy. Elsewhere in Europe, French was associated with the elite that the revolutionary ideals sought to overthrow, and intellectuals turned away from French to their own languages in an attempt to spread culture to the masses through local idioms.[12] In France, it was both the language of the elite of the *ancien régime* and the language of Enlightenment, which put France in the unique political position of being able to impose the elite language with all of its prestige, while at the same time making it seem attractive by stressing its links to progress for the people, to the ideals of the Revolution and to the republican government.

In the widely publicised report of the *abbé* Grégoire, read before the Convention on 16 Prairial, Year II (May 1794), he showed that in much of France a sound knowledge of the French language was sadly lacking, and in much of the countryside, even where French could be understood, the population could not read or write it. His recommendation, well received by his fellow revolutionaries, was to encourage an active campaign to spread French to the masses, and to rid France of the various *patois* and regional languages, the 'diversity of vulgar idioms, which prolong the childhood of reason and the old age of prejudice'.[13] Following the recommendation of the *Comité de l'instruction publique* in October 1794, the convention adopted the text of a

11 For more on education during the Revolution see Josiane Boulad-Ayoub (ed.), *Former un nouveau peuple? Pouvoir, éducation, révolution*, Québec 1996.

12 Marcel Deneckere, *Histoire de la langue française dans les Flandres (1770–1823)*, Gand 1954, 340–2.

13 The *abbé* Grégoire, quoted in Eugen Weber, *La Fin des terroirs: la modernisation de la France rurale (1870–1914)*, trans. Antoine Berman and Bernard Géniès, Paris 1983, 115. For more information on the *abbé* Grégoire's report see De Certeau, Julia and Revel, *Une Politique de la langue*.

decree which stipulated that 'All teaching will be conducted in French: the local idiom can only be used in an auxiliary manner.'[14]

The optimism, or even utopianism, of this decree was in overstating the means of the authorities to enforce such an ideal, in spite of their desire. The numerous revolutionary governments of the late eighteenth century, for a variety of reasons, including the impracticability at the time given the state of existing educational conditions in rural France and a preoccupation with other priorities, were unable to implement their plans. The many successive regimes throughout the nineteenth century which followed, independent of their political stripe and constitutional character, were all favourable to the idea of solidifying national unity and loyalty through the universalisation of the French language and to advancement in primary education, even if they differed over the inclusion of republican values.

The century following the Revolution saw gradual progress towards the dual goals of compulsory, free and secular education and the imposition of French as the sole language of teaching. The first major piece of legislation in the nineteenth century was the *loi Guizot*, passed during the July Monarchy in 1833. During the Empire and the Restoration Monarchy, many new primary schools had been established, and this new law required each commune to posses at least one primary school. The commune could provide its own public school, or utilise an existing private (usually religious) one, and the teachers could be laymen or members of religious teaching orders, as the local council saw fit. Each department was also to set up a corps of inspectors to ensure the maintenance of standards.[15] It was the Guizot law which first stated that in principle French was to be the only language used in schools, taught not as a second language, but directly through immersion. In practice, this regulation was ignored. It was not strictly enforced in the Flemish region of the Nord, due to the decision-making power of the local councils and through the influence of the clergy who favoured the continued use of Flemish.[16]

The rule that French was to be the only language used in the classroom was also an integral part of the *loi Falloux*, passed on 15 March 1850, which left possible only the teaching of catechism in regional languages or dialects. Shortly afterwards, on 27 January 1853, the *Conseil académique du Nord* issued its own decree expressly forbidding all teaching in the Flemish language.[17]

The final piece of significant legislation in the nineteenth century came

[14] Quoted in Michiel Nuyttens, 'De weerslag van de Franse onderwijswetten op de achteruitgang van de volkstaal in Noord-Frankrijk in de 19de eeuw', *DFN/LPBF* i (1976), 138.
[15] See Joel Ravier, 'Les Premiers Inspecteurs primaires du département du Nord: de la loi Guizot (1833) à la loi Falloux (1850)', *RN* lxxx (Jan.–Feb. 1998), 91–116.
[16] See Maryvonne Leblond, 'La Scolarisation dans le département de Nord au XIXe siècle', *RN* lii (July–Sept. 1970), 139–40.
[17] See Landry and de Verrewaere, *Histoire secrète*, 272.

on the heels of the republican electoral victories of 1879 in the form of the Ferry laws of 1881 and 1882. Reaffirming the position of French in schools, they made the French primary schools free, compulsory and secular, removing the control of the clergy which had been defined in the Falloux law. In the years that followed the ministry of education complimented this legislation with school curricula which included the teaching of a republican version of French history. But how far were these laws governing the language of teaching respected, and what direct impact did they have on the identity and language of the Flemish? Did the famous 'instituteurs' of the Third Republic really succeed in their mission of enlightening the masses of the Flemish and making French-speakers out of them?

Looking first at the language question, serious pressure on the *instituteurs* of the Nord to use exclusively French in the classroom had already begun during the Second Empire under Victor Duruy, who became the minister of education in 1863. His success was limited, as attested by two inspection reports to the *inspecteur général* from 1866 and 1867 which claimed that the prevailing language situation necessitated at least some study of the Flemish language: 'The knowledge of this language is still necessary for business relations with Belgium, to understand family papers and a host of other written documents for which the population has lively and perfectly natural sentimental interest.'[18] They did assure the inspector, however, that 'this study does not go beyond the simple mechanism of reading'.[19] It was considered to be a significant event that 'three communes and five schools have completely abandoned the teaching of Flemish; one other commune and two other schools have reduced it to almost nothing'.[20] The rarity is further witnessed by an inspection report dating from 1869, in which the *Inspecteur d"Académie*, J. Jarry, referred to an exceptional *institutrice congréganiste* from the community of Wormhoudt who, he wrote 'was determined to teach French to the exclusion of Flemish, and who finally succeeded'.He went on to add that 'Unfortunately, this is an isolated example.'[21]

The overwhelming difficulty facing the *instituteurs* of the nineteenth century in French Flanders was how to overcome the fact that the vast majority of their students arrived on their first day speaking not one word of French, and did not hear any language but Flemish outside the schoolroom, rendering a knowledge of Flemish indispensable for teaching. A delegation from the canton of Houtkerque in 1875, charged with finding a new *instituteur adjoint*, insisted from the start that he would have to be fluent in Flemish, otherwise he would be completely unsuited to the position.[22] In

18 Report, primary inspector of Dunkerque, 7 Feb. 1867, ADN, 1 T 80 72.
19 Letter, signature illegible, primary school inspector to 'Monsieur l'Inspecteur' (presumably *général*), 24 Oct. 1866, ibid.
20 Ibid.
21 Report to the *conseil académique*, June 1869, AN, F 17 9376.
22 Délibérations de la délégation cantonale de Steenvoorde, ADN, 6 Z 2269.

1882 the *curé* of Flêtre described the capacity of his students in French to the archbishop of Cambrai:

> Flêtre is exclusively Flemish and all of the inhabitants speak Flemish; doubt-less the classes are taught in French according to the school regulations, but once outside of the school and in their families the children speak nothing but Flemish, such that by the time of their first communion they only know French like a pupil in year five knows Latin.[23]

The inspector E. Anthoine also described the situation in the early Third Republic:

> Outside of the cities, it [Flemish] is the usual language, indeed the only one which is used; the child arriving at school must learn French like our children in secondary school learn Latin and Greek; he must (a frustrating situation), before he is even capable of understanding his teacher and being taught any-thing else at all, begin by learning French, since it is the only language which the teacher is authorised to speak with him. . . . Once out of school the child hears nothing but Flemish; he is completely re-captured by that language, the first which he spoke, and has soon forgotten French.[24]

Anthoine goes on to say that the kinds of complications that result are obvious because in spite of these circumstances, the lessons had to be short, to the point, simple and yet quick, since each student's time in school was so limited. Given these conditions, and in spite of being a representative of the central government, he claimed that he did not want to destroy Flemish, only to make certain that alongside of it French too was learned. He lamented the fact that under those circumstances 'one of the languages only seems to be able to survive to the detriment of the other' and he thought that it was unfair to hold the individual teachers responsible for the difficulties arising from that situation.[25]

These circumstances did make teaching difficult, to say the least, and given the limited time at their disposal, the *instituteurs'* ability to raise their students' French to an acceptable standard was severely limited. It was also true, of course, that having to devote so much time to the teaching of French, all other subjects suffered accordingly.[26] The temptation was to use Flemish in the classroom, in spite of the regulations, in order to succeed in communi-cating something to the students during their brief period in school.

One primary inspector at the end of the Second Empire even went so far as

---

[23] F. Van Costenoble to archbishop of Cambrai, 31 July 1882, AN, F 19 5502. 'Year five' (cinquième) was the school year in which children were 13.

[24] E. Anthoine, *L'Instruction primaire dans le département du Nord, 1868–1877: rapport rédigé en vue de l'Exposition Universelle de 1878*, Lille 1878, 13. See also idem, *À Travers nos écoles: souvenirs posthumes*, Paris 1887.

[25] Idem, *L'Instruction primaire*, 13–14.

[26] For a discussion of this aspect of the problem see report, 11 June 1872, AN, F 17 9270.

to counsel teachers that it was useful to use Flemish.[27] He considered that since the characters were identical in the two languages, and since the Flemish texts used were always accompanied by French translations, learning to read in Flemish was in fact helpful in learning French, and did not in any way hinder the progress of the language, which continued regularly.[28] He stressed that the teaching of French should come first, followed only later by Flemish. He concludes that this was the best strategy of teaching, which 'would soon be adopted by all of the instituteurs and institutrices'.[29] It should be pointed out that such an opinion was extremely rare, or at least not expressed in official reports or correspondence, among the overwhelming majority of administrative officers in the French school system.

The difficulty of the circumstances did not mean that many of the teachers did not at least attempt to force the children to speak nothing but French themselves while at school. The infamous 'signum', coming from the Latin for sign, was used in French Flanders until well into the twentieth century to punish those students who did not observe the French-only rule while at school.[30] It took several forms in the Westhoek, where it was often referred to as the 'droeven sou' and was most often 'a piece of metal or wood which the children caught speaking Flemish passed from one to another, the final holder being punished either with a verb to conjugate in sixteen tenses or with one hundred lines'.[31] Emile Coornaert describes another variety of signum, which was a ribbon or a piece of paper given out by the maître d'école on Monday morning, on which each successive holder was required to write his name. At the end of the week, each child whose name appeared lost one point of that week's mark, and the final name appearing on the list was penalised two marks.[32] Roger Taccoën, while describing his childhood experiences in a primary school in Socx (near Bergues), refers to the 'petite cube' for any student caught speaking Flemish. It had to be passed from one child to another, and he claims to have received it more often then other children because he admitted to the instituteur that he wanted to become a priest when he grew up.[33]

The direct method of teaching French through total immersion, refusing to allow any Flemish to be spoken at all, even as a means to help teach French, was criticised frequently throughout the nineteenth and even into the early twentieth century as ineffective, and sometimes even counter-

27 Report, primary inspector of Dunkerque, 7 Feb. 1867, ADN, 1 T 80 72.
28 Ibid.
29 Ibid.
30 See Emile Coornaert, 'Flamand et français dans l'enseignement en Flandre française des annexions au XXe siècle', RN liii (Apr.–June 1971), 217–21. Coornaert also distinguishes between the 'signum linguae' to punish Flemish-speakers, and the 'signum manus' to punish those caught with their hands in their pockets.
31 Landry and de Verrewaere, Histoire secrète, 274–5.
32 Coornaert, La Flandre française, 304.
33 Taccoën, Une Certaine Joie, 46.

productive. Given the little time that the children had at school, they were often unable to absorb enough French to be useful before they went off to work, and since they were not taught Flemish either, left school having learned no language at all which could be of further use to them. The fact that their other courses were taught in French also served as a handicap when trying to learn maths, history or any other subject. In a ministerial circular for the *département du Nord* in 1874, the minister expressed dismay at the fact that 'In a certain number of communes, History and Geography are not taught at all; in others only the pupils in the higher divisions have some notion of them.'[34] The system was also criticised of course by those members of the Flemish community who considered Flemish to be valuable in and of itself, and that bilingualism was the most suitable goal for which to aim.[35]

The ability to teach French to the Flemish children effectively in the nineteenth century, already made difficult by their total inability when they arrived at school, was further restricted by numerous other factors: poor teaching conditions, overcrowded classrooms, outdated teaching methods, shortage of textbooks, massive attendance problems and the quality of the candidates hired to do the teaching. A. Gandon, *inspecteur primaire* for the *département du Nord* in the early Third Republic, described too frequent cases of old, worn-out teachers or younger ones completely 'incapable, without enthusiasm and without aptitude'.[36] One of the principal causes, he wrote, was the insufficient number of teachers who were coming out of the *école normale* in Douai (founded in 1834), who were barely numerous enough to fill half of the posts which became vacant each year.[37] The *inspecteur général*, E. Brouward, in a report to the minister of education in 1880, described the recruitment of acceptable teaching personnel as an even larger problem than the objective difficulty of getting the Flemish-speakers to learn French.[38] As late as 1892, in a report to the *conseil général*, the *inspecteur d'académie* reported that

> Our primary personnel vary as much in outlook as in origin. In any case it does not have the homogeneity which only time can give. We still have numerous elderly teachers, worn out by age and professional fatigue who are no longer apt for anything but rest. . . . There comes a time, even for the valiant, when

---

[34] Circular, minister of public instruction, public worship and arts, 11 June 1874, ADN, 2 T 2403.

[35] See, for example, the references to the *Congrès Régionaliste* in prefect to minister of public instruction, 5 Jan. 1921, ADN, M 154 318, and N. Bourgeois, 'Un Tour de Flandre', in Bourgeois and others, *Flandre notre mère*, 20. These kinds of objections will be discussed in more detail in chapter 7 below.

[36] A. Gandon (primary inspector) to minister of public instruction, 14 Aug. 1873, AN, F 17 9270.

[37] Ibid. See also Richard Héméryck, 'La Congréganisation des écoles normales du département du Nord au milieu du XIXe siècle (1845–1883): l'école normale d'instituteurs de Douai', *RN* lvi (Jan.–Mar. 1974), 13.

[38] 'Rapport d'ensemble d'inspection générale de 1880', AN, F 17 9270.

weapons fall from failing hands: one should not force nature, not even in pedagogy.[39]

The older, incapable teachers were only just beginning to be replaced by younger ones, without experience but possessing 'the necessary knowledge and pedagogic vigour'. As twelve years earlier, he complained that there were still not enough of these young teachers coming out of the école normale to fulfil the needs of the department, although the school was filled to its limit every year.[40]

The classrooms themselves posed problems as well: 'Alongside of buildings which are well set up . . . one finds miserable schools, held in insufficient and unhealthy premises, which should be prohibited.'[41] E. Anthoine, the inspecteur d'académie, lamented that too often the schools were overcrowded, particularly in the junior classes, which led to a loss of enthusiasm on the part of both the teachers and the students.[42] Lack of textbooks and general class-room materials was the principal complaint made by instituteurs when asked in 1860 about the principal shortcomings facing primary instruction in rural communities from the triple point of view of school, students and teachers.[43] The second most common complaint was about the living conditions of the schoolteachers resulting at least in part from their low salaries. It is interesting to note that in their list of grievances, no mention at all was made of the language question.

In addition to the poor physical setting and teaching conditions, the teaching methods employed were not the most efficient. Robert Gildea, in his work on education in provincial France, described the realisation in the early Third Republic that the 'archaic nature of pedagogy' would have to be updated if the schools were to make any progress. He concludes that before 1880 teaching methods in primary schools were poor and the process of learning formal.[44] The child found his way around his reader 'by a combination of memory and guesswork'.[45] Much of the learning of French came through the dictée, the teacher reciting and the students attempting to write correctly. The choice of text was of course very influential and had a direct impact on what the children were to learn. One inspector complained about the subject matter, claiming that 'the choice of dictées, especially in the

---

39 Report, inspecteur d'académie, on primary instruction in the Nord, included as a part of the prefect's report to the conseil général, Apr. 1892, 557, ADN, 1 N 136.
40 Ibid. 558.
41 Gandon to minister, 14 Aug. 1873, AN, F 17 9270.
42 See Anthoine, L'Instruction primaire.
43 Francis Bailleul, 'Les Instituteurs du Nord d'après le concours Rouland de 1860', RN lxvii (July–Sept. 1985), 703–14. See also L. Mordacq (primary inspector), 'Notes pour servir à l'histoire de l'instruction primaire dans le département du Nord', MSD xvii (1871–2), 53.
44 Robert Gildea, Education in provincial France, 1800–1914: a study of three departments, Oxford 1983, 262–3, 226–7.
45 Ibid. 227.

Congregationalist schools, is not always pleasant: instead of texts within the reach of the students, family letters, one finds too often subjects with no practical utility'.[46]

Pierre Giolitto, in his discussion of teaching methods also claimed that it was not until the early 1880s that more than the most basic elements of language teaching were employed at the primary level.[47] It was not until 1882 that such elements as explanations of what was read or actual composition in French by the students became a part of the official curriculum.[48] Although teaching methods did improve towards the end of the century, the change was limited, and many teachers were never able to take their pupils beyond basic spelling and the simple recitation of grammar rules, without necessarily understanding them.[49] Due to the centralised structure of the ministry of public instruction, reform could only come from the top down. Since the bureaucrats were often out of touch with the everyday realities of the commune schoolmasters, or preoccupied with other concerns, change and improvement in teaching methods were very slow and difficult to bring about: 'Centralisation makes reform difficult . . . [and] is thus an obstacle to progress, which is authorised only in response to crises.'[50]

The final major obstacle to the effectiveness of the primary schools was students' absences from school for part or all of the year.[51] A report listing the reasons behind school absences for children who received no instruction whatsoever, be it at home or at school, included the great distance between the home and the school, 'communication difficulties', sickness which affected the potential student's mobility, insanity, insufficient family resources (in approximately 10 per cent of the cases) and, by far and away the most common, parental indifference.[52]

Although after the passing of the Ferry laws school was compulsory until the age of thirteen, it was occasionally the case that the children would only arrive at school for a year or two preceding their First Communion (made at approximately eleven years of age), which was an extremely important rite of passage for the young Flemings of the Westhoek, and then depart immediately thereafter. This reduced their overall stay in the classroom substantially and made the job of the *instituteur* that much more difficult, since the priority of those students was the learning of their catechism, and all other subjects suffered accordingly.[53]

---

[46] *Rapport général sur la situation de l'enseignement primaire*, 12 May 1876, addressed to minister of public instruction, AN, F 17 9270.

[47] Pierre Giolitto, *Histoire de l'enseignement primaire au XIXe siècle*, II: *Les Méthodes d'enseignement*, Paris 1984, 71–9.

[48] Ibid. 77.

[49] Gildea, *Education*, 263–4.

[50] Prost, *Histoire de l'enseignement*, 338.

[51] See Leblond, 'La Scolarisation', 387–98.

[52] See AN, F 17* 3160.

[53] See Gildea, *Education*, 215–16.

In addition to attending for fewer years than required, many pupils' attendance at school was seasonal, depending upon harvests and other work schedules. The industrialisation of the region, rather than helping, only served to exacerbate the problem. Parents esteemed the small wage children could earn in a factory as a greater contribution to the household than a potential education, and sent them off to work rather than to school.[54] Parents did not understand the value of anything their child could learn in school beyond what qualified them to make their First Communion.[55] Maryvonne Leblond demonstrates that, paradoxically, the percentage of children in full-time education in the Nord stagnated and even decreased after the passing of the Ferry laws, a fact she attributes directly to industrialisation.[56] In some cases school attendance was restricted because in the rural communes it was simply too far to go, or school was viewed as superfluous and unnecessary by the peasants. In other cases, both parents went to work in order to support their family, and therefore the older children did not go to school in order to be free to look after their younger siblings.[57]

Given the preceding analysis, therefore, in spite of their best efforts, restricted time, limited means and the material conditions afforded them, the ability of *instituteurs* to make French-speakers out of the young Flemish of the Westhoek was quite restricted during the nineteenth century. This assumes, moreover, that primary schoolteachers had the desire and the fortitude to persevere with the direct method of French teaching demanded by the national authorities in spite of the obvious handicaps, and this was not always the case. In 1880 the *inspecteur général du Nord* complained directly to the minister that Flemish was still being taught in primary schools.[58] After the passing of the Ferry laws, no further mention was made of language, either way, in the inspection reports. This absence of comment can at least in part be attributed to a desire on the part of the inspectors to demonstrate the loyalty of their region to the minister and to the government, and is not of itself proof that the problem had been solved.

On the contrary, writes Michiel Nuyttens, although they 'placed a heavy hand upon the language of the people . . . in the department of the Nord, the Ferry laws were never applied to their utmost effectiveness'.[59] Ludo Milis also concludes that the laws outlawing the use of minority languages were not

---

54 Circular, 30 May 1874, ADN, 2 T 2403. See also Philippe Marchand, *Le Travail des enfants au XIXe siècle dans le département du Nord*, Lille 1980.

55 See Anthoine, *L'Instruction primaire*, 12.

56 Maryvonne Leblond, *La Scolarisation dans le département du Nord au XIXe siècle*, mémoire de maîtrise, Paris 1973. See also Marchand, *Le Travail des enfants*.

57 See, for example, M. Herreman to archbishop of Cambrai, 1 July 1902, AN, F 19 5502. Herreman attributed the poor French of his catechism students to their regular absences from school.

58 'Rapport d'ensemble d'inspection générale de 1880', AN, F 17 9270.

59 Nuyttens, 'De weerslag van de onderwijswetten', 145.

completely put into effect until the dawn of the twentieth century.[60] As late as 1898 it was reported in *Le Journal* that 'Active propaganda is produced in certain areas so that teaching will continue in the existing language',[61] which presupposes that it was still going on. In 1902 a group of priests wrote to the archbishop of Cambrai, claiming that they were not opposed to the diffusion of the French language, but the schools were not doing their job and teaching French. They would have been able to eliminate Flemish from religious teaching, they complain, if only the laws had been observed in the region's schools, but at that time only 'a very small number' of the villagers could understand French.[62]

During the period following the Ferry laws, the question of schoolteachers who were still falling back on Flemish from time to time was overshadowed in the public debate by the attention particularly focused upon the teaching of catechism, which had recently been required to be in French only,[63] and the secularisation of the teaching personnel in all public schools (which caused particular outrage in the highly Catholic Westhoek, and resulted in many schools losing students).[64]

Thus, in spite of the advanced state of the Nord relative to the rest of the country, it cannot be said that the schools were universally teaching French, and certainly not effectively until at least 1890, or more likely 1900, which is directly in line with the evidence for language use presented in chapter 1. From the surveys of Dewachter, Vandekerkhove and Lauwers in the latter twentieth century, it can be seen that even the children who passed through the primary schools in 1890–1910 did not speak French as adults in any regular manner.

By the 1920s the schools had more or less accepted the national regulations and were teaching exclusively in French as required, but this did not mean that the Flemish problem disappeared, or that it ceased to be a public issue.[65] As seen in chapter 1, the Westhoek was still principally Flemish-speaking throughout the inter-war period, and as such the problems facing the *instituteur* because his students arrived in the classroom as unilingual Flemish-speakers had not changed since the nineteenth century. In 1929 we can still read the same style of comments that had appeared fifty years earlier:

---

[60] See Ludo Milis, 'Frankrijk en zijn minderhheden: politiek en cultuursbesef in Frans-Vlaanderen van de Franse Revolutie tot nu', *DFN/LPBF* vi (1981), 155–82.

[61] Untitled article, *Le Journal*, 26 July 1898.

[62] Herreman to archbishop of Cambrai, 1 July 1902, AN, F 19 5502.

[63] See chapter 5 below.

[64] See AN, F 17 9182, 9190, which contain the enrolment records for secularised schools and new private schools, 1879–88. See also *L'Indicateur de l'arrondissement d'Hazebrouck*, 1 July 1888, 1, and 13 Sept. 1888, 2, for an example of typical local reactions to secularisation; Bernard Ménager, *La Laïcisation des écoles communales dans le département du Nord (1879–1899)*, Lille 1971.

[65] See prefect to minister of public instruction, 5 Jan. 1921, ADN, M 154 318, and chapter 7 below.

'The Flemish language is as necessary for the *instituteur* as for the *curé* to teach children grammar and catechism' wrote Auguste Bergerot.[66]

Thus it can be said that the *instituteurs* of the early Third Republic did not completely succeed in transforming the Flemish of the Westhoek into French-speakers. As shown in chapter 1, many had indeed become partly, if not fully bilingual by the twentieth century, but for the vast majority the language of choice remained Flemish, in spite of what little French they may have picked up during their school days. The social and practical obstacles facing the teachers were simply too great for them to easily convert the Flemish into francophones or even into fully functional bilinguals.

As seen in chapter 1, by the mid-twentieth century French had indeed become the usual language in the Westhoek, and by the late twentieth century the use and knowledge of Flemish had been vastly reduced. As the problems of the quality of the premises and personnel were slowly resolved, and the perceived value of education increased so as to ensure higher levels of attendance not only at primary, but more importantly at secondary school, French had attained a level of universality within France such that its predominance was assured.[67]

In the post-war period the republican objective of national integration did not go away, but since levels of secondary education were increasing, and given the predominance that French had achieved among the population, the authorities could afford greater flexibility with respect to the teaching of other languages. No longer posing as great a threat, and associated mostly with nostalgia for the rural past, the various regional languages were therefore gradually able to secure some minor rights within the school system. The *loi Deixonne* of 11 January 1951 allowed for the teaching of Breton, Basque, Occitan and Catalan in public schools, although Flemish was omitted from the list.[68] By 1977–8, 21,200 out of 10 million total school population in France were taking such courses.[69] The omission of Flemish from the *loi Deixonne* can be interpreted either as evidence of the weakness of the Flemish movement that was seeking language rights, or as a sign that the number of Flemish-speakers was so small that the government did not feel obliged to make the same concessions towards them which it found necessary to make towards the other linguistic minorities.

In the Westhoek, the teaching of Dutch and Flemish in the school system would have to wait for several years before it could get going. In 1966 it

66 Auguste Bergerot, untitled article in *De Torrewachter: Maanblad voor Fransch-Vlaanderen*, 15 Mar. 1929, 3. See chapter 7 below for several more examples of articles adopting a similar position.
67 On levels of language use see chapter 1 above; on the increase of secondary education in the Westhoek see M. Codaccioni, 'Vers une renaissance culturelle', in Hilaire, *Histoire du Nord/Pas-de-Calais*, 481.
68 See Lodge, *From dialect to standard*, 219.
69 Wardhaugh, *Languages in competition*, 104.

became possible to study Dutch in secondary schools as a 'third living language', and in 1971 it could be the first foreign language (if chosen over English or German), and therefore taken as an option for the French *baccalauréat*.[70] The programme has grown slowly, from a few schools in the 1970s to over twenty in the 1990s. The number of students taking such courses, however, has remained relatively small, and it has often been difficult to recruit teachers, since until very recently Dutch was only an option for those who qualify as teachers of German, no special training and recruitment for Dutch teachers having yet been created.[71] Most of the new programmes in Dutch created in the final two decades of the twentieth century have been in the context of partnerships or exchanges with Belgium or the Netherlands, and clearly were recognising Dutch as a purely foreign rather than a regional language.[72] Their success has in many cases depended upon the enthusiasm of individuals in the specific communes.[73] A further initiative to teach Dutch in several primary schools of the Westhoek, again inspired by the Dutch and Belgians, began as a pilot in the communes of Wervicq and Bailleul, and after reasonable success was expanded to include other communes in 1996–7.[74]

As far as the teaching of the Flemish specific to the Westhoek is concerned, it was not until 1982 that it received some official recognition, and then only in the form of the Savary ministerial memorandum, which promised financial support for the teaching of regional languages for a period of three years.[75] In the wake of the memorandum, several middle schools (*collèges*) attempted to implement programmes which taught the Westhoek Flemish dialect, as distinct from high Dutch, although they were relatively few in number, and quite quickly failed for lack of interest.[76]

Thus the first part of the republican national project, the teaching of the French language which would allow all French citizens to participate in national cultural and political life, was achieved in the second half of the twentieth century in French Flanders. In terms of linguistic assimilation, the

---

[70] See Francis Persyn, 'Le Néerlandais dans l'enseignement primaire et secondaire en Flandre française', *DFN/LPBF* xx (1995), 13.

[71] See 'Flemish in France', Euromosaic Website, http://www.uoc.es/euromosaic/web/document/neerlandes/an/ i1/i1.html, consulted 14 March 2000. The CAPES, the principal qualification for teaching in French secondary schools, in Dutch was not created until the late 1990s: J. Kooijman, 'Enseigner le néerlandais dans le Nord de la France', *DFN/LPBF* xxiv (1998), 158.

[72] Persyn, 'Le Néerlandais', 13.

[73] See 'Flemish in France'. The most notable success was in the late 1990s in Bailleul, where Dutch was strongly supported by the local mayor.

[74] Kooijman, 'Enseigner le néerlandais', 148–61.

[75] See 'Flemish in France'. For more on the debate over high Dutch versus Westhoek Flemish see chapter 7 below.

[76] Persyn, 'Le Néerlandais', 17. See also Jean-Louis Marteel, *Cours de flamand: het Vlaams dat men oudders klappen: méthode d'apprentissage du dialecte des flamands de France (Westhoek)*, Dunkerque 1992, a recent textbook designed for students of the regional dialect.

Westhoek represents one of the greatest successes of the national project, the transition being so thorough that while some Flemish-speakers remain at the end of the twentieth century, popular demand for Flemish in schools has completely evaporated. To give the entire credit for linguistic assimilation to the school system itself is to overstate the case, as other structural factors also contributed to linguistic assimilation, as seen in the previous chapter.[77] It should also be made clear that the function of the schools was to transmit written language, and as long as the schools were not teaching Flemish, it was more difficult to sustain it as a written language within the Westhoek. A disadvantage, certainly, for the perpetuation of the spoken language as well, but not an insurmountable one.

In terms of the development of identity in the Westhoek, the official republican position of French only in schools continually denied the existence of a culturally legitimate regional language (introducing Dutch only as a foreign language), and did not swerve at any point during the nineteenth or twentieth centuries from the position that the cultural identity of the inhabitants of the Westhoek was French and that they had ties only to the French nation.

History and republican morals

Although it took much longer than often surmised for the republican authorities to make regular French-speakers out of the Flemish, this was not the only means at their disposal to encourage the development of a solid national identity: history courses and patriotic school manuals, as well as lessons in moral and civic virtue, also helped to shape the general attitudes of the poorer classes towards the state.[78] Those advocating it distinguished the patriotism to be taught from nationalism by its stress on faithfulness, discipline and order; those educated in the primary schools were to grow up to be respectful, loyal citizens. In his history of education in France, Antoine Prost describes how this goal was shared by the various rival factions in primary education: 'The grand unifying force, the only one which can neutralise ideological and social oppositions, is national sentiment. . . . The same patriotism invades the faculties and the primary schools, the lesson of the congregationist and the free thinker.'[79] In this way, although a teacher may

---

77 Such factors include radio, television and the perceived benefits of literacy and education in French for the changing workplace. See, for example, Monfrin, 'Les Parlers', 770, and Gildea, *Education*, 253.
78 See Marie-Christine Kok-Escalle, *Instaurer une culture par l'enseignement de l'histoire, France, 1876–1912: contribution à une sémiotique de la culture*, Berne 1988. On the importance accorded to this type of teaching, albeit in different regional contexts, see Stephen Harp, *Learning to be loyal: primary schooling as nation building in Alsace and Lorraine, 1850–1940*, DeKalb, Illinois 1998, and Reed-Danahay, *Education and identity*.
79 Prost, *Histoire de l'enseignement*, 335.

not have been an ardent nationalist, he or she was at the very least a professor of patriotism,[80] and it was via this patriotism that the unity desired through language was truly achieved.[81]

This was accomplished first of all through the creation of a uniform, continuous history of France. The current state was portrayed as the legitimate successor to an entire string of historical events and regimes, as far back as Vercingetorix and Clovis, through St Louis and the *ancien régime*, as well as the various republics, monarchies and empires of the nineteenth century.[82] Although there was a strongly republican slant to the national history which was being written, it was nevertheless inclusive of other traditions, both to discourage alienation, and to increase the overall glory of France wherever possible. Maps of France were shown to the students, in an attempt to get them to think of themselves and their current position in relation to the rest of the nation, and as the heirs to the French history that they were studying. The borders of the Third Republic (with the addition of Alsace and Lorraine) were considered to be those that corresponded to this glorious history which each and every Frenchman could claim as his or her own. The theory was to foster a sense of identity and belonging through identification with a particularly selected set of historical facts: selected to correspond with the entire nation and not with any individual region. Prost writes that the most important aspect of the integration and assimilation of the regions was not the struggle between French and *patois*, important as it was, nor that between the metric system and the various local measures, as 'no nation was completely resigned to doing without a national language', but the fact that throughout the whole of France the school system tries 'to give all of the French common memories and in so doing model a collective consciousness which is immediately national'.[83]

The second means to accomplish the integration of the regions through patriotic history lessons was the incorporation of the local or regional into the spine of common national history. Placed against the background of 'common memories', elements from local history could be integrated into national narrative, with the goal of directly associating the 'petite patrie' with the 'grande patrie'.[84] While teaching local or regional history in each village and region may seem to contradict the goal of nationalising history, the point was to 'appropriate' that local or regional history, and portray it as an integral

---

80 Singer, *Village notables*, 125.
81 See Jean-Jacques Becker and Stéphane Audoin-Rouzeau, *La France, la nation, la guerre: 1850–1920*. Paris 1995, 168–73.
82 For a description of the development of historical narratives of France see introduction; Den Boer. *History as a profession*; Maurice Agulhon, 'French historians and the reconstruction of the republican tradition, 1800–1848', trans. Laura Mason, in Fontana, *Invention of the modern republic*, 173–91; Gildea, *The past*, 1994.
83 Prost, *Histoire de l'enseignement*, 338.
84 See Jean-François Chanet, *L'École républicaine et les petites patries*, Paris 1996.

part of French national history.[85] By allowing a place for the local and regional within the larger national framework, such local history lessons could be used to show just how integrated the region was, thereby strengthening and solidifying national identity.[86] Village patriotism could thus become equated with patriotism towards the nation. Against a background of large-scale modernisation, this nurturing of such nostalgic loyalty to archaic 'petites patries' should not be seen as a sign of backwardness in the republican project of national unification, but merely of its complexity and flexibility. In terms of historical dimension, the 'petites patries' were just as much imagined communities as was the nation, but they usefully linked each village and region to the French nation. Thus history lessons served both to teach the basic elements of national history to pupils in all regions, while at the same time appropriating any local or regional history into the national, thereby strengthening national identity in the process.[87]

Necessary to the spread of the national message were patriotic textbooks, which took off and circulated widely through France during the Third Republic; such, for example, was *Le Tour de France par deux enfants*.[88] Émile Boutroux, writing in 1883, listed forty-five manuals of patriotic style, yet differing in political or religious stripe, which had appeared in the two years preceding his article.[89] The multitude of new books closely reflected the two methods described above for the instruction of patriotism: clear and unwavering praise of the French nation drawing upon a diversity of traditions from French history, and an integration of the local with the national. In her study of the place of the regions in patriotic discourse, Anne-Marie Thiesse provides numerous examples of the ways in which such textbooks made use of material from the individual histories of the various French regions in order both to ground the patriotic discourse locally, and to help to integrate the regions and their particularities into the national picture.[90]

Many of the new republican schoolbooks borrowed techniques from other traditions. Ernest Lavisse, one of the most patriotic of the writers, and the 'porte-parole' of a generation of staunch republican theorists, is a good

[85] The process of 'appropriation' of culture as well as local history will be discussed at greater length later in this chapter.
[86] One illustration of the success of this policy is the fact that by the inter-war period even the communist party was campaigning on a platform of peasants, the soil and the *patrie*: Nathanael Greene, 'National and local: rural politics, 1932–1936', *French Historical Studies* ix (1976), 507, 513.
[87] The dimension of rural nostalgia as a part of national identity continued throughout the twentieth century, most notably during the occupation, but also lay at the heart of the development of the Nord–Pas-de-Calais in the post-war period which will be examined in chapter 7 below.
[88] See Ozouf and Ozouf, 'Le Thème du patriotisme', 3–31.
[89] Emile Boutroux, 'Les Récents Manuels de morale et d'instruction civique', *Revue pédagogique* n.s. ii (15 Apr. 1883), 289–342.
[90] See Anne-Marie Thiesse, *Ils Apprenaient la France: l'exaltation des régions dans le discours patriotique*, Paris 1997.

example. Lavisse used what Pierre Nora describes as the values of neo-monarchism, transmitting the former justifications of the monarchy onto the republic: the same roots in French cultural traditions, the same cults of faithfulness to the land, heaven and the dead, and the same religious sense of unity and responsibility.[91] Lavisse himself, in his work *Questions d'enseignement nationale*, destined for the teacher training programmes of the *écoles normales*, wrote that patriotism needs to be cultivated:

> It is at the same time a sentiment and a sense of duty. All sentiments are susceptible to cultivation, and all such senses can be taught. History needs to cultivate the sentiment and specify the duty. . . . All teaching of patriotic duty can be reduced to the following: there exists a collective and continuous work which is France; each generation has its part, and, in this generation, each individual has his as well.[92]

The patriotic message conveyed through these manuals became more and more associated with pacifism as the war of 1870–1 grew more distant. Pierre Deghilage, in 1906, described the difference between 'good' and 'bad' patriotism, and encouraged schoolteachers to strive to teach the good, as he saw it, pacifist variety.[93] The rallying to the war effort in 1914 came as a surprise to many and was in the end a result of the belief that France was morally superior to the rest of the world and any French war could not be anything but a just war, a defensive war.[94]

The growing pacifism of manuals partly reflected the sense of the second important role of the primary schools, complementary to lessons in patriotism: the teaching of morals and civic virtue. The moral role of the primary schools cannot be discounted. The school system in France was divided largely upon class lines, with religious *collèges* and state *lycées* reserved for the education of the upper and middle classes, as well as some of the wealthier peasants and petite bourgeoisie.[95] The primary school was designed only for the masses, and the established order which set them up had in mind chiefly the imposition of a bourgeois ethic upon the people so they would work hard, remain disciplined, respectful and in their place, and cause the fewest problems or disruptions possible.[96] In a word, primary schools were intended more to enhance social stability than to create or encourage social mobility.

In the early Third Republic many republicans, such as the first president

---

91 Pierre Nora, 'Ernest Lavisse: son rôle dans la formation du sentiment national', *Revue historique* ccxxviii (July–Sept. 1962), 105. See also idem, 'Lavisse, instituteur national', 239–75, and 'L'"Histoire de France" de Lavisse', 851–902. See also introduction.

92 Ernest Lavisse, *Questions d'enseignement national*, Paris 1885, 208–9.

93 Pierre Deghilage, *L'Education sociale à l'école*, Montdidier 1906, 279–80. See also Mona Ozouf, *L'École de la France: essais sur la révolution, l'utopie et l'enseignement*, Paris 1984, 185, 197.

94 Ozouf, *L'Ecole de la France*, 210–13.

95 See, for example, W. R. Frazer, *Education and society in modern France*, London 1963, 2.

96 See Price, *Social history*, 339–48.

Adolphe Thiers, were in fact in favour of leaving the primary schools for the most part under clerical influence, believing that priests and members of the religious teaching orders were best suited to moralising the people. Even after this view lost favour, and it was thought important to replace religious with civic instruction, there was no change to the principle that it was the role of the primary school to encourage the peasants and working classes to 'behave', and that it was only 'the bourgeois who had the right to enlightenment'.[97] So important was this theme in the writing of the period that the moral influence of the school often overshadowed any desire for cultural or linguistic assimilation and was as important a force behind new school manuals as patriotism.[98] Gildea writes that the three main goals of both lay and religious primary schools were the imposition of a work ethic, the moralisation of the labouring classes and the encouragement of minimum standards of cleanliness.[99] Increasing levels of loyalty and obedience was a key part of the republican project for national integration insofar as social stability was necessary for the continuation of the republic, and respectful citizens would be less likely to overthrow it.

These values were what Marjio Barpagli and Marcello Dei refer to as indirect political socialisation: the transmission of values not directly political, but which impinge upon the development of the political personality of the individual (such as respect for authority).[100] This did not mean that many primary school teachers of the Third Republic were not also encouraged by central government to transmit direct political values too if they could, in particular a respect for and belief in the republic as the natural regime for France. This they did with greater or lesser enthusiasm, for not all the *instituteurs* were 'black-coated missionaries intent on colonising the countryside'.[101] Patrick Lagoueyte writes that in spite of the enduring image of the 'black hussars as the advance guard in the struggle of the republic versus the clergy in each village for the hearts and minds of the future voters, many were not republicans and even if they were they often did not do battle with the local village *curé*'.[102]

In many cases the *instituteur* was drawn from local stock, and had a strong devotion to his region; as such he may not have been an ardent centralist, although he was most often in favour of progress, insofar as education and participation in modern society could bring it about. In addition to personal convictions, *instituteurs* were often limited in their potential militant republi-

97   George Duveau, *Les Instituteurs*, Paris 1957.
98   See, for example, Felix Pécault, *L'Education publique et la vie nationale*, Paris 1897, and Boutroux, 'Les Récents Manuels'.
99   Gildea, *Education*, 235.
100 Marjio Barbagli and Marcello Dei, 'Socialisation into apathy and political subordination', in Jerome Karabel and A. H. Halsey (eds), *Power and ideology in education*, New York 1977, 423–32.
101 Singer, *Village notables*, 2.
102 Lagoueyte, *La Vie politique*, 118–19.

canism by particular local circumstances and especially by the position of the mayor. If the mayor was a republican, this made the position of the *maître d'école* much stronger *vis à vis* the clergy, whereas in the opposite situation, he usually had to give way to prevailing local opinion.[103] Since, in the Westhoek, the clergy were a particularly potent force with many of the village mayors squarely behind them, the role of the schoolmaster was often more to transmit the indirect, rather than the direct socialising values. Ultimately this served the republican project insofar as increased loyalty and patriotism to 'France' in a non-political sense, is not too far off loyalty to the republican regime as long as they are in fact one and the same.

In the end what can be said about the importance of the role of the *instituteur* and the *institutrice* in the formation of identity in the Westhoek during the Third Republic? Although they have been credited by many with being the chief perpetrators of the change, as the great colonisers of the Third Republic, their impact as language teachers was in fact, as we have seen, limited by a host of social and material conditions. Attendance problems and overall lack of time in the classroom would have also reduced the impact of the history, geography and moral lessons, which often took second seat to the teaching of the French language itself or of catechism.

The limits on primary schools left much of their impact dependent upon outside forces, such as the motivation of those coming to school, and what they wanted to get out of it. Francois Furet and Jacques Ozouf, in their analysis of literacy in France, described the secular school not as the origin but as the result of the general trend towards literacy.[104] General literacy freed the people from the priests, the elders and the notables of the community, and the end of the locally dominated oral tradition came through the written orders that came from the central state.[105] It was through the realisation of this fact that more and more demands for education were heard. Gildea writes that in spite of the efforts of the schools 'the labouring classes had no interest in being reformed; if they attended school it was in order to get on, to obtain material advantages'.[106] Weber goes further, stating that in terms of integration, the schools did not make any inroads until the parents saw and felt that these distinct material advantages for their children came through being educated, rather than by entering the workforce.[107] Particularly in the Nord, where industrialisation provided work more easily, it took longer for school to

---

103 Ibid. 119. For more information on the rivalry between the local clergy and the *instituteurs* see chapter 5 below, and Barnett Singer, 'The teacher as notable in Brittany, 1880–1914', *French Historical Studies* ix (1976), 635–59.

104 Francois Furet and Jacques Ozouf, 'L'Alphabétisation: trois siècles de métissage culturel', *Annales: économies, sociétés, civilisation* xxxii (May-June 1977), 490.

105 Patrick J. Harrigan, 'Historians and compilers joined: the historiography of the 1970s and French *enquêtes* of the nineteenth century', in Baker and Harrigan, *Making of Frenchmen*, 10.

106 Gildea, *Education*, 253.

107 See Weber, *Peasants into Frenchmen*, ch. xviii.

be seen as more than a mere road to the necessary First Communion. This argument is perhaps best summed up by Emile Durkheim, who claims that 'educational transformations are always the result and the symptom of the social transformations in terms of which they are to be explained'.[108]

In the twentieth century, while tolerating a small element of regional language teaching, the republican project to solidify national identity through teaching republican morals and a uniform French history did not lose pace. To the end of the twentieth century, the two subjects which remain compulsory at all levels of primary and secondary school are French and history, and, along with philosophy, they are included in all of the sections of the baccalaureate examinations. Throughout the twentieth century, at the summit of French republican education, the philosophy programme explicitly maintains the original objectives of the republican project, teaching 'fundamental values . . . which are *intrinsically linked to the republican ideal itself*'.[109] Although reforms have been mooted on several occasions in the latter half of the twentieth century, no one has seriously challenged the idea of the republican project of using the school system to reinforce French identity and republican values. The lack of challenge is perhaps one of the best witnesses to the success of the programme from the start. The French Flemish, who came out of the school system, even if they did not become regular French-speakers, had, through regular exposure, become more familiar with French history, geography and culture, as well as the national republican value system, such that they could identify themselves directly with the French state and nation.

Military service

A further means for republicans to advance their goals of national integration was through compulsory military service. Direct contact by certain members of the community with French culture is an obvious way to integrate a minority group and to instil a sense of loyalty and national identity. Via such military service, numerous Flemish youths had direct exposure to the French language during their compulsory military service. Years spent in a regiment transmitted the basics more effectively than their primary schooling, and they would bring both a knowledge of the language and a sentimentality towards France back to their villages after the completion of their service.[110] It is possible to exaggerate the impact of military service on the communities

---

108 Emile Durkheim, 'On education and society', in Karabel and Halsey, *Power and ideology in education*, 92.
109 Luc Ferry and Alain Renaut, *Philosopher à dix-huit ans: faut-il réformer l'enseignement de la philosophie?*, Paris 1999, 129, 19. Emphasis original.
110 Weber, *Peasants into Frenchmen*, ch. xvii, discusses in detail the role of military service in the spread of French to the provinces.

of origin from a linguistic point of view, for many of the soldiers did not return to their village or region, and of those who did, many forgot French, or did not necessarily speak French to the others when they returned, even if they had the ability to do so.[111] It is doubtful, therefore, that compulsory military service was very influential as a Frenchifying force, but it was not negligible as an opening to French society and culture which prepared the French Flemish to more readily receive and accept outside influences. It also led them to identify much more readily with France, both in military terms (who was a friend and fellow-soldier and who was an enemy) and in terms of simple awareness of other regions of what they could increasingly think of as 'their' nation.

The military in general also had some effect on the sympathies of the Flemish for the French nation, and their openness to its influence. Much of the patriotism taught at school was linked to the military defence of the nation, possible threats to French security and retribution for the war of 1870.[112] Many boys' schools instigated military exercises, if not actual 'school battalions', to help to engender the sense of national pride and unity which comes with the sentiment of defence of one's homeland.[113] While the direct military participation of the Westhoek was limited,[114] being a border region they could not help but be influenced by the wars, which were fought in their territory and contributed directly to their conception of themselves as French, ensconced on one side of the border and dependent upon the centre for protection from external enemies.

The First World War, in addition to evident sentimental contributions to identity, also increased the direct contact of many of the French Flemish with French culture through exile during the hostilities. Because of the proximity of the front, hundreds of thousands of families were forced to flee to safer regions in the interior of France.[115] For the French Flemish, this meant a greater exposure to French, contributed directly to their openness towards French culture and accelerated the trend towards bilingualism which became more marked during the inter-war period.[116] As was the case with the soldiers above, temporary exile also increased their general awareness of the rest of the country, making identification with the nation that much easier. Landry

---

111 Lagoueyte, *La Vie politique*, 120.

112 See Raoul Girardet, *Le Nationalisme français: anthologie, 1871–1914*, Paris 1983, 70–3, 80–4.

113 See Philippe Marchand, 'Les Petits Soldats de demain: les bataillons scolaires dans le département du Nord, 1882–1892', *RN* lxvii (July–Sept. 1985), 769–803. The *bataillons scolaires* were military units attached to a *lycée*, *collège* or *école primaire* which would initiate the students to military training.

114 Only one of the twenty-three *bataillons scolaires* of the *département du Nord* was in the Westhoek: ibid.

115 See R. Vandenbussche, 'La Région dans la guerre (1914–1918)', in Hilaire, *Histoire du Nord/Pas-de-Calais*, 216.

116 Dewachter, 'Sur le Front des langues', 101.

and Verrewaere write that when the *école d'Hazebrouck* took refuge in the Calvados, they brought the *signum* with them, and learning French continued as much as ever.[117] Thus the war served to increase contact and the openness of the Flemish towards the French language, in addition to the sense of Frenchness it conveyed by the direct involvement of the entire population in the fighting. Renewed invasion just over twenty years later also conveyed a heightened sentiment of attachment to France.[118]

Compulsory military service continued to serve as a means of national integration throughout the interwar period, and into the post-war era as well. It was only in the closing years of the twentieth century that the republican policy of compulsory military service, after much heated debate, was dropped. While there was talk of setting up a year-long 'civilian service' in its stead, in the end it was replaced by a simple two-day programme for men and women. The demise of compulsory military service can be attributed mostly to the changing nature of the armed forces and the perceived military disadvantages of a conscript army, rather than to any belief that the role of military service in forging national loyalty was unnecessary.

Political structure

Along with the republican project of national integration went the goal of reducing any possible political power and influence of regionalist movements concerned to foster a regional identity which could rival and potentially weaken French national identity and threaten the strength of the centralised republican nation state. The established administrative and political structure proved extremely efficient as a means to achieve this goal, through the local but centrally controlled administrative hierarchy, the tradition of multiple political representation and direct pressure by the state on local political elites. Part of the heritage from the revolutionary period was the corps of prefects named by central government, who could work to achieve the ends of government in each of the departments, and who, throughout much of the nineteenth century also controlled the nomination of the village mayors. The fact that many local political figures also combined several political mandates meant that the most influential among them also had a stake in national institutions, and were thereby discouraged from leading a regionalist movement. Finally, the republican authorities also tried whenever possible to convince or pressure any of the local traditional elites or 'notables' such that if they would not support the national project, they would at least not oppose it.

---

[117] Landry and de Verrewaere, *Histoire secrète*, 284.
[118] More will be said about the direct effects of the two world wars on the development of identity in chapter 7 below and in the conclusion. The focus here is upon the conscious policies spread by the republicans through military service.

The final decades of the nineteenth century and the first few of the twentieth have been seen as marking a major transition in the nature of local political culture in France. Up to that time, it had been the 'local notables' who were the most influential and dominant figures, particularly in the towns and rural communes and, as we have seen, local influence was extremely important in the political choices of the day.[119] The thirty-five years leading up to the First World War marked 'the beginning of the end of the notables, but they were still there. There was both hierarchy *and progress, things looked fine ahead, but M. le Maire and M. le curé, not to mention the instituteur,* were still here behind'.[120] Thus although their influence was diminishing, the attitude of the notables towards the national question was nevertheless an important factor in the determination of local trends. Barnett Singer, in his analysis of village notables, contrasts his own approach with the classic theory of Eugen Weber in 'attributing more of an active role to rural notables than he [Weber] does by stressing the in-betweeness of their function in rural society'.[121] A 'progressive' attitude on their part, in accordance with national, centralist goals eased and encouraged Frenchification, whereas resistance could retard the process. Gabriel Dessert agrees, pointing out that progress spread into the regions of France 'only if the local notables themselves were convinced of the necessity'.[122]

Each of these notables was drawn from within the Westhoek itself; the mayors, as we have seen, were local *cultivateurs* or merchants, and the priests and schoolteachers also came 'from the people'.[123] They all cared about their *pays d'origine*, but this meant that they could either choose to defend the local culture from assimilation and fight to cultivate and encourage local or regional identity, or alternatively to lead the way in national integration. Many local political figures, such as the mayors or the prefects, were at the same time agents of central government and representatives of the local community. Jack Hayward writes that such a person 'generally plays down the former role and thinks of himself in opposition to the state rather than as its servant'.[124] Singer agrees that they were 'caught between government and locality, with one foot in each of the two camps; but when it came to the crunch the centrifugal inclinations more often won out'.[125] From the point of view of republican governments, some mayors were better ignored and tolerated than opposed (or forced to resign) in spite of their defensive regional positions, because it was 'better the man should guarantee a certain village

119 See Singer, *Village notables*.
120 Ibid. 7.
121 Ibid, 1–2.
122 Gabriel Dessert, 'Alphabétisation et scholarisation dans le grand-ouest au 19e siècle', in Baker and Harrigan, *Making of Frenchmen*, 194.
123 Gérard Cholvy, 'Régionalisme et clergé catholique au XIXe siècle', in Gras and Livet, *Régions et régionalisme*, 201.
124 Hayward, *One and indivisible*, 30.
125 Singer, *Village notables*, 56.

stability than that he should adhere to orthodoxy'.[126] This was the case, for example, of twenty mayors in the *arrondissement* of Dunkerque who, in 1901, certified that their local *curés* were teaching in French when in fact they were not.[127]

In spite of their desire to be seen as taking a stance in opposition to the central government rather than acting as its mere agents, the shape of local political discourse was more of a rivalry between the various notables for local influence and control, than any systematic regional stance.[128] The nature of the politically centralised structure of France was as a sort of mutual dependency between the powers in the centre and those on the periphery; central government needing the support of the regional authorities to maintain its control, and the regions requiring the centre to provide the laws, regulations and overall authority which permitted them to govern the regions, not to mention the financial support for the infrastructure and the tariff protection so dear to the industry of the region. This system created for the local leaders a vested interest in maintaining the power that had put them there, and if possible even to garner support from higher authorities in any conflicts in their local jurisdiction. They derived 'a dual legitimacy from central government consecration and local representation'.[129] Both parts were necessary, so the local notables could attempt to preserve their local position through obtaining government grants, and in return guarantee local stability, and if not loyalty at least minimal opposition. Resistance to government regulations could be a useful menace or bargaining tool, but the local notables had to be careful not to go too far, lest they lose the support of the government altogether.[130]

State authority was always wary of mayors and other regional political figures because of the implicit threat that they might promote regional consciousness and instigate regional resistance, to the detriment of the central authority. Such was the debate in the early decades of the Third Republic over the election of mayors. Up until the end of the Second Empire, mayors were nominated, and could be recalled by the prefect, and acted as local agents for the government. The founders of the Third Republic would have liked to increase municipal responsibility, but the uprising of the Commune of Paris made them cautious, and so in the law passed on 14 April 1871, only in the smaller communes, comprising less than 20,000 inhabitants, could the mayor be elected by the *conseil municipal*.[131] It was not until 1882 that all mayors were elected, irrespective of the size of the commune

---

126 Ibid. 45.
127 Report, special commissioner of Dunkerque, 14 Aug. 1901, ADN, 1 T 123 5. See also chapter 5 below.
128 See Charle, 'Région et conscience régionale', 37–43.
129 Hayward, *One and indivisible*, 19.
130 See ibid. 18–19.
131 Law of 14 April 1871: Vandenbussche, 'La Fonction municipale', 320.

(except Paris). Even then, the change, when finally implemented, was made with a great deal of prudence, as decentralisation worried many in the national government and parliament.[132] At the same time as giving what would seem a greater legitimacy to municipal government, several specific powers were taken away from the mayor, reducing in fact his responsibilities. For example, the mayor had previously had a say in the local primary school, but with the Ferry laws, the decision was imposed from above that the schools would be lay and the teachers not members of any religious teaching order.[133]

The frequency with which individuals combined several mandates simultaneously had considerable consequences for the potential regionalism represented by these active and ambitious mayors, who could set themselves up as rivals to challenge central authority and defend local interests. In an exception to the general trends of the time, during the First World War the powers of local government were increased, and there was a marked tendency towards decentralisation.[134] After the war, these regional authorities sought to maintain their newly acquired control, and even in the parts of the Nord which had been occupied, local leaders were quick to claim the same status and increase in power enjoyed by the other regions. Subsequent demands for even greater regional scope were ignored, however, and rather than decentralisation, the trend towards reducing regional powers was resumed throughout the interwar years, weakening yet further the position of the mayor and the *conseil municipal*. Renewed occupation during the Second World War had similar effects in terms of increasing the autonomy and competence of regional elites, leading to further unsuccessful calls for greater regional autonomy after liberation.[135]

Faced with frustration in seeking greater powers for the region and in order to properly defend regional interests, a national mandate was seen as a possible alternative, and often taken as a second resort rather than increasing militancy and demands on the central government. The ability to hold two offices was thus essential as a channel to avert municipal frustration which could lead to regionalism, since ambitious local representatives had an outlet through national office.[136] Regionalism was further discouraged because it became more and more widely recognised that it was through the national

---

132 Ibid. 321.

133 See ibid. 322–6, for a discussion of the reduction in municipal powers.

134 See Henri Hauser, *Le Problème du régionalisme* (Histoire économique & sociale de la guerre mondiale), Paris 1924, and Richard Cobb, *French and Germans, Germans and French: a personal interpretation of France under two occupations 1914–1918/1940–1944*, Hanover–London 1983, 26–8.

135 See Yves Le Maner, 'Les Municipalités du Nord/Pas-de-Calais sous l'occupation: pouvoir local, pouvoir français, pouvoir allemand', *RN*, no. 2 spécial hors-série (1987), 265, and Lynne Taylor, *Between resistance and collaboration: popular protest in northern France, 1940–45*, Basingstoke 2000, 160. For a discussion of administrative decentralisation in the late twentieth century see chapter 7 below.

136 See Vandenbussche, 'La Fonction municipale', 335–6.

body, and national institutions, that local interests could best be protected, and the most effective guarantee was to ensure adequate representation by local figures, whose municipal offices added to their prestige and capacities before the government. Thus the political structure of the state itself contributed to the weakening of any regionalism which might hope to profit by championing and developing a strong regional political identity which was deliberately set at odds to the national one.

To achieve the goal of a strong national identity, one final tactic used by the French elites is what was described in the introduction as 'cultural appropriation'. When confronted with regional cultural practices which could not · be eliminated and replaced by national ones, some, after careful selection, were gradually relabelled as national ones. In this way what had formerly been thought of simply as 'Flemish' was repeatedly described as 'French' or 'northern French' until the label stuck. For example, regional festivals such as the processions of the giants and the *karnaval* of Dunkerque, or regional architecture become portrayed and thought of as characteristically and unquestionably 'French' traditions found in one particular region of France.[137] In this way important regional figures could become 'great Frenchmen' through commemoration in national histories, or in the naming of streets and public buildings, such as the Lycée Van Der Meersch in Roubaix.[138] Many of the patriotic school textbooks of the Third Republic attempted directly to integrate local or regional history into the national one.[139] Writing about traditional music in 1889, Julien Tiersot included several examples of 'Flemish' music, which included not only melodies but lyrics reproduced in the Flemish language, but presented as unquestionably examples of one style of 'French' music.[140] Even the use of the common name of the region itself was altered, indicating a shift in thinking: in the course of the twentieth century the term 'Westhoek' was used less and less frequently; the region was instead increasingly described as either 'French Flanders' or simply part of 'the north of France' in general or the more official '*département du Nord*'. The region was no longer simply 'a' region, but a 'French' region, being subsumed and appropriated into the national whole. The term 'Flanders' has itself been appropriated, becoming increasingly synonymous with 'northern France'.[141] To think of themselves as being in the 'north' and not in

137 The *karnaval* of Dunkerque has become one of the most widely known 'French' festivals, as witnessed by the success of the recent film, *Karnaval*, Thomas Vincent 1999.
138 Maxence Van der Meersch (1907–51), wrote several novels portraying life in French Flanders.
139 See p. 104 above and Thiesse, *Ils Apprenaient la France*.
140 Julien Tiersot, *Histoire de la chanson populaire en France*, Paris 1889, 32–3, 91–3, 127–30, 241. He also gives examples of 'French' music written in Breton and Basque, appropriating them into the national canon.
141 It is also used in commemorative naming (gare Lille-Flandres) and by regional societies which encompass much larger areas than the Westhoek.

the 'west' implies a reorientation, a strengthening of French identity at the expense of identification with other members of the Flemish cultural region.

The tactic of appropriation was increasingly employed after the Second World War, when French elites made a concerted effort through the ministry of culture to 'nationalise' culture and claim that even in their regional variety, most cultural traits were truly French. During the 'trente glorieuses' and thereafter, as the resources available to the state increased dramatically, more effort could be put into promoting the Frenchness of the regions.[142] It should be pointed out that appropriation as it has been defined here is not only a 'tactic' on the part of the authorities, but also part of a two-way process of negotiation between regions and the centre, as various interest groups within the region seek to influence which cultural characteristics will be appropriated and perpetuated, and how they will be labelled.[143] Nor is the process always conscious or deliberate. Its origins can, moreover, be completely cultural, in the way that Jacques Brel's *Le Plat Pays* came to symbolise northern France (for the French) and his numerous songs referring to the north and to Flanders were incorporated into the mainstream tradition of popular singing in France during the 1950s and 1960s.[144]

Thus the republican elite made the best use of the political and economic structures of the state to further their aims of strengthening French national identity, unifying national culture and identifying both as nearly as possible with republicanism. Through the school system, national holidays, compulsory military service and the ministry of culture, with some help from the political and institutional structure itself, they tried to get the Flemish to think of themselves in every possible way as French. It is also interesting to note that the assimilationist model cannot, in fact, be dissociated from a process of appropriation: important elements of regional culture were integrated via appropriation, which puts a slightly different gloss on the concept of the French melting pot.

The republican elite was not the only group which took an active interest in the identity of the French Flemish. Others had different ideas and sought to cultivate and develop other elements of French Flemish identity in ways which were not necessarily in line with those of the national elites. Their influence too needs to be considered, beginning with that of the Catholic Church.

142 Much was done subtly as well, profiting from the phenomenon of 'banal nationalism' discussed at the end of chapter 3 above.

143 See the introduction for more on the negotiation between centre and region.

144 Even though many referred to Belgium, strictly speaking, they have been integrated into French identity. See Jacques Brel, *Tout Brel*, ed. Olivier Todd, Paris 1986, 253–4, for the song referred to.

5

The Catholic Church in French Flanders

Religion played a powerful cultural part for the Flemish of the Westhoek throughout the nineteenth and twentieth centuries; the Church was the most important socialising institution for the population. It consecrated the most important rites of passage during their lifetime, marked by baptism, First Communion, marriage, as well as death. The major festivals in French Flanders were religious, marking out the year in Catholic terms. The priest played a central role in each community, as respected counsellor and adviser. The Church was in most respects at the centre of the cultural lives of the French Flemish for the greater part of the nineteenth and twentieth centuries, and thus in a position to have a direct influence on the formation of identity and the development of culture in the Westhoek.[1]

Given its powerful local position, the Church had several socially influential means at its disposal. The principal influence of the clergy was in the classroom, through congregational schools and religious education in catechism class, as well as through direct control and supervision of teachers (official for the most of the nineteenth century according to national legislation, as well as unofficial, stemming from the clergy's powerful social position and tradition).[2] Before the separation of Church and State in 1905, priests and bishops also wielded political clout, through their role in the administration and through their local prestige and authority as highly respected figures in the community.

While not among the main objectives of the Church and its representatives in the Westhoek, other priorities occasionally led them to take an active stance on questions of regional identity, language and culture. Opposition to the republican, and essentially the anticlerical dimension of the republican national project, led the Church to defend some elements of Flemish identity beyond the simply religious. A useful starting-point is to examine the evolving position of the local *curé* in the local context and the ends to which he put the influence he was able to preserve, principally in the domain of language, followed by the position of the larger Church in regional and national politics as they influenced the Westhoek.

---

[1] For more general history of the Church in France see Gérard Cholvy and Yves-Marie Hilaire, *Histoire religieuse de la France contemporaine*, Toulouse 1988, and François Lebrun (ed.), *Histoire des catholiques en France du XVe siècle à nos jours*, Paris 1980.
[2] See pp. 117–21 below for further details.

Local influence

Rivalry between the *curé* and other local notables for influence within the village was closely linked to the changing position of the Church with respect to education. For most of the nineteenth century, the Church's substantial, indeed primordial, role in education was secure, reaching its peak in the late 1870s. Although it was the state which laid the groundwork for the education system, 'the Catholic Church came to appropriate the public system of educa-tion to its own advantage, while maintaining a flourishing public sector in its own right'.[3] Education was viewed as closely linked with religion, and the Church devoted a great deal of time and effort to ensuring that the instruc-tion provided reflected this desired harmony of concepts. The national struggle to preserve Catholic influence in schools was reflected in each locality by the well-publicised conflicts between the local schoolmasters and the *curés*, especially in the closing decades of the nineteenth century.[4]

For the first half of the nineteenth century in rural society, the status of the schoolteacher was little better then that of a sub-*curé*, since education was regarded even by the general populace as subordinate to religion. Financial necessity often forced teachers to seek outside employment, very often filling the role of cantor and/or sexton at the Church, or working at any variety of other occupations in the village.[5] The first step towards bettering the teach-ers' position came with improvements in their training and salary. At the instigation of the Guizot law of 1833, each *département* was required to set up at least one special teacher training school, an 'école normale', each commune to maintain a school building and provide lodging for the school-master, and the salary for each *instituteur* was fixed at a minimum of 200 francs *per annum*.[6] The normal schools ensured a minimum standard of competence on the part of the teacher. The *loi Falloux* raised the minimum yearly stipend to 600 francs. An amendment in 1862 made it 700 for any teacher with a minimum of five years' experience. This change was brought about in response to the *concours Rouland*, in which teachers complained about the inadequacy of their salaries. In spite of these increases, by the end of the Second Empire, writes Antoine Prost, a teacher's pay was still not enough to live at an 'acceptable' standard, but was a substantial improvement neverthe-less.[7]

---

3 Gildea, *Education*, 27.
4 See Singer, *Village notables*, who discusses this conflict, as well as the rivalry between priests and mayors. For a particular example see Pierre Descamps, 'La Vie d'une paroisse au XIXe siècle: Aubers-en-Weppes', *RN* xlvi (1964), 535–73.
5 See Prost, *Histoire de l'enseignement*, 134.
6 Ibid. 140.
7 Ibid. 141. The sum earned by the teachers was less than the cost of one year's *pension* in a *lycée*.

With these ameliorations in salary and training, the quality of applicants began to increase, and, little by little, the social standing of the teacher within the village began slowly to rise. The *loi Falloux* forbade the teachers all external employment, although in practice many continued to work as secretaries to the mayor and assistant to the *curé*. Motivated partly by a fear of over-zealous republican or socialist teachers, they were made directly responsible to the local parish priest, who was given the right to have the schoolteacher dismissed or transferred.[8] Under this law, schoolteachers were also directly responsible for some aspects of the religious education of the children.

In the early years of the Third Republic, the *instituteurs* had not yet attained the level of status which they desired, but had made up a lot of ground, such that they began to rival the *curés* for influence in several areas. Correspondingly with their increased prestige, the schoolmasters sought more and more independence *vis-à-vis* the *curés*, who considered it their right to meddle in all the teacher's affairs, and hoped to preserve their measure of influence over what happened in the classroom. Teachers had to be particularly careful and tactful in places like French Flanders, since the position of the priests was so strong to begin with, if they wished to secure any measure of autonomy or independence of action. In one instance, the inspector complained directly to the minister that the teachers were regularly distracted from their job by the number of hours they were expected to spend at the church fulfilling the tasks assigned to them by the *curé*.[9]

With the new education laws in the early 1880s, the priests lost the direct legal authority over the schoolmasters they had enjoyed for the previous thirty years. They were thereafter restricted to the moral weight they carried as members of the clergy in a region with a high proportion of believers. The conflict between priest and schoolmaster was in many ways more about local influence, power and politics, than strictly about ideology, given that in the Westhoek most of the schoolteachers shared the Catholic faith of the village inhabitants.[10] While continuing to attempt to direct the teachers where they could, priests also began to pressure the people directly to boycott public schools, especially where they considered the teaching to be overly republican or anticlerical. This battle was, of course, waged all over France, and for reasons of principle in addition to those of local power.[11]

---

8 Pierre Pierrard, 'La "Petite Loi" Falloux du 11 janvier 1850 et les révocations d'instituteurs communaux en 1850', *RN* lxvii (July–Sept. 1985), 687–702, and Prost, *Histoire de l'enseignement*, 174–6. See also R. D. Anderson, *Education in France, 1848–1870*, Oxford 1975, for more information on the school system during the Second Empire.
9 'Rapport d'ensemble d'inspection générale de 1880', AN, F 17 9270.
10 See, for example, Weber, *Peasants into Frenchmen*, 362.
11 See Cholvy and Hilaire, *Histoire religieuse*, ii. 57–65. For more information, specifically on the battle in the Westhoek, see Joan L. Coffey, 'Church–State conflict: bilingualism and religious education, 1890–1905', *Proceedings of the Annual Meeting of the Western Society for*

In the Westhoek, such ecclesiastical pressure was particularly strong: some children were refused admission to catechism class or refused First Communion if they attended the public school, and in one case several mothers were refused absolution after confession because their children attended the public school.[12] The archbishop of Cambrai encouraged the heads of Flemish families to be aware of the consequences of leaving their children in a school where prayers were no longer tolerated.[13] In their sermons, the priests often depicted the schoolteachers as impious heathens of whom all loyal Christians should beware. In describing one such case to the inspector general, the primary school inspector added that in spite of this harsh treatment, the teachers continued to sacrifice their dignity 'out of devotion to their cause' and to bring their pupils along regularly to mass.[14] In 1883 the *curé* of Flers, M. Charlemagne Gailliez, went so far as to send a girl home who wished simply to attend mass, because she was a student of the local public school, and not seated in the special pews reserved for them (which were full).[15] The *curé* of Wemaers-Cappel was so unpleasant in his dealings with the *instituteurs*, complained the village mayor in a letter to the subprefect, that in the couple of years leading up to 1898 no fewer than eight different schoolmasters had asked to be transferred away.[16] The priest insisted on keeping students in his catechism class for double the time deemed 'necessary' by the teachers, in order to repeat everything twice (once in French and once in Flemish), and would not allow any of the *instituteurs* to keep students after class as a punishment, since that made them late for catechism class. The mayor himself tried to stay neutral, in order to act as an intermediary and calm both sides towards reason, but it did not work that often, as both the *curé* and the various *instituteurs* tended merely to become aggravated with him.[17]

In combating the public schools, the priests were at a significant legal disadvantage, and many were investigated and charged for their activities against the children who went to the public school, their families, or for other steps taken against the lay school.[18] The *abbé* Cabre of Bousbecque was charged in October 1900 with having refused to admit two girls to his cate-

---

French History xxii (1995), 55–66. For more on anticlericalism see René Rémond, *L'Anticléricalisme en France de 1815 à nos jours*, Brussels 1985.
[12] Academic inspector and departmental director of primary education to prefect, 24 Jan. 1902, ADN. 2 V 79; prefect to minister of public worship, 31 Oct. 1896, AN, F 19 6018.
[13] 'Lettre pastorale et mendement de monseigneur l'archevêque de Cambrai sur les ecoles & l'enseignement primaire', 29 June 1882, ADN, 2 V 117. See also 'Instruction Pastorale', 18 Jan. 1879, ADN, 2 V 115, in which the archbishop instructs the priests to defend the congregational schools at every opportunity.
[14] Primary inspector to inspector general, 3 May 1883, AN, F 17 9270.
[15] Untitled article, *Le Petit Nord*, 14 Feb. 1883.
[16] Mayor of Wemaers-Cappel to subprefect of Hazebrouck, 7 June 1898, ADN, 6 Z 2288.
[17] Ibid.
[18] Police records, 'poursuites contre catholiques', ADN, M 154 56.

chism class because they attended the public school, and for having preached sermons against the school. Similar charges were laid against M. Cerlie, *curé* of Grand Fort Philippe, in June 1901 and the *abbé* Six (a prominent member of the Flemish intellectual movement in the Westhoek) in Lannoy in January 1902. The *curés* of Frelinghem and Godewaersvelde were also both charged with preaching sermons directed against the *école laïque*. The *curé* of Wemaers-Cappel, M. Barkey, was finally charged in November 1900 on two counts – keeping children in his catechism class deliberately while the public school was in session such that they missed their regular lessons, and forbidding the children to speak any language but Flemish in and around the church (not to mention the fact that the First Communion classes and all his sermons were in Flemish).[19]

In spite of the criticisms and charges laid against them, the clergy had, nevertheless, some limited effect until the end of the nineteenth century, but the strength of persecution and pressure under the radical administrations of René Waldeck-Rousseau and particularly Émile Combes reduced clerical influence on public school attendance after the turn of the century. The percentage of children attending religious schools in the conscription of Hazebrouck declined from just under 50 per cent in 1894–5 to only 3.5 per cent in 1904–5. The corresponding figures for the conscription of Dunkerque are 35 per cent and 9 per cent.[20] These decreasing numbers represent a significant decline since the apogee of the Church's power in schools in 1878, when 26 per cent of public and 63 per cent of private schools were controlled by priests or members of religious teaching orders (the highest percentage in the whole of France).[21]

Thus the nineteenth century saw the local prestige of village *curés* in the Westhoek slowly decline relative to that of the primary school teachers, who became more and more to be considered on a par with the local priest in terms of their importance in local life. With the separation of Church and State, the Church's official say in mainstream educational matters (public) all but ceased, and it was purely through unofficial channels and religious teaching that it preserved some influence. The main priority of the priests in the decades leading up to the separation of the Church and State was to battle the secularisation of education and preserve the position of the Catholic Church in local society. In spite of the fact that the region remained strongly practising Catholic, in both of these areas the former preponderance of the priests was slowly eroded. After the separation of the Church and State, as the hostile anticlericalism of the state mellowed, and the notion of

---

19 Ibid.
20 AN, F 17 10682 for 1894–5; F 17 10717 for 1904–5. The percentages quoted are calculated from the total numbers of boys and girls attending public or private elementary schools and *écoles maternelles*.
21 Pierre Pierrard (ed.), *Histoire des diocèses de Cambrai et Lille*, Paris 1978, 241–2. The actual figures are 345 *écoles communales* out of 1,322, and 361 *écoles libres* out of 573.

'separate spheres' (religious and secular) was more and more accepted by the members of the Church, the intensity of local personal rivalry and overt conflict slowly diminished.[22]

Language

The primary goal of the Church was to preserve the place of religion in schools and society, and one of the means to this end was through persevering in the use of the Flemish language in education and in the churches of the Westhoek. The use of Flemish took several forms, including pressure on teachers, the choice of language for the recitation of the catechism and the language of sermons. The Church has been described as the last refuge of the Flemish language in French Flanders, but its significant position nevertheless gave it a decisive impact upon linguistic evolution in the region.[23] J. Jarry, writing to the Academic Council in 1869, predicted that no advance in the use of French could be hoped for in the Flemish-speaking *arrondissements* without the concurrence of the clergy, and at the time he added 'God only knows when!'[24]

While the Catholic Church supported the maintenance of Flemish in the Westhoek, that position did not mean that as individual members of an educated elite and in spite of some training in Flemish, the priests did not think of French as the superior language.[25] Gérard Cholvy claims that 'Few were the clerics who did not see the dangers of cultural and geographical uprooting, but as few those who defended popular cultures for their intrinsic value.'[26] Why then did they defend Flemish at all? Cholvy considers that it was for 'pastoral' reasons, linked to preserving a certain pre-industrial, rural and agrarian way of life which was associated by many priests with their vision of Catholicism. They were in part hoping to spare their followers from the suffering which came with 'uprooting', while at the same time protecting them from the corruption which came with modernisation and profane, secular French writing. The minister of public instruction was aware of this reasoning, as he mentioned to the minister of justice and public worship, quoting a priest as having said that 'Our Flemish language . . . is a protection from dangerous texts and a safeguard against the spirit of indifference in

---

[22] For a comparative discussion of the relationship between school teacher and *curé* in another Catholic region see Singer, 'Teacher as notable', 635–59.
[23] Luc Verbeke, *Vlaanderen in Frankrijk: taalstrijd en vlaamse beweging in Frans- of Zuid-Vlaanderen*, Leuven 1970, 33. See also Richard Héméryck, 'L'École primaire, le clergé et le recul du flamand durant la seconde partie du XIXe siècle', ACFF 1 (1992), 116.
[24] J. Jarry, inspection report, June 1869, AN, F 17 9376.
[25] Weber, *Peasants into Frenchmen*, 88.
[26] Gérard Cholvy, 'Régionalisme et clergé catholique au XIXe siècle', in Gras and Livet, *Régions et régionalisme*, 200–1.

matters of religion.'[27] The cultural links between the Church and traditional life were strong; indigenous languages 'formed part of traditional culture which has religion at the centre and which is nourished at the Church'.[28] The relationship between the Church and regionalism was, unlike its previous close connection with legitimism, symbiotic and indispensable.[29]

The position of supporting the Flemish language was only partly recognised and defended openly by the church hierarchy. The archbishop of Cambrai, in defence of his clergy, wrote to the rector of the academy that, although his priests, like those of Alsace and Brittany, regretted the fact that (through abuse) the French language had become a vehicle for irreligious and immoral propaganda, it was not true that they were systematically opposed to the spread of French in their parishes.[30] If not systematically opposed, it was nevertheless thought necessary to ensure the linguistic capabilities of priests in the Westhoek, as the prefect complained to the minister of public instruction, art and public worship:

> In order to preserve the influence of the priests in the Flemish area, he [Mgr Monnier, vicar-general of the archdiocese of Cambrai] created or preserved, if it existed before his arrival, a special section in the seminary for the clergy destined for Flanders. By maintaining the exclusive use of the Flemish language in a large part of the department in its own interest, the clergy has largely contributed to maintaining an attitude of defiance of the government among the population which causes both the agents of the government and the national interest to suffer.[31]

In this way it would be ensured that any priest who might be assigned to a parish in the Westhoek would speak Flemish, if he was not of Flemish origin already. Thus whether to protect the people from impure reading, to preserve their influential local positions by using their superior knowledge of Flemish or simply because it was the usual language of the region and the best way to communicate, many priests in the Westhoek took an active stance in defence of the Flemish language in schools, opposing the national republican project of spreading French and republican values.

The Church's defence of the Flemish language had little impact on the development of the public schools and the public school system. Of course, in the period before the Ferry laws, the clergy were in the stronger position and used their direct influence to attempt to encourage, or in some cases force, the teachers to use Flemish in the classroom. In one such case in Flêtre, in

---

[27] Minister of public instruction to minister of justice and public worship, 25 Aug. 1866, AN, F 19 5798.
[28] Le Bras, Études, i. 370.
[29] See Gildea, Education, 137.
[30] Archbishop of Cambrai to rector, 8 Oct. 1866, AN, F 19 5798.
[31] Prefect to minister of public instruction, art and public worship, 28 June 1895, AN, F 19 6018.

1869, the *curé* threatened to have the schoolmistress replaced if she continued to read in French. She had no other recourse but to complain to the inspector, who passed on the complaint to the minister, and hope that the administration could put pressure on the *curé* to change his views.[32] In an inspection report of 1873, the fact that the people spoke only Flemish at home and in the streets was a problem in itself, and only aggravated by 'the clergy [who] make an effort to preserve the use of Flemish at school as in church'.[33]

With the passing of the Ferry laws, priests were fighting a losing battle with respect to the increasingly independent public school teacher, but this did not mean that they ceased to have a major impact on the local inhabitants, and on the language question in particular through other channels. First, through the private Catholic schools, which could act more freely. In addition to the seminary, one school in the Westhoek and one in Tourcoing was still teaching Flemish as late as 1920.[34] Second, and more important, through religious education, via the teaching of catechism, the lessons in church doctrine and prayers which prepared the children for their First Communion. During the Third Republic this took place outside the schoolroom in church buildings, most often on Wednesday afternoons when the children were not in school. In this domain the clergy considered it their right to teach as they saw fit and strongly resented any infringement of their authority by government officials.

Their principal argument in this case in favour of Flemish was that it was all very well to use French in schools, where a fundamental objective was (among others) to teach French; but in catechism, comprehension of religion was the essential point. Since most of the students arrived with minimal French, they could not hope to understand anything of religious significance if they were being taught in that language. So as long as the children could only understand Flemish, they ought to receive their religious instruction in that language, or so the argument went.

Flemish catechism was permitted by the *Conseil académique du Nord* up until 1853, at which time it requested that a French text appear opposite the Flemish one, and as of January of that year the diocese first published a bilingual catechism. The educational authorities desired that the two languages would be at the very least taught simultaneously to Flemish children, and hoped for the co-operation of the religious authorities. The primary inspector wrote to the academic council that the academic administration had dared to request that the diocesan authority support their efforts to spread the French

---

[32] Report to *conseil académique*, June 1869, AN, F 17 9376.
[33] A. Gandon to minister of public instruction, 14 Aug. 1873, AN, F 17 9270.
[34] Camille Looten, speech to the *Congrès régionaliste*, text of which included in a letter from the prefect to the minister of public instruction, 5 Jan. 1921, ADN, M 154 318. The schools were St Winoc of Bergues and Sacré-Coeur in Tourcoing.

language with clear, formal written instructions to each of the priests.[35] By 1864 even Duruy, the minister of education, began to petition the archbishop of Cambrai, Cardinal Régnier, to try to convince him to encourage his priests to use the French version of the text exclusively, and if they could not use exclusively French, to at least follow the guidelines and use both languages.[36] The archbishop utterly refused to interfere, and indeed later complained that Flemish was under particular pressure, and not given the same leniency as Alsatian and Breton by the government.[37] Duruy's request was followed up shortly, on 1 July 1866, with an official ban on the use of Flemish catechism in schools.[38] Mgr Régnier, writing a letter of complaint to the rector in reaction to the new regulation, asserted that the decision over which language would be used in catechism lay 'incontestably with the Episcopal authorities', and that the government had no right to have anything to do with religious instruction and teaching, which was in every respect the responsibility of the Church alone. He asserted plainly that 'catechism must therefore be in Flemish in every parish where preaching is done in Flemish'.[39]

These early exchanges were the beginnings of a long series of disputes between the archbishops of Cambrai and the prefects and ministers of public instruction. The general tactic employed by the archbishops, as outlined by the prefect in a letter to the president of the council, was to refuse to give any written instructions on the subject of language of catechism to their priests, and to show a copy of these instructions to the prefect (which many prefects had requested of the archbishops). Such written instructions would have permitted the government to monitor what directives were really given to the priests of the Westhoek; it could then have used them as leverage against any local *curé* found to be errant. The prefect complained as well about the linguistic tolerance and the use of Flemish for the explanations accompanying the recitation of catechism.[40] In this way the blind eye of the diocesan authorities allowed Flemish catechism to continue 'unofficially', and in some cases they even supported its use. In 1882, in a town called Zerezeele, the archbishop of Cambrai, Mgr Alfred Duquesnay, declared to a group of his faithful that: 'Flemish is the language of God! Not only should catechism be taught in Flemish, but it is even necessary to ensure that the children do not speak any other language in the streets.'[41] It should be pointed out that although the archbishop considered Flemish the language of heaven, he himself did not speak it. He repeated his position adamantly to the minister

---

35 J. Jarry, describing his position to the *conseil académique*, June 1866, AN, F 17 9374.
36 Coornaert, *La Flandre française*, 304.
37 Archbishop of Cambrai to rector, 22 Oct. 1866, AN, F 19 5798.
38 Verbeke, *Vlaanderen in Frankrijk*, 30.
39 Archbishop of Cambrai to rector, 22 Oct. 1866, AN, F 19 5798.
40 Prefect to *président du conseil*, 22 Aug. 1902, AN, F 19 5502.
41 Quoted by representative (signature illegible) of the subprefecture of Hazebrouck to prefect, 16 Oct. 1882, ADN, 2 V 76.

of justice and public worship, arguing that in the communes where Flemish was spoken, catechism would be in Flemish until such a time as French became the 'language of daily use'.[42]

If the higher clergy were defending the use of Flemish, the local priests were doing doubly so. As seen in the previous chapter, French was not effectively taught in the schools until extremely late in the nineteenth century; for catechism, Flemish persisted longer, and was much more difficult to dislodge. In the 1860s, says one report, in two-thirds of the communes religious instruction took place in Flemish, covering the region in which Flemish was spoken 'in all of the ordinary circumstances of life'.[43] In another report from the same period, the primary inspector was only able to say that Flemish was in widespread use and the only remedy for the situation that he could see was goodwill on the part of the ecclesiastical community.[44] In a report from the subprefectures of Hazebrouck describing the situation in 1882, the communes are listed in which only Flemish (fifteen in total), both languages (ten), or only French (the remainder) were used in the recitation of the First Communion service (and in all three of the groups, oral explanations were still given in Flemish).[45] Concerning the *arrondissement* of Dunkerque, a representative of the Académie de Douai (the local administrative office of education) wrote to the subprefecture in 1882 that since the academic authorities were no longer responsible for religious teaching, it was no longer their job to fight Flemish catechism, but went on to say 'But it is not less true that the *curés* continue to insist on Flemish catechism for the children preparing their first communion.'[46]

It is evident that although in some places what was recited may have been in French, in the whole of the two *arrondissements* the explanations were given in Flemish, and the position of the *curés* was supported by the archbishop. In a letter to Mgr Duquesnay in the same year, F. Bailleul, *curé* of Caestre, affirmed that in spite of the fact that every one of his fifty-four students could understand Flemish and only three of them had sufficient understanding of French to permit them to follow a lesson, he still had them recite their catechisms in French. He was obliged, however, given these circumstances, 'to provide the explanations in Flemish, for fear of not being understood by two-thirds of my young listeners'.[47] F. Van Costenoble, *curé* of Flêtre, had divided his students into two sections: one for those native speakers who could speak only Flemish, and another in French for those

---

[42] Archbishop of Cambrai to minister of justice and public worship, 8 Aug. 1882, AN, F 19 5502.
[43] Report to inspector (*re.* Dunkerque), 24 Oct. 1866, ADN, 1 T 80 72.
[44] Primary inspection report, June 1866, AN, F 17 9374.
[45] Representative (signature illegible) of office of subprefecture of Hazebrouck to prefect, 14 Aug. 1882, ADN, 2 V 76.
[46] Representative (signature illegible) of academy of Douai to subprefect of Dunkerque, 10 Aug. 1882, ibid.
[47] F. Bailleul to Mgr Duquesnay, 2 Aug. 1882, AN, F 19 5502.

children who had come 'from elsewhere' and could speak only French (he had three classes of each). In response to an accusation that he refused to let a child into the French catechism class despite a request from the parents, he replied to the archbishop:

> It is true, Monseigneur, that Mr. Savage is Flemish, as is his wife, and they only speak Flemish in their home. To give in to Mr. Savage's request I would thereby do a disservice to the children who know no more than a few words of French and who could not usefully follow the French catechism.[48]

In 1895–6 the new archbishop, Mgr Sonnois, was also pressured to encourage the teaching of a French-only catechism in the diocese. The prefect wrote to request that the archbishop intervene in the twenty-one communes in which French was denied the inhabitants and the thirty-six others in which Flemish was accorded a clear priority.[49] Like his predecessors in the post, Mgr Sonnois refused to recognise the authority of the government over such matters.[50] He also complained, as did his vicar-general, that the Flemish were not given as much freedom in the question of language as the Basques, Bretons and Provençaux, and were more harshly pursued by the government.[51]

In 1897 the *curé* of Steenbecque, M. Barbier, in response to the subprefect's queries about catechism stated that of the 420 households in his commune, at the very least 380 were exclusively Flemish, and although he took pains to be sure that he did not impose Flemish upon anyone, it was his duty to make sure that all his students understood. That is to say, he spoke principally in Flemish.[52]

In the closing years of the nineteenth century, government officials began to enforce the regulations applying to the language of catechism. The debate was not restricted to local priests and officials in the Westhoek, but went right to the highest governmental authorities. The will to pursue cases was more an indication of heightened national anticlericalism than of an increased hostility towards the Flemish language itself, but it was sufficiently strong to initiate change.[53] It was a prominent enough issue that the *président du conseil* in 1896, Léon Bourgeois, took the time himself to write to the staunchly anticlerical minister of public instruction and worship, Émile Combes, about the persistent teaching of catechism in Flemish by certain

---

48 F. Van Costenoble to archbishop of Cambrai, 31 July 1882, ibid.
49 Prefect to archbishop of Cambrai, 16 Feb. 1896, ibid.
50 See Coornaert, *La Flandre française*, 323.
51 See archbishop of Cambrai to prefect, 12 July 1902, ADN, 1 T 123 5; Em. Lobbeday, vicar-general of diocese of Cambrai, to director at the 'Direction Général des Cultes', 24 July 1902, AN, F 19 5502, both of whom express this opinion.
52 M. Barbier to subprefect of Hazebrouck, 9 Apr. 1897, ADN, 6 Z 2108.
53 For a discussion of the extent of anticlericalism in the period see Eugène Defeuille, *Anticléricalisme avant et pendant notre république*. Paris 1911, and Theodore Zeldin (ed.), *Conflicts in French society: anticlericalism, education and morals in the nineteenth century*, London 1970.

priests in the Nord, stating that 'it is important that we put an end to this state of things without delay, since a prolongation would constitute a real danger for national unity'.[54] Under the regime of Waldeck-Rousseau, who viewed priests merely as functionaries of the state and problems with them as purely administrative, the government increased its pressure and began to withhold the salary of any priest who was reported to be teaching all or part of his class in Flemish.[55] Several years later, when himself president of the council, Combes was of the same opinion as Bourgeois, continuing his predecessor's politics of pressure, and stating in 1902 with reference to allowing explanations in Flemish to aid in comprehension that 'such tolerance could only lead to a rebirth of ancient abuses'.[56]

Several complaints were received from a handful of parents who wished, for whatever reason, to have their child make his or her First Communion in French. These complaints could then be used as a evidence against the *curé* in question. One such letter was signed 'an old republican from Cassel' who complained generally that the *curé* of Ste Marie Cappel taught and preached in Flemish 'in spite of the parents' protests', and concluded that 'a little warning would do some good'.[57] It was often the case that the letters which arrived in the offices of the minister were written in exactly the same handwriting, with only the signatures different, indicating that the 'unhappy' parents were either illiterate, or could not speak (or write) French themselves.[58] It may also have been that they were encouraged to complain by local officials hostile to the *curé*, who presented them with the letter already written and ready to sign. One letter came from the *instituteur* of Lederzeele, complaining in 1900 that the new *curé* of the parish, after previous *curés* had tolerated both languages, was imposing the Flemish language on all the children without exception: 'From thence, general discontentment on the part of the parents who constantly call for [French] but are not listened to.'[59]

One of the best-publicised incidents, beginning in 1900, took place in the village of Killem, which lies not far from the Belgian border in the *arrondissement* of Dunkerque. The *instituteur* of the commune wished to have his son recite his lessons in preparation for his First Communion, and to receive

---

[54] President of the council and minister of interior to minister of public instruction, art and public worship, 11 Mar. 1896, AN, F 19 5502.

[55] For information on Waldeck-Rousseau's position see Pierre Sorlin, *Waldeck-Rousseau*, Paris 1966, 423. For details of the legal action of suspension of pay see AN, F 19 5502.

[56] President of the council and minister of the interior and public worship to prefect, 5 Aug. 1902, ADN, 1 T 123 5.

[57] 'Un vieux républicain de Cassel' (signature illegible) to prefect, date illegible (most probably 1901), ADN, 6 Z 2288.

[58] There were numerous letters of this sort, for example one from Richard Laleur, an agricultural day-labourer in Merkeghem, who had a letter written for him by the mayor to the minister of justice and public worship which he signed with an 'X', 24 Apr. 1898, AN, F 19 5502.

[59] *Instituteur* of Lederzeele to *inspecteur d'académie*, 20 Nov. 1900, ibid.

explanations of the texts uniquely in French, but was refused by the local *curé*. Reports varied as to the true details of what happened: one of the inhabitants of the village, a Madame Schapman, wrote to the subprefect saying that the priest had apparently told her that he had received direct instructions from the archbishop to deny the use of French in religious instruction, which cannot be substantiated by other means.[60] It was at first unclear whether the *instituteur* in question was himself Flemish- or French-speaking. In several papers, such as the *Figaro*, it was portrayed as an outrage that a French-speaker had his son denied a French catechism. The *curé* maintained, however, that the family were Flemish, and that the general level of French in the community was so poor as to render any teaching impossible if it were not in Flemish.[61] It was later confirmed that the *instituteur* and his family were in fact Flemish. In an undated transcript of an interview with the *instituteur* himself, he claimed that his family spoke only French at home, yet he agreed that his children, like himself and his wife, were native speakers of Flemish.[62] No one seems to have asked how the children came to be native speakers of Flemish in a household in which French was allegedly the sole language.

Frustrated with the lack of consistency in the reporting of the Killem case in the rest of the press, the *Echo du Nord* sent a reporter to Killem to find out what lay at the bottom of the story. The *instituteur* did not deny that his family were Flemish-speakers, but considered that Flemish was more of a *patois* and not fit to be taught in any kind of class, religious or otherwise. The *curé*, when asked to comment, claimed that he was given one hour per week in which to have thirty students recite their lessons, and to give accompanying explanations; with the time available he could not repeat the explanations in more than one language and therefore had to choose, selecting the one universally understood. For the recitation itself French was optional and Flemish obligatory, since that was the language in which the students were able to function. When criticised because in the neighbouring commune of Hondschoote each child was given a choice of language, the *curé* replied that that was true, but that they had the benefit of more than one priest to do the teaching.[63]

As a result of this incident, the *curé* of Killem, along with many other priests of the Westhoek who found themselves in similar situations, had his monthly stipend withheld on the grounds that he did not follow ministry regulations for language in catechism. In a letter to the archbishop, the prefect L. Vincent apologised for the inconvenience of lack of pay and

---

60 Madame Schapman to subprefect of Dunkerque, 14 Nov. 1900, ibid.
61 Archbishop of Cambrai to minister of public worship, 24 Dec. 1900, ibid. Mgr Sonnois defended the priest's position, and denied having issued any direct instructions to use only Flemish.
62 Found ibid.
63 'Français et Flamand – le conflit de Killem – le catéchisme en flamand – Notre enquête', *L'Echo du Nord*, 11 Apr. 1901.

explained that if he (the archbishop) had made a move sooner he could have perhaps prevented the lamentable situation; but as it stood, pay could not recommence until the priests began to give a French-only catechism classes.[64]

On top of the legal charges, several elements of the anticlerical press made use of the material as well. In the *Progrès du Nord*, an article was published condemning a priest who apparently insisted that the son of an *instituteur* learn Flemish (which he did not know) before he would even be allowed to start attending catechism class.[65] This situation left the archbishop with no alternative but to include, in his forthcoming circular to the priests and religious congregations of his diocese dated 22 August 1902, the principle that 'We will now teach catechism, text and explanations, exclusively in French.'[66]

In addition to using the testimonies of citizens such as the *instituteur* of Killem, requests were sent out through the ministry of the interior to the mayors of each commune, requesting that the mayor certify that the priest was teaching catechism in French. The mayors were not, however, in all cases as co-operative as the ministry had hoped. In 1901 a special commissioner from Dunkerque was sent out to tour the rural communes of the Westhoek in order to verify the language used by priests. He reported that in twenty cases in which the mayor had certified that the local *curé* followed the regulations, and was using French, the commissioner discovered the use of Flemish.[67] In one case, George Tible, mayor of Ochtezeele, was suspended for one month because he demonstrated no respect for the superior levels of the administration and continued to certify that the local priest taught in French, when it had been clearly established in the investigation that he was using Flemish.[68]

In a chart summarising the results of a further enquiry into language use in 1902, only four communes were found to be restricted exclusively to Flemish, along with a dozen others in which the religious teaching was still carried out in both languages.[69] By the period 1904–7, most priests had 'come on board', as it were, and were officially listed as conforming to the regulations, thereby having their pay restored. It is most probable that explanations continued to be given in Flemish to those who really could not understand, since the authorities were less active in the monitoring process after the achievement of the separation of the Church and State. Several sources testify that

64 Prefect to archbishop of Cambrai, 8 July 1902, AN, F 19 5502.
65 Untitled article by E. Lagrillière-Beauclerc, *Le Progrès du Nord*, 13 Nov. 1900.
66 Episcopal circular, 22 Aug. 1902, AN, F 19 5502.
67 Packet of reports by a special commissioner from Dunkerque, representing the ministry of the interior, dated 14 Aug. 1901, ADN, 1 T 123 5. See also prefect to minister of the interior, 7 Sept. 1901, AN, F 19 5502.
68 Certificate of suspension, 29 July 1902, ADN, 6 Z 2279. Similar certificates exist for several other mayors.
69 Unsigned chart, dated '1er trimestre' 1902, ibid. Several mayors were shown as still offering information which contradicted the results of the enquiry.

although in a significant part of the region religious instruction had been changed to French, some Flemish-language catechism continued well beyond the First World War.[70] The diocese continued to publish a bilingual cate-chism manual regularly up to 1926, and at least one further bilingual version was edited at Lille in 1932, proving that some use must still have been made of them.[71] Describing the early 1920s in his village, Maurice Houvenaghel reveals that: 'At that time we had a very good priest in Boeschepe: the abbé Emile Huyghe, a native of Morbecque, and he taught catechism in French and Flemish; he preached likewise in Flemish.'[72] Writing in 1931, although one would have expected it to have been a given by that time, Jules Dewachter still found it worthwhile to note that in French Flanders 'teaching is done, by the way, in French', and added 'except for catechism in certain communes which is done in Flemish'.[73] Gérard Landry and Georges de Verrewaere claim that after the separation of Church and State, the Flemish language followed religious life closely, remaining in use until nearly the end of the Second World War, when, in 1944, it quite suddenly disappeared almost completely from catechism teaching and the 'pulpit of truth'.[74]

In addition to catechism, these writers make reference to another hotly contested issue: the language of sermons. A further means for the *curés* to attempt to preserve their linguistic hold on the people (and consequently retard the advancement of French), much of the preaching in the Westhoek was done in Flemish throughout the period in question. According to de Coussemacker's survey of 1856, the only one to include the language of sermons as a question, in seventy-three of the communes Flemish was the exclusive language of preaching, as compared to twenty-six where French was the only one, and sixteen in which both languages were used alternately.[75] Legally speaking, Flemish in the pulpit was banned by Duruy at the same time as Flemish in catechism, in 1866.[76] In spite of this, and just as with catechism, it was the attitudes of the individual priests alone that determined their choice of language. In the period of massive pressure against the teaching of Flemish catechism, the language of sermons was also monitored and criti-cised, although never used as a reason for the suspension of pay. Throughout the latter half of the nineteenth century most priests preached in turn a certain number of services per month in each language, depending upon the particular linguistic composition of the parish. Although the authorities

---

70 Verbeke, *Vlaanderen in Frankrijk*, 34. According to Verbeke some priests continued to teach in Flemish right up to the Second World War.
71 Landry and de Verrewaere, *Histoire secrète*, 274.
72 Houvenaghel, *Boeschepe*, 118.
73 Dewachter, 'Sur le Front des langues', 102.
74 Landry and de Verrewaere, *Histoire secrète*, 274. The two exceptions were Abeele and Steenvoorde.
75 E. De Coussemacker, 'Instructions relative aux dialectes flamands et à la délimitation du français et du flamand dans le Nord de la France', ACFF i (1854–5), 62–9.
76 Verbeke, *Vlaanderen in Frankrijk*, 23.

grumbled, they did not take any decisive action against the language of sermons, as they were generally more concerned with the content (that they did not openly criticise the lay schools or the republic itself for example).[77] Because of the lack of strict enforcement, some priests, such as Fr Dupont in Abeele, continued to preach exclusively in Flemish for several years after the conversion of catechism to French, as did his successors.[78] As we have seen, Flemish sermons persisted until the inter-war period and did not disappear from the Westhoek until after the Second World War.[79]

Of course the Church's involvement in the language question was not that of an institution directly interested in the defence of Flemish for its own sake. Its primary motivation was to use language to combat the republican anticlerical authorities by thwarting their nationalisation project and to prevent the spread of what they considered to be immoral values to the Catholic population of the Westhoek. It was also interested in the defence of a traditional way of life closely associated with local languages. Nevertheless, the religious press, with papers such as *La Croix du Nord* and *L'Indicateur*, in addition to diocesan publications, did not generally take up the cause of the Flemish language directly, except in certain particular cases to defend the actions of individual priests accused of not using French in catechism. Even then the primary intention was to combat republicanism and anticlericalism, and to defend the Church against attacks from the government or municipal authorities through commentaries about such issues as the secularisation of schools. It should also be stressed that it was anti-Catholic and secular values, rather than the strictly national ones which the Church opposed, and thus the emphasis was not on building a solid regional or anti-national identity in the hearts of the French Flemish. On the contrary, most of the Church's attitudes and teachings manifested overt French 'patriotism', which it hoped could include religion. The Flemish language was only preserved insofar as it helped the Church to communicate its religious message and to prevent itself from becoming the tool of authorities whose values it did not share.

Politics

In addition to battles against secular schools and the control and interference of the republican anticlerical authorities, the Catholic Church also sought directly to influence the results of elections in the Westhoek. As seen in chapter 3, maps showing Catholicism in the north often coincided with electoral preferences, a trend many members of the Church sought to perpet-

---

[77] ADN, 6 Z 2108; 1 T 123 5.
[78] Report on M. Dupont, 22 Mar. 1905, ADN, 6 Z 2288. See also Landry and de Verrewaere, *Histoire secrète*, 274, quoted above.
[79] Interview with *abbé* Depoers, Hazebrouck, France, 20 Dec. 1993, who heard Flemish sermons regularly as a child in the 1920s and 1930s.

uate.[80] In spite of its best efforts, there was little the government could do to reduce constant 'meddling' in politics by local priests. A special commissioner from Lille lamented the fact to the minister, writing that 'The clergy of the diocese of Cambrai, a mix of French and Flemish, constantly involved in the breach of political and economic struggles, has developed a habit of independence such that they do not easily bend at the knee.'[81] Their activities took various forms, including preaching sermons in favour of certain candidates, ignoring legal restrictions. Public preaching was not the most important means of influence at the clergy's disposal, however, and it declined as the ministry became stricter in monitoring and enforcing the rules governing the pulpit. Reduction of politics in the pulpit did not, however, imply a reduction in the clergy's influence. In 1889 the subprefect of Hazebrouck explained the situation to the prefect:

> In answer to your confidential letter of 26 October, I have the honour to inform you that the attitude of the *arrondissement*'s clergy during the electoral period did not present any differences from their usual attitude. . . . The necessity of maintaining God in the schools was preached more or less everywhere on two Sundays: that is the most typical theme of local sermons. I have been informed that in none of the communes were the sermons accompanied by allusions to the candidates or to the upcoming elections. On the other hand, everywhere the clergy was in action; the *curés* multiplied the individual visits to their parishioners.[82]

By visiting their parishioners in their homes, the priests could exert political influence without risking an altercation with the law. After all, continued the subprefect, 'their influence is used in a milieu so favourable that they do not need to further their cause with compromising public acts'.[83]

In 1895 the minister of public worship wrote to the archbishop of Cambrai, Mgr Sonnois, who was noted for his co-operation with the government, asking what action the archbishop intended to take against his priests who were violating the law of 18 Germinal, Year 10, by writing political letters which were later published in a newspaper.[84] The archbishop responded that he intended to do nothing whatsoever, since the priests in question 'did not speak, write or act in the exercise of their official functions, nor in official conditions as ministers of a religion recognised by the state'.[85] If they had truly broken the law, then they could be prosecuted in due course, but as far as the archbishop was concerned

---

[80] See chapter 2 above and Legrand, 'La "Gauche" ', 29–33.
[81] Report of M. Romard, special commissioner of the *police des chemins de fer*, to minister of the interior, 7 June 1895, AN, F 19 6018.
[82] Subprefect of Hazebrouck to prefect, 29 Oct. 1889, ADN, 2 V 56.
[83] Ibid.
[84] Minister of public worship to archbishop of Cambrai, 16 May 1895, AN, F 19 6018.
[85] Archbishop of Cambrai to minister of public worship, 19 May 1895, ibid.

What they have done, they have done as French citizens and voters, using the rights which the French republican constitution recognises and guarantees to all citizens, by which I mean the right to freedom of thought, speech and publicity.[85]

Mgr Sonnois sent a copy of these two letters to his deans, stating that they were absolutely confidential and not to be published, but they none the less leaked out into the press.[87] They won him a great deal of support from among his priests, and he had to answer to some criticism from the minister (who was not happy, but had no legal basis to do more than complain). The involvement of priests 'unofficially' in politics continued unabated.[88] The domination of the priest in the political debate, according to another police commissioner sent to investigate the situation in the Westhoek, forced the republicans to be discreet in their publicity, and efforts to win support had to be out of the public eye. In referring to the elections of 1904, he wrote in March 1903 that 'the electoral campaign has already begun, everything is done here in shadow and mystery'.[89]

The archbishop's attitude remained constant with respect to public authority when it came to the inventory taken of all church property ten years later, following the law of 9 December 1905. He told priests not to open the church at hours when it would not normally be open, nor should they sign any inventory themselves or aid anyone in opening the sacristies; but they should not hinder the process by any other means (which would have been illegal).[90] With this simple strategy, several priests did manage to frustrate the public authorities required to administer the inventory, forcing them to procure the services of a locksmith to enter the church or to put up with peaceful but noisy protests from local parishioners. In only one town in French Flanders – Boeschepe – was there a serious incident. On the day of the inventory 150–200 people came to protest in front of the *percepteur*, and one protester was shot and killed by the gendarmes.[91] The clergy also protested vigorously against the separation of the Church and State in 1906, and there were literally hundreds of infractions of the rules on public manifestations.[92] The political influence of the Catholic Church in the Westhoek, while declining, nevertheless persisted after the separation through the twentieth century. Such movements as the Christian Democrats or the *Action Catholique* had a large following in the region which endured well after the

86 Ibid.
87 Archbishop of Cambrai to *Les Doyens*, 22 May 1895, ibid.
88 See archbishop of Cambrai to minister of public worship, 30 May 1895, and prefect to minister of public instruction, art and public worship, 28 June 1895, ibid.
89 Report, police commissioner of Roncq, 31 Mar. 1903, ADN, 1 T 123 5.
90 Instructions from archbishop of Cambrai to parish priests, published in *La Semaine religieuse du diocèse de Cambrai*, 6 Jan. 1906, 7–9, F 19 1974 2.
91 Untitled reports by parish, 1906, AN, F 19 1974 2.
92 See ADN, 2 V 601.

Second World War.[93] In 1981, when the first socialist government of Pierre Mauroy (also mayor of Lille) tried to abolish partial state support for those Catholic schools which were 'under contract' and to create a unique state school system, a huge wave of demonstrations, openly supported by the church hierarchy, swept through France.[94] Among the largest manifestations were those in the north of France, where the tradition of Catholic education remained strong and successful (more than 20 per cent of students to the end of secondary school attend Catholic institutions)[95] and the subsequent repeal of the proposed legislation marked their success.

Thus the Church had a great deal of influence in the Westhoek and was certainly politically active, but what sorts of candidates did they support and how did their politics affect the question of regional and Flemish identity? Their first priority was clearly the question of religion and the Church's power, both in society and education, as seen above over the question of rivalry with schoolteachers for local influence. The political influence of the Church was primarily used to support or resist individual candidatures and meant that all the candidates to benefit from their support had to be Catholics. However, they did not necessarily have to support a strong sense of regional Catholic identity in accordance with the Church's stance in support of Flemish language, culture and identity. Thus the Church does not at any point seem to have supported overtly *flamingant* candidates, although it did make use of Flemish and regional culture in its political platforms.

Arguably the most significant position taken by the Church in the region was the association of a large number of Catholics with the social Catholic movement. French Flanders in general and the *arrondissement* of Hazebrouck in particular were prominent in support of the national movement which arose towards the end of the nineteenth century known as the *Démocratie chrétienne*. Founded after the death of the Legitimist heir, the comte de Chambord, the movement sought to reconcile the Catholic Church with 'the people', in part at least through outright acceptance of the republic as a form of government.[96] It believed that the best way to maintain and strengthen religion in France was through co-operation with the state. The *abbé* Lemire, the first priest to be elected as a deputy in the Third Republic was one of the founding members of the movement.[97]

Lemire, in spite of the opposition of the archbishop of Cambrai, Mgr Sonnois, to the very idea of his candidature for public office, was vigorously

---

[93] See Hilaire and Vandenbussche, 'Mutations idéologique', 452–5. *Action Catholique* was founded in 1922, and reached its peak in the north between 1945 and 1960.
[94] See Cholvy and Hilaire, *Histoire religieuse*, III: *1930–1988*, 362–3.
[95] Duriez, 'La Religion', 19.
[96] Jean-Marie Mayeur, 'Les Abbés démocrates', *RN* lxxiii (Apr.–Sept. 1991), 240.
[97] For more on the *abbé* Lemire see Jean-Marie Mayeur, *L'Abbé Lemire, 1853–1928: un prêtre démocrate*, thèse pour le doctorat ès lettres présentée à la faculté des lettres et sciences humaines de l'université de Paris, Paris 1968.

supported by the clergy of the Westhoek. All but two or three were actively involved in his campaign, and the prefect had cause to lament that it was the clergy who 'ignoring his authority and deaf to his advice, solicited the candidature of the abbé Lemire and made it triumph'.[98] Lemire's success was achieved in a region characterised by Pierre Lévêque as 'clerical democrat: that is to say one of direct rapport between the priests and a peasantry of small and medium-sized landholders'.[99] Although he was born in Vieux-Berquin, a Flemish-speaking area neighbouring the linguistic border, Lemire did not learn the Flemish language until he was in his twenties and attending the seminary, but used it to his advantage in campaigning. In an election poster in Flemish, Lemire summed up the attitude of the *Démocratie chrétienne* towards the government: 'It is no longer a case of fighting against the Republic. It has been, for many years now, the government of our France. The pope has spoken, it is done.'[100]

As an illustration of some Christian Democrat politics, Lemire was not directly opposed to the separation of the Church and State, provided that it meant greater control and autonomy for the Church in strictly religious activities, since in any case relations with the state should be seen as of secondary importance to the question 'of faith and its sincerity'.[101] As a further example, he was also not opposed to the existence of the secular public school in principle. He considered universal, free education to be genuine progress, but wanted at the same time to guarantee the Church its rights to continue to control and maintain religious private schools for those who wanted a religious education for their children.[102] Lemire always included working conditions and salaries as a part of his campaign and also wrote about the need for workers to find support through Catholic unions, which he argued had served the workers for centuries, associating them historically with the trade gilds of the Middle Ages and their patron saints.[103] His electoral victory in 1893 was described as 'in one word the reconciliation of the priest and the worker who has finally seen that only through religion will he find support'.[104] His parliamentary work and support of the 'workers' gardens' was also oriented toward the role of unions and support for workers and their families.[105] Hostile reactions on the part of some workers,

---

98   Prefect to minister of public instruction, art and public worship, 28 June 1895, AN, F 19 6018.
99   Pierre Lévêque, *Histoire des forces politiques en France*, II: *1880–1940*, Paris 1994, 35.
100   'Stemmers van Vlaender', election poster, 1893.
101   *Abbé* Lemire to *abbé* Birot, 22 Dec. 1901, quoted in Mayeur, *L'Abbé Lemire*, 274.
102   Ibid. 276–9.
103   J. Lemire, 'Confréries ouvrières d'Hazebrouck ou les corporations de cette ville considérées du point de vue religieux', ACFF xx (1892), 14–40.
104   *Le Fermier des Flandres et de l'Artois*, 5 Sept. 1893, 1.
105   Mayeur, *L'Abbé Lemire*, 367.

syndicalists and radicals were less a result of the content of Lemire's programme than of simple anticlericalism.[106]

The *Démocratie chrétienne* formed a part of social Catholicism, which was particularly widespread among the Flemish. The vitality of faith in the region, relatively early industrialisation and the important presence of workers helped to create a territory which favoured the relatively rapid development of social Catholicism.[107] Although it was particularly widespread in this area, the movement had no specific position on regionalism or assimilation, one way or the other, and was indeed very international in its outlook, forging numerous connections with similar movements in Belgium and Germany.[108] The primary goal of the movement was to reconcile the Church and the people, and it could even be considered that at its root Christian Democracy was really more of a social than a political movement, 'founded with apostolic motivations: reconquering the people, bringing the Church closer to the people, bringing the masses back to the church and rebuilding a Christian society'.[109] The idea was that through reconciliation with democracy, the Church would liberate itself from the old political debates in order to concentrate on the growing social problems confronting workers at the turn of the century and thereby be brought back closer to the population. Caroline Ford, in her book *Creating the nation in provincial France*, argues indeed that Christian Democracy in Brittany was the most important integrating force bringing Bretons into the French nation, through its role as an intermediary in Breton society, creating an identity which was at the same time regional and national.[110]

In French Flanders, while Christian Democracy had considerable influence, it did not have the primary role which Ford describes for Brittany. Although sharing numerous cultural characteristics with Brittany, the political situation in the Westhoek differed significantly. Immediately adjacent in the industrial and mining centres was one of the most important bastions of the socialist Left in all of France, both in terms of political and trade union activism.[111] The proximity of leftist propaganda and success, including that from over the border, meant that the Christian Democrats' position was regularly challenged, and they were not the only successful group seeking to influence regional identity and vying for the role of intermediary between the local population and the nation. In terms of securing workers' loyalty, the Catholic unions and the *Démocratie chrétienne* had a tough fight, since they

106 Ibid. 390.
107 Nadine-Josette Chaline, 'Le Catholicisme social dans le Nord au début du XXe siècle', *RN* lxxiii (Apr.–Sept. 1991), 305. See also Lévêque, *Histoire des forces politiques*, ii. 34–6.
108 See Alain-René Michel, 'Les Catholiques sociaux du Nord et les modèles belges et allemands', *RN* lxxiii (Apr.–Sept. 1991), 321–8.
109 See Mayeur, 'Les Abbés démocrates', 239.
110 Ford, *Creating the nation*.
111 See chapter 6 below.

were up against not only their anticlerical socialist adversaries, but the paternalistic Catholic *patronat* and elements of the church hierarchy as well,[112] to say nothing of the disadvantage of arriving later in urban working-class areas than the socialists.[113] Thus it can be said that while both Flemish and Breton Christian Democrat movements sought to create an identity which was both national and contained a specific regional and Catholic element, the important variations in strength of the movements in each region can partly explain the difference in impact. In the Nord, unlike Brittany, no politically strong regionalist movement emerged out of Christian Democratic circles, and their legacy was more to merge gradually with socialism from the 1970s onwards once anticlericalism was no longer the main issue.[114] It is worth pointing out that the political heir to the old-school socialist mayor of Lille, Pierre Mauroy (previously a 'secular' public school teacher), is Martine Aubry, a former student of the well-known Couvent des Oiseaux in Paris who has strong family as well as political links to the Christian Democratic tradition.

The long-term weakness of the Church's defence of regional culture in the Westhoek can also be explained by its fundamental political strategies at the national level. The primary goal of the Church was the preservation of religion and of its position within French society. For this reason it opposed the particular nationalist message of anticlerical republicanism, but never opposed the French nation or national culture *per se*.[115] To preserve its influence, the national Church never went so far as to officially endorse the regionalist cause, nor did it give its support to any regionalist political movement, even if some individuals within the church hierarchy did so.[116] The French Catholic Church as a whole chose gradually to accept the consequences of the separation of the Church and State, and to focus more upon religious and spiritual, as opposed to strictly political questions. It sought to preserve the role of religion in French life not by contesting the nation, but by creating and promoting a religious version of French national identity.[117]

---

112 See Florin, 'Présentation des forces politiques', 168.

113 Robert Talmy, 'Les Tendances anti-cléricales des socialistes dans le département du Nord (1860–1900)', Mémoire de licence, université catholique de Lille 1952, 116. By the time Catholic trade unionism got moving the socialist unions had already been in place for several decades: idem, *Le Syndicalisme chrétien en France (1871–1930): difficultés et controverses*, Paris 1965.

114 Gille, 'Quarante Ans d'Action Catholique', 154.

115 A stance very different from that of the Irish Catholic Church, for example, when confronted with British nationalism.

116 See the examples given in chapter 7 below.

117 This involved the development of the cult of patriotic saints and heroes from the Middle Ages such as Joan of Arc or Bayard, 'le chevalier sans peur et sans reproches', initiatives such as the consecration of France to the Virgin Mary, with accompanying patriotic and religious hymns including 'Sauvez, sauvez la France au nom du sâcré coeur', and was expressed in the motto 'Français sans peur et chrétien sans reproche' of the Collège

This patriotic but Catholic version of the French nation could remain fundamentally opposed to republican France or partially in agreement with it, depending upon the particular strain within the Church that was articulating it. Such choices on the part of the French Catholic hierarchy could not but have deterred regional elites in conservative regions such as French Flanders from adhering to strongly regionalist anti-French political movements. In general, the Church encouraged conservatism and moderation and acted as a brake on radical changes and departures from the *status quo* which was globally favourable to its position within Flemish society, and helped it to oppose the rising challenge from the Left within the greater Nord–Pas-de-Calais region.

Stanislas in Paris, where many of the future economic leaders of the Nord went to study after their *baccalauréat*: P. Pouchain, *Les Maîtres du Nord*.

6

The Labour Movement

The major economic transformation of the nineteenth century described in chapter 4 led to the formation of a proletariat in the north of France, which in turn spurred on an organised workers' political movement.[1] The Nord as a whole was a particular hotbed for socialist and syndicalist activities, particularly in the densely populated, working-class Lille urban area, but the large numbers of agricultural workers and small-town industries in the Westhoek meant that it was not excluded, and unions had already been formed in several Flemish towns by the middle of the nineteenth century.[2] A prominent political issue throughout the nineteenth and twentieth centuries, the development of this movement is worthy of careful examination, to determine the attitude and position of its leaders towards the questions of ethnic, cultural, national and regional identity within the class struggle.

The high population density of French Flanders throughout the nineteenth and early twentieth centuries was a major contributing factor to the early and rapid development of the economy. While the large number of workers may have encouraged industrialisation, at the same time it helped to keep wages down. E. Levasseur remarked upon the disadvantageous situation of the worker in the north of France relative to other regions, given the extremely low salaries resulting from competition in the job market.[3] The low salaries, combined with long working hours, limited the political interests of the working classes in the short term to changing one or the other of these two, as any labour activism which defended any other position was 'guaranteed to fail'.[4] In Halluin, a mostly Flemish-speaking, textile-producing village on the Belgian border, more than 60 per cent of the strikes before 1914 were motivated by simple calls for higher wages.[5] This meant that, for the workers

---

[1]   For a good general overview see Roger Magraw, *A history of the French working class*, Oxford 1992; Claude Willard (ed.), *La France ouvrière: histoire de la classe ouvrière française*, Paris 1995; Gérard Noiriel, *Workers in French society in the 19th and 20th centuries*, Oxford 1990.

[2]   Levasseur, *Histoire du commerce de la France*, ii. 695.

[3]   *Ministère du commerce, de l'industrie, des postes et télégraphes: office du travail, salaires et durée du travail dans l'industrie française* (1897), quoted in E. Levasseur, *Questions ouvrières et industrielle en France sous la Troisième République*, Paris 1907, 527. One can also find specific descriptions of working-class conditions in the north in Victor Hugo's poetry.

[4]   Robert Pierreuse, 'L'Ouvrier roubaisien et la propagande politique 1890–1900', *RN* li (Apr.–June 1969), 273.

[5]   Michel Hastings, *Halluin la rouge, 1919–1939: aspects d'un communisme identitaire*, Lille 1991, 97.

of the Nord, political interest was, as Robert Pierreuse described for Roubaix, completely unrelated to the major issues of the day facing the France of the Third Republic; to these they were perfectly indifferent.[6] The working classes of which the French Flemish were a part lacked the economic strength and security, as well as the political culture, to be particularly interested in national labour struggles. In this sense, although for different reasons, workers' political attitudes resembled those of the general voters of the Westhoek who, as seen in chapter 2, were concerned primarily, if not exclusively, with the economic consequences for themselves and their immediate area.

To understand the question of worker identity in French Flanders, one must examine first of all the Lys valley and the Lille industrial basin, not only because of its proximity to the Westhoek, but also as a significant centre of 'Flemish' immigration from both French and Belgian Flanders. Numerous communities within the Lille basin remained Flemish-speaking throughout the nineteenth century; Firmin Lentacker writes that Flemish was the current working language for workers in many of the factories in the valley of the Lys along the southern edge of the Westhoek, and even those who had lost the use of it in their school days relearned it at the factory.[7] Since large numbers of the workers were Flemish-speaking, trade union and socialist movements were directly confronted with the question of language in disseminating their propaganda, and their numerous contacts with the Belgian-Flemish socialist movement had to be contended with. Most of the written propaganda was in French, although there were several exceptions to this rule.

In the context of specifically local interests, and given the perpetuation of identifiable cultural characteristics in the industrial areas, ethnic and regional consciousness seemed to have had a great deal of potential as a source of support among the Flemish workers of Lille and the Westhoek, and yet was rarely cultivated or developed during the nineteenth or twentieth centuries. To answer the question why requires an investigation of the character of socialism and syndicalism in the Nord and of the leaders of the movement and their relationship with both Belgian socialists and their opponents in northern France (among both employers and Catholics).

For the period 1870–1914, Herman Balthazar described the Flemish working-class community in the Lille conglomerate, drawn from both French and Belgian Flanders, as having a separate existence in terms of socialism, more or less apart from the rest of the workers' movement, and holding their own meetings without the French present.[8] This did not mean that there was not a great deal of contact, cooperation and information-sharing between the two groups at the higher level, for indeed there was; only that in day-to-day

6 Pierreuse, 'L'Ouvrier roubaisien', 249–50.
7 Firmin Lentacker, 'En Marge d'une métropole: hier et aujourd'hui dans "la vallée de la Lys" ', *RN* lxiv (Apr.–June 1982), 283–341.
8 Herman Balthazar, 'Betrekkingen tussen het socialisme in Vlaanderen en Noord-Frankrijk (1870–1914)', *DFN/LPBF* iv (1979), 25–6.

terms, the Flemish were living in 'a living micro-world' within the greater working-class community.[9] Given the level of segregation between the communities and the fact that the large numbers of Belgian immigrants helped to keep overall wages down, it should also be noted that the communities coexisted relatively peacefully and the kind of xenophobic violence against immigrants which surfaced in other areas of France was comparatively less common in the region.[10]

Given the large numbers of Flemish-speakers, trade union material was circulated in both French and Flemish, since 'syndical publications needed to be bilingual in order to be read'.[11] Written propaganda was also forthcoming from the Belgian socialist movement. A number of Belgian Flemish pamphlets circulated in the Westhoek and Lille,[12] as did the principal Belgian socialist newspapers in both languages: *De Werker* (The Worker), *De Volkswil* (The People's Will) *Le Suffrage Universel* (Universal Suffrage) and *La Voix de l'ouvrier* (The Worker's Voice).[13] Meetings and word of mouth were the principal means of spreading information, and meetings were held throughout the Westhoek and the Lille basin in both languages on a regular basis. Here again, much of the Flemish contribution came from Belgium. Belgian socialist leaders gathered in France once a fortnight and occasionally every Sunday through the latter decades of the nineteenth century.[14]

Recent scholarship has shown that the Flemish-speaking Belgian trade unionists and socialists had a much greater influence upon the character of the workers' movement in the Nord than was previously thought.[15] In spite of occasional problems among the leadership of a party which contained both Flemish and Walloons, many of the socialist leaders in Belgium were generally sympathetic to the Flemish movement and came more and more to favour linguistic demands on the part of the working class and to unite the concepts of class with race or culture.[16] Speaking to a meeting of the *Comité*

---

9 Ibid. 26.
10 This was the case even though Belgian workers were sometimes deliberately brought in by factory-owners to weaken trade union activity.
11 Lentacker, 'En Marge d'une métropole', 307.
12 See ADN, M 154 58.
13 See Talmy, 'Les Tendances anti-cléricales', 10.
14 Ibid. 8; Charles Lefebvre, 'Socialistes belges et français de la fin de l'Empire au début de la IIIe République', *RN* xxxvii (1955), 196–7.
15 See Carl Strikwerda, 'Regionalism and internationalism: the working-class movement in the Nord and the Belgian connection', *Proceedings of the Annual Meeting of the Western Society for French History* xii (1984), 221–30, who argues that much of the character of socialism in the north of France can be attributed to the Belgian influence. For the opposite position see Jean Puissant, 'Relations socialistes sans frontière: Belgique et le Nord de la France', in Bernard Ménager, Jean-François Sirinelli and Jean Vavasseur-Desperriers (eds), *Cent Ans de socialisme septentrional: actes du colloque, Lille 3–4 décembre 1993*, Lille 1995, 79–87, who argues less convincingly that although there were 'non-negligible' contacts, Belgian socialism had little impact upon that of the Nord.
16 Shepard B. Clough, *A history of the Flemish movement in Belgium: a study in nationalism,*

Flamand de France in December 1897, M. A. Vermast quoted the Belgian socialist leader Anseele as claiming that the Flemish movement was a class struggle and that his party therefore supported it, and warned that while such was not yet the situation in France, it could certainly become so.[17] The Belgian case thus demonstrates that, in spite of the theoretically internationalist stance of all socialists, their position was not necessarily inherently opposed to cultural, ethnic, nationalistic or regionalistic claims. Since the Belgian syndicalists and socialists, who had such an impact upon the working class in France, clearly made use of Flemish consciousness in order to establish a clear link between class and the Flemish culture or race, to oppose 'Flemish' workers and the 'French' bourgeoisie, the possibility existed for such ideas to cross the border into France along with other elements of their propaganda.[18]

Among the different political organisations which were attempting to cultivate a following among the workers of the Nord in the twenty-five years preceding the First World War, the greatest success was that of Jules Guesde and the socialists, firstly as the *Parti Ouvrier Français* and later the *Section Française de l'Internationale Ouvrière*.[19] The leaders of the movement, unlike their followers, were interested in more than salaries and were very much involved in socialist and Marxist theories of the day. The question of how the message was spread from the leaders to the workers is difficult to answer. It was not an easy task, since the average worker, after the long tedious working day, did not have sufficient time, energy or instruction to study the complex doctrines seeking to influence him or her.[20] Claude Willard, in his analysis of the Guesdist movement, writes that 'in Flanders in particular . . . a dialect was spoken which rendered the region impenetrable to propaganda written in French'.[21] This did not mean that in the urban setting the still numerous Flemish-speakers were ignored or unimportant. On the contrary, writes Patricia Hilden, 'the Guesdist method of assimilating Flemish popular culture

New York 1930, 133–4. This was true for both socialist and Christian trade unions: Emmanuel Gerard, 'The Christian workers' movement as a mass foundation of the Flemish movement', in Kas Deprez and Louis Vos (eds), *Nationalism in Belgium: shifting identities, 1780–1995*, Basingstoke 1998, 127–38.

17 M. A. Vermast, *Le Mouvement flamand en Belgique* (pamphlet: communication faite à la séance du CFF le 20 décembre 1897). This was a mild overstatement on Vermast's part of Anseele's position on the Flemish movement.

18 For more on Belgian socialism and the Flemish movement see chapter 8 below and Carl Strikwerda, *A house divided: Catholics, socialists and Flemish nationalists in nineteenth-century Belgium*, Lanham 1997, who shows that the link between socialism and the Flemish movement was spurred on mostly by the rank-and-file of Belgian socialism, rather than by the national leadership.

19 See 'Le Socialisme Guesdiste et la S.F.I.O. dans la région (1894–1914)', in Trénard, *Histoire des Pays-Bas français: documents*, 366–8, and Jean-Marie Mayeur, *La Vie politique sous la Troisième République, 1870–1940*, Paris 1984.

20 Pierreuse, 'L'Ouvrier Roubaisien', 273.

21 Claude Willard, *Les Guesdistes: le mouvement socialiste en France (1893–1905)*, Paris 1965, 224.

to socialist ends necessarily drew all members of the working class community into contact with socialism at least at some point in their lives'.[22] The Guesdists, she argues, were able to pick up on the natural Flemish sense of community and portray socialism as an extension and solidification of the existing community. The leaders were encouraging the Flemish to participate, but rarely using that language themselves, and certainly not implying that culture or ethnicity were linked to the class struggle, or that Flemish workers could find solidarity as a group in opposition to any perceived 'French' bourgeoisie.[23]

Much of the passing on of socialist information and propaganda occurred at the local *estaminet*, cabaret or music hall. There were more than 1,000 of these in Tourcoing alone in 1898, one for every seventy inhabitants.[24] The singing in these cafés has been particularly well studied, but for the Lille area was mostly in either French or Picard dialect, rather than in Flemish. It was not that the Flemish did not sing, as workers' songs were extremely common in Ghent,[25] and the Flemish in Lille did write songs and poems at least through the first half of the nineteenth century.[26] L. Marty describes one example of a Roubaix cabaret featuring an exclusively Flemish repertoire, opened by a M. Vandenbroucke in 1873, although she describes it as unusual.[27] Pierre Pierrard adds that the songs in Lille were principally apolitical in theme, describing life, work and daily misery, and not treating the idealistic, contemplative or mythical themes as found in traditional Flemish singing.[28] Armand Audiganne confirms his findings, describing the subjects as arising either from daily life or from pure fantasy.[29] Thus neither through the leaders in the French workers' movement nor spontaneously in local

---

[22] Hilden. *Working women and socialist politics*, 273. Assimilation, primarily in the sense of appropriation, was discussed in the chapter 4 above.

[23] The French socialist leaders were in a difficult position when faced with Belgian immigrants, since by actively recruiting them they were open to criticism for lack of patriotism and indifference towards French workers, but if they ignored or marginalised them they were left open to accusations of betraying their internationalist principles.

[24] Ardouin-Dumazet, *Voyage en France*, 39. The density of *estaminets* was high for the whole of the region, both in the cities and in the villages. See also chapter 1 above.

[25] See Hendrick Vandecuveye, 'Het proletarierslied: een sociaal-kulturele verschiedingsvorm van de socialistische arbeidersbeweging', *Belgische Tijdschrift voor Nieuwste Geschiedenis/Revue belge d'histoire contemporaine* xi (1980), 171–204.

[26] Armand Audiganne, *Les Populations ouvrières et les industries de la France dans le mouvement sociale du dix-neuvième siècle*, Paris 1854, 36–9.

[27] L. Marty, *Chanter pour survivre: culture ouvrière, travail et techniques dans le textile Roubaix, 1859–1914*, Lille 1982, 77.

[28] Pierre Pierrard, *Les Chansons en patois de Lille sous le Second Empire*, Arras 1966, 233. For examples of Flemish language songs see Jean-Paul Sepieter, *La Musique du peuple flamand/ De muziek van het vlaamse volk*, Dunkerque 1981. Marty attributes the lack of politics/ work in songs to the alienation of factory work, although this does not account for the cross-border differences.

[29] Audiganne, *Les Populations ouvrières*, 37–8.

gatherings did ethnic or cultural consciousness blend in with the class struggle.

Several factors can account for the absence of a greater development of Flemish consciousness among workers. One of the primary reasons is of course the cultural and linguistic diversity of the urban working class. Although entire sections of the Lille basin, large parts of Dunkerque and most of Hazebrouck and Bergues were Flemish-speaking, a variety of patois and quite a bit of French was also to be found. As a platform for action, unity or consciousness among workers, therefore, one could argue that Flemish lacked the sheer numbers in the urban setting to be effective. A similar point could be made for Belgium, however, which also had a diversity of languages in urban settings, but where Flemish consciousness did develop among the workers. The Flemish-speakers themselves could not be considered a cohesive group, since they often identified only with others from their immediate locality, and considered themselves just as ethnically different from other Flemish as from Walloons: 'Flemish speakers in Ghent . . . found only minimal common ground with inhabitants of Antwerp or Leuven – and, in fact, a distinct dialect of Flemish was spoken in each city.'[30] Thus diversity of language alone is not sufficient to explain the absence of a Flemish dimension to the workers' movement in northern France.

A second reason is that the leaders of the socialist movement in France were French-speaking themselves, and proud of that aspect of their scholarship: 'unlike the anarchists, who delighted in "argot", . . . Guesdists systematically employed formal language'.[31] In some cases they even overtly supported assimilation into French, since this was their language of operation and publication. When it came to general worker solidarity in France, the Flemish workers followed Guesde or other French-speaking leaders without reference to or great concern over language.[32] In addition to their simple lack of Flemish, the practice of using French can in part be linked to the genuinely national aspirations of the leaders, whose goals encompassed more than simply French Flanders. It came also in part from their theoretically international position, which while not necessarily incompatible with regionalism, as we have seen from the example of Belgium, certainly did not encourage a regional stance. Finally, this position was also an opportunity to combat local industrialists and the clergy. Several of the factory-owners themselves could speak Flemish, and tried to use that to their advantage by addressing their workers in Flemish,[33] and the case of the clergy was even more obvious.

30 Patricia Penn Hilden, *Women, work, and politics: Belgium, 1830–1914*, Oxford 1993, 43.
31 Robert Stuart, *Marxism at work: ideology, class and French socialism during the Third Republic*, Cambridge 1992, 43.
32 Eric Vanneufville, *Apprenons notre histoire de Flandre*, 2nd edn, Steenvoorde 1989, 79.
33 Jules Brenne, 'Les Candidats ouvriers dans le Nord', *RN* lvi (Apr.–June 1974), 190. More will be said about the attitude of the *patronat* as a whole in chapter 7 below which deals with local interest groups.

Anticlericalism provided a weighty reason for not adopting Flemish consciousness as a part of the socialist or syndicalist platform in the Nord. Particularly strong among the socialists of Lille, anticlericalism reached its peak with the election of Gustave Delory as mayor from 1894 to 1904, in the period partly coinciding with the strong anticlerical ministries of Pierre Waldeck-Rousseau (1899–1902) and Emile Combes (1902–5).[34] The anticlericalism manifested by socialist leaders in the Nord was heightened by their early and influential contact with the Belgian socialist movement: 'The dynamism of the Belgian socialists at the same time as their hostility towards all religion can largely explain the orientation of their action as well as their success among the workers of the Nord.'[35] The socialists attempted to link religion with capitalism, and present it as another form of exploitation and tyranny.[36] Since several elements within the Church had directly associated themselves with the Flemish movement, anticlerical socialists would never have wished to be even remotely associated with it themselves, let alone contribute to or aid its development in any way.[37] Thus the socialist workers' movement kept away from any sort of regionalist stance, and class, ethnicity and language were not associated with one another in northern France.

A final explanation for the absence of an ethnic or regional dimension to the class movement in the north of France, given the close association with the Belgian socialists, is the 'national' orientations of the socialist movements in the two countries. During the nineteenth century the level of co-operation had remained high, but beginning in the early years of the twentieth century, what Carl Strikwerda described as a new nationalism was adopted by members of the socialist movement which led them to accentuate the differences between French and Belgian socialists, driving the two groups further apart.[38] As the socialist parties grew more concerned with elections and political power during the twentieth century, they also naturally focused more upon their own countries and tried to work within their different political systems. Divergent policies on tariffs, transportation, wages and working conditions further encouraged working-class leaders to devote their energy to specific questions within their own state structures, and heightened the division.[39] In this way, at the same time as the Belgian socialist movement was encouraging the association between working-class and Flemish ethnic and

34 On anticlericalism in the Lille region see Pierre Pierrard, *Histoire de Lille*, Paris 1982, 221–3.
35 Talmy, 'Les Tendances anti-cléricales', 8, 11–12.
36 Ibid. 117.
37 More will be said in chapter 7 below on links between the clergy and the regional Flemish movement.
38 See Carl Strikwerda, 'France and the Belgian immigration of the nineteenth century', in Camille Guerin-Gonzales and Carl Strikwerda (eds), *The politics of immigrant workers: labour activism and migration in the world economy since 1830*, New York 1993, 122–3.
39 See Balthazar, 'Betrekkingen', 26, and Strikwerda, 'Regionalism and internationalism', 228.

cultural identity, it was drifting apart from its socialist counterparts in the north of France.

Partly explained through the long-standing Belgian connection, northern socialism remained characteristic within France well into the twentieth century, beyond the period of heightened contacts with Belgian socialists, and included characteristics of the workers themselves, their political positions, attitudes towards work, their values and their *mentalité*;[40] regional characteristics did not, however, include any consciousness of their very regional character. After Guesdism, the socialism of the north was characterised by moderation, desire for genuine elected office and respect for the democratic principle of alternation, with markedly little success for the internationalist communist Left.[41] The moderation of the Left in the Nord comes as no surprise, given the general political characteristics of French Flanders (*see* chapter 2). From the end of the First World War onward, the large numbers of immigrants from diverse ethnic origins meant that the proportion of Flemish workers in the area decreased, and the potential for any serious development of an ethnically-based working-class consciousness grew more remote.

Thus in spite of the sizeable Flemish-speaking community in the main urban centres of the Nord and contacts with Belgium in the period preceding the First World War, the potential for using cultural or ethnic consciousness as a means of increasing solidarity among workers through the association of workers' grievances with Flemishness was not developed. A key distinction between the north of France and Belgium was, therefore, the differing positions of the respective socialist parties *vis à vis* the place of Flemish ethnic and regional consciousness in the workers' struggle. In France, for a variety of reasons, but perhaps due more to their anticlerical position and French background than to their internationalism or any diversity among the population, Flemish consciousness was never utilised as a platform to attract workers by socialist and syndicalist leaders, who focused uniquely upon the cultivation of a class-based identity.

---

[40] See Robert P. Baker, 'Socialism in the Nord, 1880–1914: a regional view of the French socialist movement', *International Review of Social History* xii (1967), 357–89, and Brenne, 'Les Candidats ouvriers', 193.

[41] See Jean-Louis Robert, 'Eléments sur la scission dans la France du Nord', Patrick Oddone, 'Socialistes et communistes dans l'agglomération dunkerquoise, 1945–1981', and Antoine Prost, 'Conclusion: les légitimités du socialisme septentrional', all in Ménager, Sirinelli and Vavasseur-Desperriers, *Cent Ans de socialisme*, 91–119, 315–29, 401–5. See also Gille, 'Quarante Ans d'Action Catholique, 139–57.

7

Local Interest Groups

Among the population of the Westhoek and the surrounding regions, several other groups with an inherently local focus also adopted positions on the development of identity in French Flanders during the nineteenth and twentieth centuries. This chapter will examine first of all the local press, both from the point of view of language employed in production and any position adopted specifically with respect to the region, the nation or ethnic and cultural identity. Second, a variety of organisations which sought explicitly to encourage the development of a specifically Flemish cultural or regional identity in the Westhoek will be described and their influence analysed. Attention will then be turned to the *patronat*, the loose grouping of industrialists and business leaders, to examine the extent to which their collective influence had any impact upon identity formation. The chapter will conclude with a discussion of the development of a broader regional identity for the whole Nord–Pas-de-Calais and the place of Flemish identity within the greater region.

The press

No discussion of regional identity would be complete without a discussion of the popular press. Both reflecting and describing the issues of the day, the press could also serve as a leading force, influencing local opinion. Newspapers were among the first means whereby information spread through the small towns, reached rural inhabitants, and brought rural communities into contact with the world at large.[1] Especially since the final decades of the nineteenth century, a political press developed which aimed at the masses and sought to convince them 'not through syllogisms, but questions of principle and gross effects of sentimentalism'.[2] This made the press a particularly influential way of fostering a sense of regionalism, be it culturally, ethnically or politically based or a sense of nationalism, since all are highly susceptible to sentimentalism.

One point worth noting is that at no time during the nineteenth or twentieth centuries was there official anti-Flemish censorship, nor was it ever

---

[1] Maurice Agulhon, 'Réflexions sur l'image du bourgeois français à la veille de 1848', *Quarante-huit quatorze: conférences du Musée d'Orsay* vi (1994), 4–13.
[2] Winock, *Nationalisme, antisémitisme et fascisme*, 81.

illegal to publish in any other language than French. The freedom of the press as far as language was concerned was complete, and outside of the schoolroom linguistic tolerance prevailed.[3] It was the opinion of Émile de Girardin, one of the most prominent national press barons of the nineteenth century, that censorship of the press had the exact opposite of the effect desired. The best way to nullify a contrary position, according to Girardin, was to permit it freedom to publish (so that it could not gain support through a quasi-martyrdom) and swamp opinion with views to the contrary. The more different opinions appear in a widely diverse press, the weaker each one becomes individually, reducing their potential impact.[4] In this way, any claim to be an oppressed minority was taken away from the press ahead of time, and publishing in Flemish could not be an act of defiance.

As a general rule, the press of the Nord, like the politics of the Nord, was moderate.[5] It was also one of the only regions in France during the late nineteenth century to boast a newspaper labelled at the same time 'Catholic' and 'Republican': the *Patriote des Flandres*. Most of the newspapers in the Nord were written in French throughout the nineteenth and twentieth centuries, not only in Lille and Dunkerque, but also in Hazebrouck, Bergues, Steenvoorde and other Flemish communities. This is a sign that direct access to the press was restricted to the educated elite and that important political discourse was restricted to French. Often it was the mayor of the village who would communicate the news to the rest of the inhabitants who could not read for themselves, further emphasising his role as an intermediary between the local inhabitants and the state.[6]

A few Flemish-language newspapers were published in the Nord. A primary example is *Het Vlaamsch Kruis* (The Flemish Cross) published in Lille beginning in the year 1892, later becoming *Het Volk* (The People).[7] The subtitle of this daily paper was 'Voor de Vlamingen van Frankrijk – 'for the French Flemish'. Upon closer scrutiny, it is obvious that this paper was written by Belgian expatriates and was much more concerned with events and issues on the Belgian side of the border. The main articles and news columns dealt with Belgium, while French news was relegated to the 'foreign' news column, along with England, Germany or America. A special 'North of France' column appeared each day, but, rather than treating any real political issues of the day, dealt exclusively with petty incidents such as burglaries, accidents, fires, and occasionally brief mentions of strikes, but only to say they were happening. The odd feature articles discussed the Flemish move-

---

3 Agulhon, 'Conscience nationale', 257. See also Jean-François Chanet, 'Les Instituteurs et le régionalisme dans l'entre-deux-guerres (1918–1940): premiers résultats d'une enquête par questionnaire', mémoire *ad hoc*, DEA de sciences sociales, EHESS – ENS 1991.
4 See Pierre Pellissier, *Émile de Girardin: prince de la presse*, Paris 1985.
5 See Néré, 'Les Elections Boulanger', 7.
6 Singer, *Village notables*, 39.
7 See ADN, 1 T 222 24.

ment in a positive light. In July 1892, 'Onze toestand' (Our situation) compared the Flemish nationalist movement with nationalism in Ireland.[8] Several years later an article discussing literature described the Flemish: 'And our Flemish people love their language, with their whole heart and their whole soul.'[9] The author goes on to say that if Flemish were to disappear, their very existence would be negated. A further article cried out in nationalist tones that Flemish was distinct from Dutch, and they should not be confused, but respected as unique and different.[10]

The general impression or feeling given by this paper is one of attachment to the Belgian Flemish movement, rather than any particular appeal to the French Flemish for themselves in any capacity other than as neighbours and co-sufferers (supposedly). It is unlikely that if these papers made it out of the circle of recent Belgian immigrants or migrant workers, they had a great impact, or inspired the French Flemish to feel associated with any calls to join or support the Flemish movement, given their lack of genuinely local references to the Westhoek. The weekly version of *Het Volk* was expressly for Belgian expatriates, bearing the title *Het Volk der Franschmans*.[11] This being the only fully Flemish paper in the department, its association with the Church could not help but reinforce the link between the Catholic Church and the Flemish movement in the minds of the people of the north. It is likely that this was supplemented by other newspapers published in Belgium and brought across the border, nevertheless restricting the reading options in Flemish with Westhoek content.

Among the other papers of the region, some did contain some small articles in Flemish. The weekly *Patriote des Flandres*, coming from Steenvoorde, had a small column in Westhoek dialect in almost every issue. They were usually set up as a dialogue between two Flemings, 'Kô Tasse and Pier Fynoore', who either told jokes or made very general observations about something related to religion which was reported in the main French articles.[12] On weeks when Kô and Pier did not appear, they were replaced by a column of either jokes of witty proverb-style humour or short humorous fiction. *Le Cri des Flandres*, a newspaper founded by the *abbé* Lemire also contained the odd small article in Flemish, again exclusively humorous subjects.[13] A Dunkerque paper, *L'Ami des Flandres*, describes itself in its first issue with the statement: 'Inhabitants of the region, knowing both of its languages, its morals, habits and its most legitimate aspirations, we have

8 'Onze toestand', *Het Vlaamsch Kruis: voor de Vlamingen van Frankrijk*, 13 July 1892, 1.
9 'Wetenschappelijk onderhoud: eene leemte in onze vlaamsche letterkunde', *Het Vlaamsch Kruis: voor de Vlamingen van Frankrijk*, 19 Mar. 1898, 1.
10 'Vlaamsch, NIET Nederlandsch'', *Het Volk*, 8 Feb. 1911, 1.
11 The full title is *Het Volk Der Franschmans: Orgaan der Franschmans – en Steenbakkersgilden van Oost-Vlaanderen*.
12 See, for example, 'Kô Tasse en Pier Fynoore', *Le Patriote des Flandres: journal de Steenvoorde et de l'arrondissement d'Hazebrouck*, 4 Dec. 1910, 2.
13 See, for example, 'Hy was te moe', *Le Cri des Flandres: journal républicain*, 3 Oct. 1926.

founded this newspaper.'[14] In spite of this encouraging debut, only issue number 4 contained even a word of Flemish – one small article.[15] In this paper, as well as others such as *L'Echo de Flandre* or *Le Petit Steenvoordois*, which claimed to be 'of local interest', there were no articles with the slightest regional slant, nor in any way did they attempt to promote cultural or regional consciousness among the people of the Westhoek.[16] In a report to the prefect, who wished to be informed of the political stripe of the press of the department as a forewarning of potentially dangerous quarters, no mention was made of any threats of regionalism, nor were any Flemish titles cited.[17]

As far as other sorts of publications in Flemish are concerned, the *Comité Flamand de France* published *Tisje-Tasje's Almanak*, but little else in Flemish, and otherwise only the catechism was bilingual. Other books would have been available from Belgium, but, as in the case for newspapers, would have sustained the language, but been a poor basis for sparking political discussion or regional consciousness.

Therefore those French Flemish who could read had the choice between the Belgian-oriented press, with little Westhoek content, or the French-language local press which did not explore the question of cultural or even regional identity. In a newspaper entitled *La Chronique des Flandres: organe de défence à Paris des intérêts du département du Nord*, no mention was made of cultural issues, and outside of defending economic interests, little sense of cohesion in the region was even suggested.[18] Among the local French press of the Nord, however, the occasional article was written in support of the French language and the republican position of national cultural integration.[19] Where they were not supporters of national cultural integration and assimilation, the press of the region treated questions of cultural or regional identity with relative indifference. For the most part, the press of the Nord reflected the principal national political currents of the time in France, with a bit of unpolemical local content as well.

After the First World War, a newspaper entitled the *Mercure de Flandre* began to publish regionalist articles with the aim of promoting 'nordism' and

14 'L'Union', *L'Ami des Flandres: journal de Dunkerque & de la région: organe républicain, indépendant, littéraire, commercial, agricole et d'informations*, 11 Nov. 1911, 1.
15 'van tisje-tasje', *L'Ami des Flandres*, 2 Dec. 1911, 2. The BN has only twenty copies altogether, the final one being no. 53 (10 Nov. 1912).
16 See *L'Echo de Flandre: journal politique, d'intérêt local, agricole & littéraire*, and *Le Petit Steenvoordois: organe d'intérêt local commercial, agricole & littéraire de Steenvoorde & du canton*.
17 Report, 1880, ADN, 1 T 217.
18 *La Chronique des Flandres: organe de défence à Paris des intérêts du département du Nord*, 15 Dec. 1906. The BN holds only this first issue, so it is possible that it did not survive. Issue 1 clearly sets out their objectives, and they did not include cultural issues.
19 'Demain', *Le Journal d'Hazebrouck et de l'arrondissement*, 1 Jan. 1888. This article claimed that French was the only 'true' language.

criticising 'literary and artistic centralisation'.[20] Edited by Valentin Bresle, a young free-thinking intellectual, the paper hoped to spawn a greater regionalist movement which was not centred around Catholicism. Including Flemish cultural demands, this paper did spawn a few groups and contributed to the growth of the Flemish movement in the inter-war period, although it did not achieve wide notoriety nor detach the bulk of the Flemish movement from its close links with the Church.[21]

In the late 1920s a small group attempted to cultivate regional identity and strengthen regionalism in the Nord through a newspaper entitled *Le Nord fédéral: organe régionaliste*. Their platform was purely political and had no basis whatsoever in cultural matters. Led by Henri Lauridan, a member of the central committee of the *Parti Fasciste Révolutionnaire*, the group did have several connections with the Flemish movement in Belgium and published some Flemish articles in their paper, but due to their vehement anticlericalism had little or no contact with the leaders of the French-Flemish movement.[22] Their positions were in general so extreme that they did not have much appeal to the inhabitants of the Nord. A special commissioner wrote to the prefect in 1929 that 'In sum, even if it might be worthwhile to watch this group and the men who started it – there is no need for alarm over the appearance of the "Nord Fédéral" which has left the population indifferent.'[23]

With the exception of *Le Nord fédéral*, which was extremist, marginal, and not concerned with the French Flemish or regional culture, the only example of true regional sentiment in the press came after the First World War with publications under the auspices of the local *flamingant* societies which will be discussed in the remainder of this chapter.

Flemish societies before the First World War

Several societies came into existence in northern France in the latter half of the nineteenth century with the preservation of Flemish language, history, culture and identity as their express goals. For the largest part, these were upper- and middle-class groups, particularly, although not exclusively, intellectuals. The various groups attempted, through their publications and meetings, to increase awareness of, spread knowledge of and garner support for the Flemish movement in France, as well as to keep Flemish consciousness alive by instilling a pride in the regional culture such as would ensure its survival.

By far and away the most important of the societies in French Flanders was

[20] See Olivier Engelaere, 'Le Mouvement Flamand en France de la libération au "renouveau" du début des années 70', maîtrise d'histoire contemporaine, université de Lille III, 1989, 22–5.
[21] See pp. 158–63 below for a discussion of the Flemish movement in the inter-war period.
[22] See 'Vlamingen', *Le Nord fédéral: organe des droits de la région du Nord*, 1er année, no. spécial, 18 Mar. 1929, 1.
[23] Special commissioner to prefect, 1 May 1929, ADN, M 154 318.

the *Comité Flamand de France* (CFF), which was founded in 1853 by Louis de Baecker, a philologist, and Edmond de Coussemacker, a justice of the peace in Bailleul, the man who had initiated the survey of Flemish-speakers in 1856 (*see* chapter 1). Outside the Church, the *Comité* was the only real defender of Flemish in France before the First World War.[24] Membership was drawn principally from the well-educated segment of the population living in the Westhoek, although quite a number of members came from across the border, and a disproportionately high percentage were members of the clergy.[25]

The express goal of the founders of the CFF was to act as agents for the defence and preservation of the Flemish language and culture in French Flanders. Their motto was 'Moedertaal en Vaderland': Mother tongue and Fatherland (referring to Flanders). They held regular meetings in various parts of the Westhoek, and published both a regular *Bulletin*, and *Annales*. Their meetings and work in general tended to be of an erudite, elitist nature, however, and not geared towards more popular pursuits. In the second article of their statutes, the *Comité* outlined its objectives as the study of Flemish literature, research and the conservation of historic and literary documents written in Flemish.[26] It is worthy of note that although their goal was to preserve Flemish culture, and most particularly its literary culture and language, their motto alone was expressed in Flemish; their main publications, with the exception of only a handful of articles in the whole 140–year history of the *Comité*, appeared in French, which apparently was also the principal language used at their meetings.[27]

The one exception is a series of almanacs written by J.-B. van Grevelynghe, which the CFF began to publish in 1900, first in Flemish, and then in a new edition after the First World War with Flemish and French appearing side-by-side.[28] These were called *Tisje-Tasje's Almanaks* and contained jokes and amusing stories written in Westhoek Flemish. Unfortunately, it is difficult to determine what sort of circulation they might have had, since they cannot be found in any libraries or archives, nor in library of the *Comité* itself, and it therefore seems likely that they were not too widely circulated.[29] Luc

[24] Verbeke, *Vlaanderen in Frankrijk*, 65.

[25] A. Withoeck, 'Proeve tot typologie van de Belgische leden van het Comité Flamand de France, 1853–1914', *DFN/LPBF* xix (1994), 116–39.

[26] See 'Allocution prononcée par Mgr. Dehaisnes 20 novembre 1888 à Hazebrouck', *ACFF* xviii (1889–90), 1–8, where he outlines the objectives of the CFF as purely academic, and Louis De Baecker, *Les Flamands de France: études sur leur langue, leur littérature, et leur monuments*, new edn, ed. Gérard Monfort, Brionne 1975, as a sample of the work of the early members.

[27] See 'Comité Flamand de France', *L'Indicateur de l'arrondissement d'Hazebrouck*, 13 Sept. 1888, 2, which gives a detailed description of the contents of a typical meeting, with academic papers presented, discussion, and reviews of the most recent research under way.

[28] Coornaert, *La Flandre française*, 325; *Tisje-Tasje's almanak 1901*; *Tisje-Tasje's almanak voor Fransch-Vlaanderen 1929*, Hazebrouck 1929.

[29] The two copies cited in n. 28, one a photocopy, were consulted by the author in the the private collection of M. Staes of Hazebrouck.

Verbeke writes that the largest number printed in a single year between 1900 and 1914 was 6,000.[30]

Thus the *Comité* sought to preserve Flemish through purely academic pursuits, such as histories of popular songs, or grammatical or idiomatic comparisons between regions or through history. They were followed by several other learned societies, such as the *Société Dunkerquoise*, with similar goals. To the question of the extent of their collective impact on Flemish society, and the ability of these various organisations to inspire pride in and a desire to preserve traditional Flemish practices, including the Flemish language, Jean Chocqueel summed up in 1920 that their work was insufficiently circulated, had not succeeded in reaching the mass of the people and only interested 'a restricted number of dilettante and amateurs'.[31] He noted that the work of the *CFF*, *l'Union Faulconnier* and the *Société Dunkerquoise* was somewhat scattered, but nevertheless considerable in quantity.

Culturally, therefore, local organisations such as the *CFF* were primarily geared to the elite and had limited impact upon the population. Willem Meyers identifies the pre-1914 aspirations of the *CFF* as purely cultural and lacking any political dimension.[32] This did not mean that they did not come out in favour of the teaching of Flemish in primary schools or of Flemish catechisms or make public statements in defence of Flemish as a popular idiom, as they most certainly did, but that they remained extremely cautious in all domains not directly academic.

The striking and yet pervasive feature of everything that the *Comité* did was its avoidance of anything even slightly political in nature. In any public utterances or writings about the importance of the preservation of Flemish and its culture, they always included clear statements about their loyalty to France and the importance of being at the same time both Flemish and French. They always 'truly desired to remain good French citizens'.[33] In the *Bulletin* of the *Comité* in 1864, one of the original members, the *abbé* D. Carnel wrote in an article entitled the 'Revue du Mouvement Flamand' that in Belgium the Flemish movement had gone out of its 'natural domain' and into politics.[34] In a speech at the fiftieth anniversary celebration in 1903, the chairman of the *Comité*, the *abbé* C. Looten, stressed how pleased the members of the *Comité* were to both preserve and support the Flemish language through study, while at the same time remaining faithful to 'La

---

30 Verbeke, *Vlaanderen in Frankrijk*, 63.
31 Jean Chocquel, *Les Chambres de rhétorique en Flandre française* (editions du *Beffroi de Flandre*, revue régionaliste, 1920), 3.
32 Willem C. M. Meyers, 'Les Collaborateurs flamands de France et leurs contacts avec les milieux flamingantes belges: les visées territoriales sur la Flandre française pendant la Seconde Guerre mondiale', *RN* lx (Apr.–June 1978), 377.
33 Verbeke, *Vlaanderen in Frankrijk*, 50.
34 D. Carnel, 'Revue du mouvement Flamand', *BCFF* iii (session of 3 Mar. 1864), 245–6.

Grande Patrie'.[35] Almost twenty years later, in 1921, Looten further asserted with pride that what distinguished the Flemish movement in France from that in Belgium was that groups such as theirs or the *Société Dunkerquoise*, did not pose any threat to the authorities and were not in any way political or disloyal.[36] The long-standing deputy for the region, the *abbé* Lemire, was a participating member of the CFF as well as of several other Flemish organisations, but did not act as a political representative of the movement. He did intervene on three occasions in parliament in defence of Flemish, but it was hardly a major part of his political platform in Paris, and he certainly could not be described as a regionalist.[37]

The best description of the collective position of the CFF is to be found in a letter written by Louis de Baecker, one of its two founders, to the rector of the Douai Academy, in charge of administering the schools of the district.[38] The rector had requested that de Baecker advise him on the best way to deal with the language problem in the schools, and how to overcome the hurdle of teaching French to children whose knowledge of that language was non-existent when they arrived at school. De Baecker began by explaining that Flemish was not merely a *patois*, but a full-fledged language employed 'from Gravelines to Königsberg', which had 'its literature and its admirers'.[39] He advised that while the teaching of French was of primary importance, it would be much to the benefit of the French state to attempt to preserve what could be seen as a valuable resource: native speakers of Flemish. After all, who better than such native speakers, when well educated, to enter the diplomatic corps for service in Dutch-speaking countries, or to foster commercial interaction? He advocated a bilingual primary school to encourage at the same time the cultivation of both French and Flemish, which would, he argued, in no way threaten the advancement of the French language or the loyalty of French-Flemish citizens to the republic.

His argument was quite subtle, claiming that 'the Latin of the Middle Ages is the French of today'.[40] He maintained that science had been greatly retarded in the Middle Ages by the restriction to Latin and that the teaching of other languages 'was the first step by the peoples of Europe on the road to general civilisation'.[41] The next step to other languages could only be to the

---

35 Camille Looten, *Le Comité Flamand de France 1853 à 1903*, Arras 1904. This is the text of a speech delivered at the fiftieth anniversary celebration.

36 Idem, 'La Question du Flamand', BCFF (1921), 266–75.

37 Lemire spoke on 18 Feb. 1902, 11 Mar. 1910 and 11 Dec. 1921: Landry and Verrewaere, *Histoire secrète*, 274. His regionalism was limited to an opposition to centralised secularism, which became less and less important to him as his career progressed: Michiel Nuyttens, 'Priester-volksvertegenwordiger Lemire (1853–1928) en het regionalisme', DFN/LPBF vii (1982), 10–32.

38 Louis de Baecker to rector, 14 Apr. 1856, ADN, 2 T 767, dossier 1856.

39 Ibid.

40 Ibid.

41 Ibid.

further benefit of mankind. He claimed that the result of the system as it stood was that

> the child of the Flemish worker, who only knows how to speak Flemish like his father and mother, being forced by the schoolteacher to forget his mother tongue in order to learn to read and write French, yet unable to consecrate enough time to this study in order to truly possess this new idiom, this child will leave school knowing neither Flemish nor French.[42]

De Baecker's advice, being merely advice, was not followed, and the schools of the Westhoek remained officially French only. The CFF's position of encouraging Flemish in schools was also supported by the Church (*see* chapter 5) and occasionally by others, such as Charles de Gaulle (uncle of the famous general), who along with two others sent a petition to the legislature in early 1870 also calling for the introduction of Flemish and other provincial languages in schools.[43]

The CFF never got beyond giving advice to officials and urging upon its own members the importance of preserving Flemish through scholarly pursuits. Even so the *Comité* itself published in French, held meetings in French and never made public statements about the importance of Flemish for children, preferring instead mere private suggestion, and the hope that the authorities would eventually acquiesce. Their chief goal was to safeguard 'literary life' as distinguished from the general survival of the spoken idiom.[44] Thus the chambers of rhetoric also went into decline, as the pure literary and translation aspects took over from public performance and general interest. The limit of 'Flemish' patriotism in their writings can be found in a review by A. Bonvarlet of a book published by the *Société Brugeoise* about famous men of West Flanders. Bonvarlet attempts to show which of those famous men could also be claimed by the French Flemish, because they were born in the Westhoek, or had some other connection to it. An example is Philippe de Comines, a fifteenth-century seigneur under Louis XI, and himself an historian possessing land in what is now the *arrondissement* of Hazebrouck.[45] In the whole of the review, Bonvarlet's tone could not be said to be 'patriotic' in a popular sense, although he did refer to 'Flanders, our dear fatherland'.[46] Without a harder, political line, little sense of urgency was created or conveyed to the peasants and working classes of the Westhoek, to encourage more widespread active determination to preserve Flemish on the local level.

[42] Ibid.
[43] See 'Charles de Gaulle réclame l'enseignement du flamand', *Le Lion de Flandre* 3rd ser. xiii (Jan. 1942), 35–7; Landry and de Verrewaere, *Histoire secrète*, 272.
[44] See Deprez, 'Over Gezelles briefwisseling', 228–45. The poet Gezelle translated old words and Flemish proverbs for the CFF. He was particularly interested in the preservation of the West Flemish variation spoken on either side of the Franco-Belgian border.
[45] A. Bonvarlet, 'Un Mot sur ce que la biographie des hommes remarquables de la Flandre occidentale contient au point de vue des flamands de France', *BCFF* ii (1862), 344–5.
[46] Ibid. 341.

It is not difficult to understand that, given the position it adopted, the *Comité Flamand de France* was not known outside elite circles and had little popular appeal, such as might have lead others outside to seek actively to hold onto their language and identify themselves more closely with their Flemish cultural traditions. De Baecker himself, the author of this letter and one of the co-founders of the organisation, resigned from the *Comité* in 1866 because he felt that they should be more politically active and not restrict their activities to archaeology and folklore.[47]

The other learned societies in the region were equally apolitical in their motives, and several ignored the question of contemporary culture and language altogether. In the published *Mémoires* and *Bulletin* of the *Société Dunkerquoise*, another nineteenth-century learned society calling itself 'Flemish', even articles discussing education in French Flanders did not include mention of the language question.[48] The situation was similar for the *Union Faulconnier*.[49]

In writing about the learned societies in the nineteenth century, Robert Fox shows that a conflict for funding and support existed between the regionally centred societies and the centralised ones.[50] 'By the early 1870s the struggle was all but over', the universities the victors, and regionalist societies on the losing end, becoming more dependent than ever on governmental funding for their publishing efforts.[51] By the 1890s government interest in societies was much reduced, and their financial troubles only increased until the war. Since they were dependent upon the central government for funding, the societies predictably did not take hard-line regionalist, anti-centralist positions in their policies, knowing what the repercussions would be.

In addition to the learned societies originating in the Westhoek, several associations from Belgian Flanders took an interest in the fate of their linguistic compatriots across the border. Two of the most prominent Belgian Flemish societies in Belgium had offshoots in the Westhoek – the *Willemsfonds* and the *Davidsfonds* – each named for prominent Flemish activists from the early and mid-nineteenth century. Such Belgians as Paul Fredericq, a professor at the university of Ghent, were keen to lend support to the French Flemish whenever they could.[52] These groups succeeded in mustering a great deal of

47 Pierre Brachin, 'Un Pionnier: Louis de Baecker (1814–1896)', *DFN/LPBF* xiii (1988), 65.
48 See, for example, Mordacq, 'Notes', 36–65, and M. Tronchet, 'La Place des langues dans l'enseignement', *MSD* xxi (1877–80), 187–99, neither of whom make any mention of the question of the native language of the pupils arriving at school or the Flemish question in general.
49 See the *Bulletin de l'Union Faulconnier*, which contains similar material to the *MSD*.
50 Robert Fox, 'Learning, politics and polite culture in provincial France: the *Sociétés savantes* in the nineteenth century', in Baker and Harrigan, *Making of Frenchmen*, 543–64.
51 Ibid. 552.
52 Coornaert, *La Flandre française*, 324–5.

support for the Flemish movement in Belgium, but never really took off in French Flanders, which was perhaps viewed as a bit peripheral by many of the central members, while from the Westhoek they were seen as 'too Belgian'. The French Flemish maintained a close contact for literary purposes with Belgian activists, but seldom responded politically.[53] With respect to this interaction, Willem C. M. Meyers differentiates the prewar aspirations of the French Flemish from those of the Belgians as being above all cultural; as yet they did not have political aspirations.[54]

Towards the end of the nineteenth century, one of the principal figures in the Belgian Flemish movement, Guido Gezelle, attempted to found a review for the Flemish of France, designed for both the man on the street as well as the cultural elite. It was entitled *Ons oud Vlaemsch* ('Our old Flemish') and met with problems right from its inception: it only ever printed one issue, at Christmas 1885, principally due to lack of subscribers.[55] Dirk Beirens describes three other problems for the review: no businessman, Gezelle had financial difficulties from the outset. Moreover, a lack of co-operation on the French side of the border at the organisational level (he found only two people to help him) made distribution and publicity difficult. Finally, Gezelle's illusion that 'French Flanders was completely Flemish', caused practical difficulties.[56] The fact, for example, that Gezelle insisted that all address labels be in Flemish only (using the old Flemish place-names) meant that many of those who did subscribe never received their copies, since the French post office was unable to deliver them.

Other Belgian political pamphlets supporting the Flemish movement, and written in Flemish, did circulate in France, but, like the Belgian newspapers, particularly among Belgians living abroad. Such writings were geared primarily to garner support either for the socialist movement in general, or particularly oriented towards Belgium, rather than towards France.[57] Thus the Flemish societies founded in the Westhoek in the period before the First World War, in spite of their interest in the preservation of Flemish culture and identity, chose to remain aloof from politics as a platform to defend their interests, and made little progress in popularising their efforts beyond the restricted circle of an educated elite.

[53] See, for example, Deprez, 'Over Gezelles briefwisseling'.
[54] Meyers, 'Les Collaborateurs flamands', 337–46.
[55] Dirk Beirens, 'De geschiedenis van "Ons oud Vlaemsch", tijdschriff van Guido Gezelle voor Frans-Vlaanderen', *DFN/LPBF* vii (1982), 130–52.
[56] Ibid. 152.
[57] ADN, M 154 58. This carton contains many Flemish pamphlets seized in Lille, mostly published in Ghent, although one, *Algemeen Steemrecht* (Universal Suffrage) came from the Netherlands, and was intended for the French. As, however, it is rather poorly written, it is difficult to ascertain exactly what their intention was, besides speaking generally about hunger and togetherness and socialism in a mild way. The others are for the most part Belgian political tracts dealing with the Belgian socialist and workers' movements.

From the inter-war period to collaboration

In the inter-war period, the role of the learned societies began to change. Fox shows that, by the 1920s, their previous function as a regional elite had largely been replaced by other institutions and they suffered from a 'professionalisation of culture and the systematic assumption of their diverse functions by bodies better suited to the tasks they had once filled almost as a monopoly'.[58] In this way their role became further marginalised from mainstream society, as they were neither 'popular' nor 'professional'.

The CFF continued its activities throughout the inter-war period in the same spirit of academic interest devoid of political aspirations that had characterised it before the war. In an evaluation of regionalist strength in 1921, the prefect of the department said of Camille Looten, president of the CFF since 1899, that 'his attitude is irreproachable; he has never uttered the slightest unsavoury remark from the point of view of the nation, and has absolutely no relations with the "Flemish separatists" of Belgium'.[59]

The prefect's comments about Looten's loyalty came in response to a speech he gave at a meeting of the *Fédération Régionaliste du Nord et du Pas-de-Calais*, held in December 1920. In spite of what is conveyed by the title, the *Fédération* was not separatist, nor even regionalist in the strict sense of the word.[60] At the 1920 meeting they were particularly concerned with the rights of regions devastated by the war and with reclaiming from the government (and ultimately from Germany) 'integral reparation for their damages, via application of the law of 17 April 1919'.[61] This focus did not prevent Flemish regionalists from attending, participating and putting some items up for discussion. Monsieur Mabille de Poncheville put forward three propositions which were all accepted unanimously: that a Flemish literature course, as well as a course in regional history, be instigated at the university of Lille, that regional authors be studied and regional songs sung in the schools, and that the schools teach local and regional history.[62] In spite of the occasional other item on the agenda, little else was forthcoming from the *Fédération* which dealt with Flemish culture, identity or regionalism.

While in the pre-1914 period the CFF was the principal Flemish organisation in the Westhoek, the inter-war period saw the foundation of several new *flamingant* organisations, and renewed efforts to promote Flemish culture in France, occasionally venturing into the political arena as well. This new

---

58 Ibid. 560.
59 Prefect to minister of the interior, 5 Jan. 1921, *re* the 'Congrès régionaliste du Nord et du Pas-de-Calais', ADN, M 154 318.
60 Prefect to minister of the interior, trade and liberated regions, 14 Dec. 1925, ibid. This organisation was described briefly in the section dealing with the *patronat*.
61 Central commissioner to prefect, 10 Jan. 1921, ibid.
62 This was reported in prefect to minister of the interior, 5 Jan. 1921, ibid. See also Dewachter, 'La Situation du français et du flamand', 31.

activity was primarily centred around the Catholic seminaries, preserving the religious character of the Flemish movement. Not unlike their predecessors, these 'Flemish circles' hoped to spread knowledge of Flanders through literature and history, as well as through the defence of the Flemish language. They were organised by and for the seminary students and encouraged the study of all things Flemish. Two were founded by Antoon Lescroart at the seminary in Annappes in 1919 and at the theological seminary in Lille in 1921. Jean-Marie Gantois founded another at the academic seminary of Lille in 1923 which was called the 'Michiel De Swaenkring' after a prominent Flemish writer of the seventeenth and early eighteenth centuries. A fourth was founded at the small seminary of Haubourdin by Marcel Dupont in the same year.[63]

Led by Jean-Marie Gantois and Antoon Lescroart, with the supportive encouragement of Camille Looten, the *Union des Cercles Flamands de France* became the *Vlaamsch Verbond van Vrankrijk* (VVF) in July 1924. The VVF was designed as a broader movement, to embrace not only seminary students, but the wider population as well. Its goals were outlined by its first secretary, J.-M. Gantois:

> The VVF groups together all of the Flemish from the French Low Countries who want to have the personality of their region respected, preserve its unique appearance, develop its genius, recreate a Flanders worthy of its genius, wake its soul, give it free and proud expression, defend and cultivate its language, develop its literature, renovate its artistic traditions.[64]

The VVF brought together much of the youth and energy of the Flemish movement. Looten encouraged the young Flemish to found this separate organisation and steered many into it, rather than into his own CFF, in order to bring fresh life and a new approach to the Flemish movement, which had grown complacent and conservative.[65] In this way the long-standing pattern of compliance and pure loyalty set by the CFF did not burden the new organisation, and the VVF was free to join in the regionalist movement which was expanding throughout France and to associate itself with the *Fédération Régionaliste Française*, led by figures such as Charles-Brun.[66] They forged contacts with other regionalists in Lorraine, Bretagne, Alsace and the south, in the hopes of lending strength to their cause and taking it out of the exclusively clerical milieu.[67] Writing in 1920, Jean Chocqueel described some of

---

63 Verbeke, *Vlaanderen in Frankrijk*, 83–4.
64 Jean-Marie Gantois, quoted in Landry and de Verrewaere, *Histoire secrète*, 285.
65 See ibid. 280–1.
66 Landry and de Verrewaere, *Histoire secrète*, 285. The CFF also had links with the *Fédération Régionaliste Française*, beginning in 1903.
67 Several of these organisations were cultural rather than political as the CFF had always been: see Joe Roza, 'The *Félibrige rouge* and pan-latinism: ethnic identity without separation', *Proceedings of the Annual Meeting of the Western Society for French History* xxii (1995), 128.

the aspirations of the movement which was already crystallising immediately after the Great War:

> The regionalist movement which counts so many ardent champions among us, will it ever see the renaissance of Flemish and of our old customs? . . . The regionalist movement which is beginning, if it is well understood and well-led, could very well lead us towards this long-awaited renaissance.[68]

The 1920s was a good time to begin to spread regionalist ideas, due to the pacifism and anti-nationalist sentiment of the inter-war years, although it often led to internationalism rather than regionalism.[69] Other regional cultural groups which were not affiliated in any way to the Catholic Church began to form in the 1920s around the paper the *Mercure de Flandre*, but they were never able to occupy a central space in the inter-war Flemish movement.[70]

In terms of actual activity, the VVF began in a similar sort of vein as the CFF, with the sponsorship of cultural and literary endeavours. Their work did, however, make an attempt at being more popular, and they tried to use Flemish in a more concrete way than their predecessors, rather than making French the practical working language. They revived and sponsored yearly literary competitions for the best original compositions of poetry and theatre in Flemish, as well as awarding prizes for the best translations of selected texts. They also began a course in Flemish by correspondence and encouraged various post-secondary institutions to include Flemish among their options.[71]

The publications of the VVF, in both languages, were prolific during the inter-war period.[72] In the early 1920s the principal French-language paper was *Le Beffroi*, replaced at the end of 1928 by *Le Lion de Flandre*. They were both organs which printed regionalist articles, in addition to general culture, history, folklore and geography, and had more appeal to the cultural elite than to the general population of the Westhoek. In Flemish they published the short lived *De Vlaemsche Stemme in Vrankrijk*, (The Flemish Voice in France) and a monthly paper called *De Torrewachter: Maanblad voor Fransch-Vlaanderen* (The Belfry: Monthly newspaper for French Flemish), which produced its first number in 1929, and survived until the end of the Second World War. *De Torrewachter* was written completely in Flemish; its goal was to speak to the French Flemish in their mother tongue, particularly about their 'fatherland'.[73] By way of encouragement, in the second issue one article

---

68 See Chocqueel, *Les Chambres de rhétorique*, 4.
69 See Agulhon 'Conscience nationale', 259–60.
70 Engelaere, 'Le Mouvement Flamand de la libération', 22–5.
71 Dewachter, 'Sur le Front des langues'.
72 See Verbeke, *Vlaanderen in Frankrijk*, 95–7, for a discussion of the publications of the VVF.
73 H. Ryngaert, 'Wat wil de Torrewachter', *De Torrewachter: Maanblad voor Fransch-Vlaanderen*, 15 Jan. 1929, 1.

suggested that 'As Flemish, your thoughts and your feelings should be Flemish. But that is not enough. Your business and outings, and also your speech, writing and work should be Flemish.'[74] Although these publications did have Flemish patriotic sentiment right through them, they suffered in part from the clericalism and intellectual elitism of the movement which published them and did not reach the wider public audience for which they were intended.

The VVF also sponsored yearly regional congresses, the 'Flemish Regionalist Festivals'. On the programme for June 1929, entitled the 'Flemish Day in Eecke', was a mass with a Flemish sermon, a reception with Flemish speeches, an exhibition of works of art and costumes from the archives of the local chamber of rhetoric, a banquet and a Flemish play performed by the members of the 'Verblyders in het Kruis' (the chamber of rhetoric, 'Joyous in the Cross') with the assistance of the local youth dramatic club.[75] On that day, Eecke was 'solemnly toasted by the whole of French Flanders . . . for its perseverance in maintaining one of the most noble of our traditions'.[76]

The VVF had high hopes and aspirations to spawn increased consciousness among the Flemish and to forge a strong regionalist feeling among the inhabitants of the Westhoek, as well as to establish further rights for the Flemish as a group, particularly in education. Like those of the CFF before them, the members of the VVF were particularly interested in the question of education in Flemish. Justin Blanckaert, the first president of the VVF, wrote in one of their publications, Le Lion de Flandre, that

> Our cultural regionalism puts at the first rank of our demands *an educational structure* which respects the originality and responds to the needs of the Flemish people. This concern is expressed in the very statutes of the Vlaamsch Verbond. This subject of the utmost importance is discussed, one can say, in each of our meetings.[77]

One of their yearly congresses (1930) was devoted entirely to 'bilingualism in education' and their attempts to reinstate Flemish in schools at all levels. In a *resumé* of conclusions from the conference, it was generally accepted by the participants that what was needed was the 'abandonment of the direct method which is so detrimental to the development of minds, and use of the mother tongue to pass from the known to the unknown'.[78] In addition to claims of the need to preserve the 'treasure' of the Flemish language, the VVF

---

74 'Taal en zeden', *De Torrewachter: Maanblad voor Fransch-Vlaanderen*, Feb. 1929, 1.
75 See 'Communiqués', *Le Lion de Flandre* i (Mar.–Apr. 1929), 31, for the full programme of the day.
76 Despicht, 'La Littérature flamande', 109.
77 Justin Blanckaert, 'La Flandre française réclame le régime de l'Occitanie, du Pays Basque et de la Bretagne: l'Enseignement de sa langue', *Le Lion de Flandre* viii (Mar.–Apr. 1930), 1–2 (emphasis original).
78 Idem, 'Le Bilinguisme scolaire en Flandre française', *Le Lion de Flandre* xi (Sept.–Oct. 1930), 7.

put forward arguments demonstrating the advantages to France as a whole of having bilingual citizens. A great deal was written in their various publications on the subject, none of which had any effect in terms of the government policy of unilingual primary education.[79]

The VVF were hopeful that they would succeed in increasing regional consciousness among the Flemish of the Westhoek, acting themselves as the spearheads for a political regional movement which would surpass anything the CFF had achieved and secure true rights for the Flemish as a group. First and foremost they were concerned with rights to education and with the encouragement and promulgation of the cultural and literary aspects of the Flemish movement which, as already shown, were extremely important for the VVF. They went beyond mere cultural progress, though, and hoped to make limited political gains as well. They hoped that through politics they could expand outside the Church and make the Flemish movement in the Westhoek not merely 'a minuscule and unexpected outgrowth of the old regionalist and clerical tendency which the schools question spawned during the Second Empire'.[80] Their success in this field was limited, for even in the Flemish literary competitions which they sponsored, many of the participants were students in the seminary, and several of the themes treated by others were religious.[81]

To fully understand the development of the Flemish political movement in the 1920s and 1930s, it is imperative that we take some time to examine the main figure behind *Vlaamsch Verbond van Vrankrijk*: Jean-Marie Gantois. Born in 1904 of Flemish-speaking parents in Watten (near St Omer), Gantois was raised principally in French and learned his Flemish at the Catholic seminary of Annappes where he began his studies in 1922. He quickly joined the Flemish circle, which 'had as its goal to stimulate love and familiarity with the history, as well as the "zeal of the Flemish people", and to give them a knowledge of the Flemish which they would need in their future pastoral activities'.[82] Gantois was particularly susceptible to the ideas circulating in the seminary and quickly adopted the Flemish cause as his own. He founded the short-lived paper *De Vlaemsche Stemme in Vrankryk* (The Flemish Voice in France) and became more and more involved in Flemish organisations, until the founding of the VVF, by which time he was the principal force behind the new organisation and its first secretary. In the late 1920s and the 1930s he wrote profusely, using a large number of pseudonyms, both in the journals of the VVF and in other publications in France and Belgium. He was

79 See chapter 4 above.

80 Étienne Dejonghe, 'Un Mouvement séparatiste dans le Nord et le Pas-de-Calais sous l'occupation (1940–1944): le "Vlaamsch Verbond van Frankrijk" ', *RHMC* xvii (Jan.–Mar. 1970), 50.

81 See 'Rapport sur les concours de langues et littérature Flamande 1929', *Le Lion de Flandre* vi (Nov.–Dec. 1929), 13–19.

82 Eric Defoort, 'Jean-Marie Gantois in de vlaamse beweging in Frankrijk, 1919–1939', *Ons Erfdeel* v (1974), 684.

particularly caught up in the regionalist movement in France and cultivated numerous personal contacts with other regional leaders around the country, especially in Lorraine, where he had done his military service.[83]

Gantois and the VVF began slowly to work more political material into their discourse. In Gantois's style of regionalism he was willing to remain within and recognise France only insofar as France recognised and respected his region.[84] On a political level, however, Étienne Dejonge considers that right from its inception the founders of the VVF, 'without clearly admitting it, were already pursuing separatist goals'.[85] They gradually reduced their involvement with the French regionalist movement and became increasingly linked with the pan-nederlands movement known as 'Groot Nederlandisme', which considered Dutch, Belgian and French Flemish as all belonging to one race, the 'Dietse volk'.[86] It was important for the members of the race to stick together: in a letter to Vital Celen, Gantois wanted to find out if a certain Pierre Hans, an engineer and composer who had come up with a new style of notation, was Walloon or Flemish, in the hopes that he would prove to be the latter so as to utilise his talent and notoriety in the Flemish movement.[87] Opinion is divided as to the early goals and intentions of the members of Gantois's entourage; in light of what happened during the Nazi occupation of the region during the Second World War, its separatist tendencies in the inter-war period are at best opaque. At least one official investigation of Flemish separatism in the late 1920s concluded that while some of the Flemish separatists in Belgium hoped to attract French Flemish participation, and in spite of the strength of Flemish language and traditions in the Westhoek, 'no trace' of a separatist movement could be found in French Flanders.[88]

After the capitulation of France, Nazi Germany divided France into several zones. The two northernmost departments, Nord and Pas-de-Calais, were attached administratively to Belgium under the *Oberfeldkommandantur* (OFK) 670.[89] Customs barriers between the Nord and Belgium were

[83] Ibid. 689.
[84] Ibid. 685.
[85] Dejonghe, 'Un Mouvement séparatiste', 50.
[86] Defoort, 'Jean-Marie Gantois', 692–3; Jacques Julliard (ed.), *Les Conflits*, Paris 1990, 496.
[87] J.-M. Gantois to V. Celen, 1 Nov. 1933, in *Brieven van J-M. Gantois aan V. Celen I. 1925–1939*, ed. Eric Defoort and Els Lion, Kortrijk 1979, 45–7.
[88] Special commissioner to the subprefect of Dunkerque, 24 Mar. 1927, ADN, unclassified documents on Flemish separatism. It should also be noted that Gantois's pre-war activities were considered so suspect that many of his papers were seized and burned in 1939. A detailed account of the affair can be found in ADN, 1 W 2330.
[89] For a general overview of the occupation in the north of France see Étienne Dejonghe and Yves Le Maner, *Le Nord–Pas-de-Calais dans la main allemande, 1940–1944*, Lille 1999; Jean-Marie Fossier, *Nord–Pas-de-Calais 'zone interdite' mai 1940–mai 1945*, Paris 1977; Michel Rousseau, *Le Nord et le Pas-de-Calais 'zone interdite' dans la guerre 1939–1945*, Le Coteau 1985, and Taylor, *Between resistance and collaboration*.

removed, and access, travel and trade were easier with Belgium than with Vichy France. The OFK 670 also eliminated much of the economic legislation of Vichy France as it applied to the parts of France under its control. The initial results of the military control for the Nord–Pas-de-Calais were not only to arouse suspicion and unease at the prospect of future permanent annexation, but also meant a much more onerous occupation than other areas because of the heavy burden imposed by strict military authority.[90]

As in other parts of France, workers were deported, and the population was subject to a multitude of fees and requisitions by the military authorities which constituted an abuse of their power. These inflictions, as well as shortages of food and coal and general widespread social misery, were more pronounced than in other area of free France.[91] These conditions made the inhabitants of the Nord and the Pas-de-Calais feel much more as if they continued to live in a state of war, rather than of mere occupation.[92]

One of the motives of the occupying forces was eventually to reclaim former Germanic territory which had been 'Frenchified' and hopefully to re-establish the borders to coincide with the Lotheringia of the Middle Ages.[93] They attempted to play on dislike of Vichy, which had 'abandoned' the north, but the real effect of the harsh occupation was to increase pro-England, gaullist or communist tendencies among the population. By the second year of the occupation, the harshness was toned down, and travel to Vichy France as well as the distribution of Vichy propaganda were tolerated in the hope of reducing local opposition and resistance.[94]

In line with their policy of a possible future re-creation of Lotheringia, the authorities of OFK 670 based in Lille authorised the teaching of 'dialects' in the primary schools of the region on 24 December 1941.[95] Although they attempted to get the French authorities to enforce the regulation for French Flanders, after a great deal of stalling, the inspector declared that no teachers in the region were qualified to do so, and that it was therefore impossible to comply and no action would be taken to teach Flemish in schools.[96]

Early in the occupation, claiming membership of the Flemish 'race' had one clear and decided advantage for the inhabitants of the Westhoek and the

90 Dejonghe, 'Le Nord et le Pas-de-Calais, 687.
91 See ibid. 693–704, and Michel Rousseau, 'La Répression dans le Nord de 1940 à 1944', RN li (Oct.–Dec. 1969), 709–33.
92 Étienne Dejonghe, 'Le Nord isolé: occupation et opinion', RHMC xxvi (Jan.–Mar. 1979), 51.
93 Fossier, Nord–Pas-de-Calais, 47.
94 Étienne Dejonghe, 'Les Délégués de la propagande dans le Nord/Pas-de-Calais (1942–1944)', RN lxxiii (Jan.–Mar. 1991), 87.
95 Arrêté, 24 Dec. 1941, ADN, 1 W 998, on the Flemish language in primary schools, 1942.
96 Dr Muller, veraltungschef OFK 670 (head of administration) to the prefect, 18 Mar. 1942; inspector to the prefect, 2 June 1942; prefect to Dr Muller, 17 June 1942, ADN, 1 W 998.

Lille area. The possibility of instant release for those prisoners of war certified of 'Flemish race' sent hundreds of family members rushing to their local authorities for such certification. Several enterprising mayors had form letters drawn up in French, Flemish and German stating that the individual named was born in Flanders of Flemish parents who had also been born in Flanders and requesting his immediate release from the German prison or hospital where he was being held.[97] Although at least twenty-nine village halls would sign any form on request, several others refused point blank to do so, while others wrote to the prefect asking for direction as to how to act.[98] A special police commissioner sent to report upon the situation found that the practice had begun in Belgium and spread across the border. He could only find one person, from the village of Warhem, who claimed actually to have been liberated for reason of being Flemish (along with three others in the same German camp).[99] Although a specific case and for clearly pragmatic reasons, this situation did nevertheless have large numbers of the population of the Westhoek scrambling to assert their Flemish identity.

During the occupation, the VVF was able to take up its prewar activities in the cultural and literary sphere, as well as in politics.[100] Jean-Marie Gantois was made vicar of Notre Dame de Roubaix after the armistice, but Cardinal Liénart, bishop of Lille, displeased with Gantois's political activities, forced him to choose between the priesthood and politics. Gantois chose the latter and was duly stripped of his rights as a priest, allowed still allowed to say mass in private, without witnesses.[101] This conflict was not new, for during the inter-war period Gantois had already been forced to limit his actions in politics because he wanted more freedom from the church authorities.[102]

In 1941 *De Torrewachter* and *Le Lion de Flandre* reappeared, and contributors began to make references to the greater Flemish community that had been artificially divided by the border. In February 1943 an 'Institut Flamand' was founded at Lille, designed to promote cultural activities. A weekly conference was held until the end of the war, and many people came to attend these cultural events, at which propaganda was spread in favour of the pan-Flemish cause (although it was not a big part of the programmes and did not concern or affect many of the participants).[103] Much of the material written at the time was overtly racist in its promotion of the Flemish 'race'. This did not, however, prevent a split in the VVF in 1943, when several anti-intellectuals and anticlericals attempted to turn the movement into an

---

97 ADN, 1 W 1464, contains several examples. See also untitled article in the *Reveil du Nord* (23 Mar. 1941) describing the procedures.
98 Mayor of Hazebrouck to prefect, 21 Mar. 1941, ADN, 1 W 1464.
99 Divisional commissioner of special police to subprefect of Dunkerque, 29 Mar. 1941, ADN, 1 W 1464.
100 See Dejonghe and Le Maner, *Le Nord–Pas-de-Calais dans la main allemande*, 101–4.
101 Dejonghe, 'Un Mouvement séparatiste', 52.
102 See Meyers, 'Les Collaborateurs flamands', 338.
103 Dejonghe, 'Un Mouvement séparatiste', 56.

auxiliary of the Nazi party, but did not succeed. A schism ensued.[104] Jacques Julliard asserts that although the leaders of the Flemish movement 'foolishly' claimed links with Nazism in the name of their cause, they remained Catholic and conservative at heart, such that 'their true ideology had few similarities with that of Hitler'.[105]

In spite of the tremendous progress made in general popularity and the large increase in the number of people participating in Flemish cultural activities, the Flemish movement during the Second World War remained an elitist, intellectual group, not directly associated with the workers or their conditions.[106] It also suffered from the timing: the experience of occupation and terrible living conditions were hardly conducive to convincing people that association with the greater Flemish community brought any advantages, or was in any way worthwhile.[107]

At the end of the war, Gantois and forty-nine other members of the *Vlaamsch Verbond van Frankrijk* and the *Zuid Vlaamsch Jeugd* (Southern Flemish Youth) were arrested and charged with collaboration.[108] The main evidence was a letter which Gantois had supposedly written to Hitler expressing the devotion of the Flemish to 'his' Europe, and asking, along with an accompanying fifty-seven page memoir explaining why the Westhoek and surrounding territory were a part of greater Flanders, to be reunited with Belgium and the Netherlands in a single state.[109] Although it has been accepted by many scholars, there was some question as to the authenticity of the letter, which was typed and unsigned; forty-six pages of the accompanying memoir had also disappeared. Even the style is debatably not Gantois's.[110] Although the prosecution requested the death penalty, Gantois was eventually sentenced to five years in prison, 'national indignity for life' and forbidden to reside in any one of a number of potentially regionalist departments. In fact he was released within two years, and was even able to continue writing until his death in mysterious circumstances in May 1968.[111]

The question of the real motives of the members of the VVF during the ten years leading up to the war, and even during the war itself – separatist or otherwise – is a difficult one to answer. In the atmosphere of hatred for collaborationists of the immediate post-war period, the case against them was somewhat exaggerated, although in their writings in the 1930s and 1940s one

104 Ibid. 64–5.
105 Julliard, *Les Conflits*, 500.
106 See, for example, 'Rapport sur la mentalité actuelle en Flandre Française' included with commissioner of special police to prefect, 26 June 1941, ADN, 1 W 1216.
107 Dejonghe, 'Un Mouvement séparatiste', 68–9.
108 South Flanders was another term for the Westhoek, used with respect to greater Flanders.
109 See Meyers, 'Les Collaborateurs'.
110 See Landry and de Verrewaere, *Histoire secrète*, 290.
111 See ibid, 291–5, and Olivier Engelaere, 'Le Mouvement flamand en France de la libération à la mort de Jean-Marie Gantois, 1945–1968', *DFN/LPBF* xvi (1991), 83–6.

can certainly find examples of racism and comments that the border sepa-rating French from Belgian Flanders was artificial.[112] There can be little doubt that they hoped for some real political gains for the Flemish in terms of regionalism as it was viewed in the 1930s, nor that during the war they prof-ited from the situation in order to popularise Flemish culture, folklore and language to a greater extent and with much more success than had been achieved by any of their predecessors. The VVF had achieved 'a level of influ-ence which would be the envy of many cultural associations today'.[113] On a political level, they were certainly envious of the linguistic concessions won by the Flemish movement in Belgium, although Belgian Flemish aspirations for a future reunification with the Westhoek had more or less ceased after the First World War.[114] When the opportunity presented itself during the war, the French Flemish were not outwardly hostile to being annexed to the Belgian provinces, although the claim that it was among their overt goals, or that they had been separatists all along, is of dubious validity. As late as 1943, police reports to French authorities concluded that the VVF was not a threat and 'demonstrated no excessive autonomism'.[115]

The post-war Flemish movement

Whatever they may really have been thinking, the entire episode surrounding the occupation and its aftermath was to deal a severe blow to the Flemish movement in the Westhoek. What progress had been made in increasing popular consciousness and participation in Flemish culture and cultural events was instantly lost, due to the overwhelming antipathy for all that was identified with collaboration. Some parents even ceased to speak Flemish with their children, because the post-war environment made speaking Flemish all the more embarrassing, in addition to being merely backward.[116] Although the VVF was disbanded forever and its publications discontinued, the CFF survived, but had to lie low for some years after the end of the war and to dissociate itself from the collaborationist aspects of the Flemish movement. The slow rebuilding of the Flemish movement in France after 1945 was characterised primarily by conflict and division between a variety of groups, partly due to generation, partly to personality, and partly to the objectives of the movement, including the way in which Flemish culture and even language were defined for the Westhoek.

---

112 See Dejonghe, 'Un Mouvement séparatiste', 51–4; Defoort, 'Jean-Marie Gantois', 692–3; C. Debusschere, 'La Bataille idéologique', *Le Lion de Flandre* xx (Aug. 1942), 366–78.
113 Landry and Verrewaere, *Histoire secrète*, 289.
114 Meyers, 'Les Collaborateurs', 338.
115 Police report on authorised parties and organisations, 27 Jan. 1943, ADN, 1 W 2545.
116 Interview with Mme Mortelette, 21 Dec. 1993.

The initial impulse to get the Flemish movement restarted in the post-war years came from a younger generation, centred in Lille, who had little contact with Jean-Marie Gantois. The young 'Lille group', which included Jan Klaas, Edward Corsmit, Lode Hoex and Lucien Demey, sought to rekindle a move-ment around a new and authentically 'French-Flemish' publication. They had difficulty at first in finding a printer in France, but *Notre Flandre* finally began publication in 1952.[117] While several of those involved hoped to keep Gantois on the margins, by the third issue he had succeeded in working his way into the primary position.[118] Up until then Gantois had continued writing, having been allowed to start publishing again in 1948, but for the first few years he found outlets principally in Belgium rather than French Flanders. Once his foot was in the door at *Notre Flandre*, he dominated the publication until its demise with his death in 1968, and it would remain essentially a vehicle for the expression of his own personal and increasingly outmoded ideas. Using the journal as a base, Gantois also organised a society, called the *Vlaamse Vrienden van Frankrijk* (Friends of French Flanders) which had the same initials as his earlier organisation, VVF. This never progressed beyond an extremely small nostalgic circle of elderly former members of the first VVF. Although Gantois continued writing, he became more and more marginal to the rest of the Flemish movement, which espoused a 'softer' regionalism.[119]

Much of the support for the renewed Flemish movement in French Flan-ders came from a Belgian organisation, founded in 1947, called the *Komitee voor Frans-Vlaanderen* or *KFV* (the Committee for French Flanders).[120] Founded by André Demedts and Luc Verbeke. the association was designed to promote cultural contacts and exchanges between French and Belgian Flanders and to provide some concrete aid and support to the French Flemish who desired to maintain their language, culture and historical consciousness. One of their primary activities was the organisation of annual 'French-Flemish culture days' in the Belgian town of Waregem, featuring presenta-tions and discussions about the cultural and artistic life of French Flanders.[121] After initial success, further culture days were also held in Esquelbecq in the Westhoek itself as of 1962.[122] In a similar vein, the *KFV* helped to

---

117 Engelaere, 'Le Mouvement flamand de la libération', 60–4, 76–84.
118 Ibid. 88–92.
119 See Engelaere, 'Le Mouvement flamand à la mort de Gantois', 99–103.
120 The name *KFV* was not adopted until 1979; the organisation was until then known as the more unwieldy 'Committee for the French-Flemish Culture Days'. For a summary of their activities see Luc Devoldere, 'Een uitgestoken hand, 50 jaar "Komitee voor Frans-Vlaanderen" ', *DFN/LPBF* xxiii (1998), 65–75; Luc Verbeke, *De Nederlanden in Frankrijk en het Komitee voor Frans-Vlaanderen*, Wareghem 1978; Dirk Verbeke and others (eds), *Een halve eeuw werking voor en in Frans-Vlaanderen: Komitee voor Frans-Vlaanderen jubileumboek, 1947–1997*, Waregem 1997.
121 Devoldere, 'Een uitgestoken hand', 66–7.
122 Engelaere, 'Le Mouvement flamand de la libération', 118.

encourage the French town of Nieuwpoort to organise annual two-week programmes of contact and cross-border exchanges between French and Belgian Flanders beginning in the mid-1970s. Reaching a somewhat wider public than the culture days in Waregem, activities in Nieuwpoort have included cross-border contacts between town and village mayors, and seek to encourage mutual awareness and communication between the respective communities.[123]

In addition to cultural co-operation, the KFV has directly supported numerous publications on both sides of the border. Its support was essential in getting Notre Flandre off the ground in 1952, although subsequent disputes with Jean-Marie Gantois over objectives and direction meant that the relationship between the respective groups and their work cooled considerably.[124] The KFV then supported another initiative for a publication by a younger generation of Flemish, Ons Erfdeel–Notre Patrimoine (Our Heritage) which began publication in 1957 under the direction of Jozef Deleu. It kept the French part of the title for only three years and gradually took the direction of interest in all sorts of Dutch culture from French Flanders to the Netherlands.[125] Over the years the KFV supported the launching of numerous other publications, including the revue De Franse Nederlanden/Les Pays Bas français in 1976, organised numerous Dutch courses in the Westhoek, and progressed to the support of other French-Flemish media, including Radio Uylenspiegel.[126]

While the financial and other support of the KFV has contributed significantly to the Flemish cultural movement in French Flanders, from the outset the KFV maintained that it could only assist and encourage what enthusiasm and interest came from within French Flanders. Belgian support did not create the movement, only helped to build upon and accelerate what was already present. There can be little doubt that without their help, the post-war Flemish cultural movement would have taken a great deal longer to get going and never attained even the modest success which it has achieved.

May 1968 marked a double turning-point for the Flemish movement in France: the death of Jean-Marie Gantois liberated younger members and allowed them to go in their own direction, and the national-scale 'social revolution' meant that it was no longer perfectly incompatible to call oneself a regionalist opposed to Jacobin centralism and still be on the Left. Numerous

123 See Dirk Verbeke, 'Nieuwport: twintig jaar fraans-vlaamse veertiendaagse', DFN/LPBF xx (1995), 181–201.
124 Devoldere, 'Een uitgestoken hand', 67–8; Engelaere, 'Le Mouvement flamand de la libération', 100–1.
125 Devoldere, 'Een uitgestoken hand', 68–9.
126 For general information on the publications supported by the KFV see Luc Verbeke, 'Initiële doelstellingen: belanstelling wekken, een tijdschrift oprichten: van Notre Flandre tot Ons Erfdeel, tal van andere publicaties van verenigingen en de KFV-Mededelingen', in Verbeke and others, Een halve eeuw, 31–70. See also Pierre-Yves Le Priol, 'La Flandre se découvre franco-belge', La Croix, 2–3 Oct. 1994, 6.

groups with an interest in Flemish culture or regionalism would appear on the scene for a short time, make their mark upon the Flemish movement, and then disappear to be replaced by others. The specific objectives of the different groups often led them to disagree and the movement as a whole could not escape repeated fragmentation.

Out of the university in Lille sprang a group called *Les Étudiants Fédéralistes Lillois* (Federalist Students of Lille) under the leadership of François-Xavier Dillmann. With links to the European Federalist Party led by Guy Héraud, they adopted the position that centralism hurt regional universities, cultures and languages, and was at the root of the economic crisis and unemployment which was touching the region.[127] None of the original members were from the Westhoek, but they quickly took an interest in Flemish culture and linked up with younger members of the French-Flemish movement as well as other regionalist and federalist movements.

The younger members of the French-Flemish movement who were now able to express their opinions freely after the disappearance of Gantois did not lose much time before founding in 1971, in conjunction with some students from Lille, the *Cercle Michel de Swaen*. Founded spontaneously without contacts from either Belgian organisations or other Westhoek societies, under the leadership of Pascale de Leersnyder, the *Cercle* was a grass-roots movement which focused fundamentally upon Flemish culture. Among their demands was yet again the instigation of compulsory Dutch classes throughout the Westhoek, for fear that the language would die if left exclusively to the voluntary teaching current at the time.[128] The journal *Notre Flandre* had been revived as *La Nouvelle Flandre* in 1969, edited by Jan Kaas, and it was supplemented by various other works treating the culture and history of French Flanders. When de Leersnyder went for his military service, the *Cercle* was taken over by Nick Nierynck, who was a much more prolific writer, while being less interested in the public profile of the society.[129] Much of his writing was a general critique of modern society and its ills, with regionalism as a pretext.[130] Nierynck left in 1976, and while the organisation theoretically continued to exist, all activity ceased shortly after.

In 1974 a rival organisation called *De Hekkerschreeuwen* was founded by a former member of the *Cercle* which focused specifically upon Westhoek Flemish.[131] From that time forward a debate which had been around since the nineteenth century became much more central to the Flemish movement in the Westhoek: which language exactly was the true native language of the

---

[127] See Engelaere, 'Le Mouvement flamand de la libération', 144–65.

[128] See ibid. 165–91.

[129] Ibid. 183–4.

[130] See, for example, Nick Nierynck, 'Qu'est-ce l'enracinement?', in *Le Régionalisme?* (pamphlet: dossier d'étude no. 3, Cercle Michel de Swaen), Dunkerque 1976, 5–25. Note that he spelled Dunkerque 'Duinkerke'.

[131] The name means the cry of the 'Hekker', a legendary monster of the Westhoek.

Westhoek? It was not merely a question of *patois* (spoken only) and high language (written), as one might at first be led to believe. Though this was indeed partly true for many of the inhabitants of the Westhoek, for even though they may have been able to read it, Flemish was the spoken idiom, and the vast majority of their literate culture was French. In her memoirs, the novelist Marguerite Yourcenar described Flemish as the 'language of childhood' for her aristocratic father, who spoke Flemish up to the age of about twelve, and French thereafter.[132] Thus for many of the earlier members of the Flemish movement the only objective was to establish that it was a written language, not simply a *patois*.[133]

By the second half of the twentieth century, however, the Flemish were acutely confronted with several versions of their language to choose from as the 'written element'. The language which they spoke was a dialectical version of West Flemish, and several publications and other material could be found written in this form, in the 'old Flemish as it had been taught prior to the reforms of 1865'.[134] The Dutch language had undergone several reforms, and the standardised version which emerged, known as 'ABN' (*het Algemeen Beschaafd Nederlands* or high Dutch) was often not easily understood by those who could read and write Westhoek Flemish.[135] While many of the French Flemish wanted to follow the leadership of the Flemish in Belgium, who used ABN as their standard language, several others, including prominent writers, intellectuals and poets, were in favour of keeping to the old way.[136] They preferred to protect what they considered their own language from the 'for-

132 Marguerite Yourcenar, *Le Labyrinthe du monde: souvenirs pieux, archives du Nord, Quoi? l'éternité*, Paris 1990, 1990, 444.
133 See, for example, Louis de Baecker to rector, 14 Apr. 1856, ADN, 2 T 767 dossier 1856; J. J. Carlier, 'Nouvelle démonstration de l'utilité de la langue flamande', BCFF vi (1872–75), 28–36; C. Looten, 'La Langue des flamands de France', *Revue de Lille* i (1890), 278–94, 435–61; N. Bourgeois, 'Un tour de Flandre', in Bourgeois and others, *Flandre notre mère*, 20. See also Nicolas Bourgeois, *"Les hexagons": de la Gaule à la France et de la France à l'hexagone*, Dunkerque 1970, glossary.
134 Dewachter, 'Le Flamand et le français', 99. An example is *Tisje-Tasje's almanak*, published by the *Comité Flamand de France*. See also Ryckeboer and Maeckelberghe, 'Dialect', 129–52, where they discuss the differences in spoken and written language between the Westhoek and West Flanders.
135 The differentiation occurred largely with the rapid evolution of the nineteenth and twentieth centuries: Hugo Ryckeboer, 'Het Vlaams van de Westhoek in het geheel van het nederlandse taalgebied', DFN/LPBF iv (1979), 139. See also Tozzi, *Apprendre et vivre*, 45. For a description of the characteristics of the Flemish language and its evolution see O. Vandeputte and J. Fermaut, *Le Néerlandais: langue de vingt millions de néerlandais et de flamands*, Rekkem 1990, 5–19, 43–54.
136 Some Belgian poets such as Guido Gezelle also wanted to preserve their old regional dialects, but they lost out within Belgium: Beirens, 'De geschiedenis van "Ons oud Vlaemsch" ', 130–52; Landry and de Verrewaere, *Histoire secrète*, 278–9. For a discussion of the Belgian decision to adopt ABN and not develop written Flemish see Kas Deprez, 'The language of the Flemings', in Deprez and Vos, *Nationalism in Belgium*, 96–109.

eign' influences of the Netherlands, which derived from a culture as different from their own as that of the French.[137]

This distinction between the two levels of language is extremely important with respect to the question of Flemish identity, connected as it is to the definition of the larger Flemish community. Either the Flanders to which they belonged was defined simply locally, in which case Flemish was the dialect of the Westhoek, or if defined more broadly, Flanders included their co-linguists across the border and the language of the Westhoek needed to keep up with the reforms and ABN should be adopted for writing and language courses. The leaders of the Flemish movement in France, by and large, attempted to continue to use Westhoek Flemish until the First World War, and during the inter-war period the younger generation of Flemish activists began to use ABN. In the post-war period, the *KFV* and the members of the *Cercle Michel de Swaen* also preferred ABN, but several of the groups which took off in the 1970s and early 1980s returned to 'authentic' Westhoek Flemish as that which should be chosen. Such were *De Hekkerschreeuwen* a spin-off group *Menschen Lyk Wyder* (People Like Us), *Tegaere Toegaen* (Forward Together), and *Het Reuzekoor* (The Giant's Choir), which forwarded Westhoek Flemish via traditional songs.[138] Of these conflicts and the turnover of various Flemish groups, the *CFF*, *KFV* and *Het Reuzekoor* were the only survivors. The one constant of the various groups was the desire to cultivate a stronger cultural identity among the French Flemish through increased consciousness of local history and the maintenance of local traditions. To this end, numerous publications originating from the various organisations sought to promote Flemish identity in the Westhoek, with the goal of informing the French Flemish about their heritage and culture,[139] and to promote language classes, in either standard Dutch or Westhoek Flemish. While such classes met with a reasonable amount of success, particularly in the late 1990s, no accompanying development of Flemish identity has followed, and indeed a resurgence of language learning of this nature can be interpreted as a sign of the final stages of language disappearance.[140]

---

[137] See Milis, 'Frankrijk en zijn minderhheden', 170, who contrasted the Flemish language – Catholic and hot – with Dutch – Protestant and cold.

[138] Engelaere, 'Le Mouvement flamand de la libération', 192–5. See also James Minney, 'The Flemish movement of French Flanders and the maintenance of *Vlaemsch*', unpubl. PhD diss. Southampton 1999, 194–207.

[139] See, for example, Régis Dericquebourg, 'L'Identité culturelle des flamands de France: comment peut-on être flamand?', *Plat Pays* 3–4 (1986), 1–15; Vanneufville, *Apprenons*; Philippe Despriet, *La Patrimoine historique de la Flandre française*, Courtrai 1979; E. H. Descamps, *De Vlamingen in Frankrijk*, Antwerpen n.d.

[140] See Roland Willemyns, 'Language shift through erosion: the case of the French-Flemish "Westhoek" ', *Journal of Multilingual and Multicultural Development* xviii (1997), 60. On the resurgence of Dutch and Flemish language classes see Minney, 'Flemish movement', 272–321. Unlike Willemyns, Minney argues (at p. 362, not too convincingly), that it is not too late to save Westhoek Flemish.

It was not until 1982 that an organised co-ordination of the various Flemish regional societies that were still active produced a joint manifesto.[141] This, bilingual with French first, gives a brief description of the history of French Flanders and states the desire 'to have their right respected to be recognised as Flemish', to be able to protect and propagate their cultural heritage, and to have their language revived.[142] By 1987 a publication of *Menschen Lyk Wyder* claimed that it was the only Flemish society still active in French Flanders besides the CFF.[143]

In addition to the post-war cultural movements, a Flemish regionalist political party was created in 1976 by Jean-Paul Sepieter, called the *Parti Fédéraliste Flamand/Vlaemsch Federalistische Partij*. A one-man show at the start, it reached the peak of its popularity in 1990 with a few hundred members (by its own estimation), and suffered from the incoherence of its ethno-cultural Flemish stance which it promoted in the whole of the Nord–Pas-de-Calais region.[144]

Thus the effects of Flemish societies during the nineteenth and twentieth centuries were limited as far as preserving elements of Flemish culture and generating a popular culturally-based identity were concerned. Not at all interested in promoting regionalism, most did not discourage assimilation into mainstream French culture, but hoped only to preserve some elements of local language and culture along the way. The lack of a stronger political resistance to assimilation can be explained by several factors: the elite status of much of the leadership, belonging as it did to a class which was already itself immersed in French and which had no particular interest in spreading its ideas among the labouring classes; their association with clericalism and the Church, which brought them instant disfavour in large segments of the working-class population; their drifting away from the pan-Netherlandish movement and its institutional and cultural support structure; the nature of their dependent status *vis-à-vis* the French state; numerous internal divisions and rapid changes of leadership; and finally their association with collaborationists in the Second World War, which drastically reduced any popularity Flemish had, and made it an embarrassment for some to be known as Flemish.

---

141 *Les Flamands de France: Qui sont-ils? Que veulent-ils?*, 4. The manifesto retained the names of several societies which were still technically in existence, but no longer 'active'.
142 Ibid. 6–7.
143 Franck Allacker, *La Flandre en France* (pamphlet), n.p. 1987, 2. The author also comments that the CFF has kept itself extremely discreet.
144 See Minney, 'Flemish movement', 242–53.

The *patronat*

The *patronat* is the collective term to describe 'the bosses', those industrialists and capitalists who were behind the great industrial expansion in the north during the nineteenth and twentieth centuries.[145] Overlapping in many cases with the political elite of the region described in chapter 2, this economic elite had a great deal of sustained influence and decision-making power throughout the nineteenth and twentieth centuries. Their base of economic and political strength meant that their position with respect to the identity of the region, the position of culture and ethnicity within it, and the relationship between the region, the centre of France and greater Flanders needs to be considered.

The *patronat* shared a sufficient number of characteristics to render a consideration of the group as a whole feasible. The genuine homogeneity of the class is the first striking feature. Interlinked as families through marriage, the *patronat* of the Nord gained its importance through its collective action, and it was connections rather than personal achievements, the family rather than the individual, which conferred status.[146] Studies abound which describe specific families and their place in the complex network of connections, and the class as a whole has even been the object of works of fiction.[147]

Socially conservative, the preoccupation of the *patronat* was with economic questions. They demonstrated considerable adaptability to pertaining conditions which accounts in part for the persistence of their dominant position in the region down to the end of the twentieth century.[148] The vast majority of the *patronat* were practising Catholics, often representing the most fervent tendencies within the Church.[149] The Catholicism of the *patronat* extended well beyond the Westhoek; it was an identifiable shared cultural characteristic of the French Flemish and the economic elite of the greater region.

The Catholicism of the *patronat* was a significant contributing factor in their paternalist attitudes towards the workers of the region.[150] Through

---

[145] For a good general work describing the *patronat* of the Nord through the two centuries see Pouchain, *Les Maîtres du Nord*.

[146] Bruno Duriez, 'La Bourgeoisie répertoriée: le livre des familles du Nord', *Ethnologie français* xx (jan.–mars 1990), 71.

[147] Ibid; Pouchain, *Les Maîtres du Nord*; Pierre Pierrard, *Histoire du Nord*, Paris 1978, 356–62, and 'Un Grand Bourgeois, 381–425. See also Maxence Van der Meersch, *Quand les sirenes se taisent*, for an example of a novel describing the *patronat*.

[148] Pouchain, *Les Maîtres du Nord*, 318–21.

[149] Jean Lambert Dansette, *Quelques Familles du patronat textile de Lille-Armentières (1789–1914)*, Lille 1954, 750.

[150] See *Rapport présenté au Congrès catholique de Lille à la séance générale du 30 novembre 1888 par M. Bayart, industriel à Roubaix* (pamphlet), Lille 1888, for a detailed description of the attitudes of the bosses towards the workers, overtly expressing the links to Catholic origins of their thinking.

174

various organisations, as well as in their capacity as factory owners, the *patronat* sought Christian ways to improve 'the material, intellectual and moral conditions' of the workers of the region.[151] While their priority was always the overall state of the economy, and it was extremely unusual to see unilateral gestures to the workers on the part of an individual factory owner, as a group they did petition for legislation which would help their workers without jeopardising individual industrialists, including the simple calls for protectionism.[152] Their opposition to the spread of socialism was vehement, and they hoped to combat it via their paternalistic gestures and in some cases through the encouragement of Christian unions as well.[153]

A good example of the success of the *patronat*'s paternalist position is Eugène Motte in Roubaix. Defeating Jules Guesde himself as mayor in 1898, during an intense wave of anticlericalism, Motte went on to hold the city hall until just before the First World War.[154] His success bears witness to the genuine popularity which progressive members of the *patronat* could achieve with the population, even in the heart of Guesdist socialist territory.

In spite of the Catholicism which they shared with the workers and farmers of the Westhoek, and the fact that many of the industrialists were of Flemish origin and Flemish-speakers themselves, the *patronat* as a whole did not adopt a specific viewpoint with respect to Flemish identity.[155] Willing in some cases as individuals to support Flemish cultural activities, they certainly did not adopt a position in defence of ethnic or cultural identity in the region that could be seen as threatening to the republican centre. Their priorities were solidly economic, with the well-being of the inhabitants of the region, and they considered belonging to France a key to that economic well-being. Thus although in a position to influence identity formation, like the workers' movements examined in the previous chapter, the priorities of the *patronat* were decidedly elsewhere.

Alternatively, in terms of a more broadly based regional identity, the *patronat* as a whole, interlinked well beyond the Westhoek to the greater region of the north of France, did contribute to the development of a sense of this region. Already closely linked themselves, solidarity across the region

---

151 See *Discours sur la réduction des heures de travail prononcé par M. Edouard Crépy, conseiller municipal dans la réunion publique tenue Salle Meurisse le 20 février 1881* (pamphlet), Lille 1881, 4.
152 Dansette, *Quelques Familles*, 754–7.
153 See Talmy, *Syndicalism chrétien*. This characteristic of paternalism remained a distinguishing feature of firms in the north of France, such as the Mulliez family's Auchan, which has an extensive personnel development programme: Pouchain *Les Maîtres du Nord*, 346–7.
154 See David Gordon, 'Liberalism and socialism in the Nord: Eugène Motte and republican politics in Roubaix, 1898–1912', *French History* iii (1989), 312–43.
155 Jules Brenne, 'Les Candidats ouvriers dans le Nord', *RN* lvi (Apr.–June 1974), 190. Some of the Flemish-speaking factory-owners came from Belgian Flanders, and others from French Flanders.

was seen as key precursor to defending its economic interests (such as protectionism). Newspapers had been published since the late nineteenth century with the economic interests of the larger region at their core, and such organisations as the *Fédération Régionaliste du Nord et du Pas-de-Calais*, led by M. Vancauwenberghe, the president of the *conseil général du Nord*, included many of the important politicians and businessmen of the Nord and the Pas-de-Calais who got together to discuss economic, commercial, industrial and agricultural questions from the point of view of their region.[156] The establishment of an elite economic and political network across this greater region, although not consciously aimed at the general population, was an early step towards the growth of consciousness of belonging to the 'Nord–Pas-de-Calais' region during the second half of the twentieth century, which is the subject of the final section of this chapter.

Economic regionalism and the post-war rise of the Nord–Pas-de-Calais

In the second half of the twentieth century, a third level of identity began to develop in French Flanders, between French and Westhoek Flemish: that of the greater Nord–Pas-de-Calais region.[157] What originally held the region together were economic questions, especially protectionism. An economic and political elite which had been loosely integrated since the nineteenth century took an interest in the affairs of the wider region and petitioned the national government on economic questions common to them all, gaining in strength from numbers.[158] Greater administrative decentralisation and the rise in regional governments, especially following the post-1981 socialist reforms, only served to increase the importance of this greater region for political and economic questions and to reinforce the need to develop a regional identity to serve as a base for making further economic and political arguments.[159]

---

156 See, for example, *La Région du Nord: journal industriel commercial & financier: assurances, mines, metallurgie, chemins de fer*, which appeared in 1879, and had its name changed to *Le Moniteur financier de la région du Nord* in 1882. For a description of activities of this federation see prefect to minister of the interior, trade and liberated regions, 14 Dec. 1925, ADN, M 154 318.

157 For the purposes of this study, French Flanders has been defined as the Westhoek, which is only a part of the *département du Nord*. See introduction and chapter 1 above.

158 On the *patronat* as a regionalist organising force see Wagnon, *Identités*, 23–59.

159 It can even be argued that the Nord–Pas-de-Calais was not a coherent region economically (with Lille as the urban centre), but that several selective segments of region stood to benefit from collective action, which was never as thorough or as co-ordinated as it could (or perhaps should) have been. See for example Philippe Pinchemel, 'De la Région du Nord à la région lilleoise', *HTN* (1963.2), 118. On the political process of regionalisation in France see André Gamblin, 'Le Choix: les 22 régions administratives', in André Gamblin (ed.), *La France dans ses régions*, 2nd edn, i, Paris 1998, 13–40.

Although forming a vaguely coherent entity from an economic point of view, the various elements of the larger region of the north had little in common culturally or historically. The diverse regions of Flanders, Artois, Boulonnais, Hainaut and Cambrésis were held together principally by historical accident and the fact that they were the bit of France east of Normandy and north of Picardy.[160] The greater region did not have even the traces of an identity up to the Second World War, and the best name that could be thought of was simply the united names of the two departments – the Nord–Pas-de-Calais. The war itself was the first powerful contribution to greater regional consciousness, since it was a specifically regional experience to have been detached from the rest of France and united with Belgium throughout the occupation. The result was that the inhabitants of the forbidden zone, as it was called, developed a feeling that they had suffered more intensely than other Frenchmen, and their extra loyalty set them apart from their fellow countrymen and made them more truly French than the rest.[161] They were also able to hold their heads up as not having been involved with Vichy France. The war experience can be considered a defining characteristic of the Nord–Pas-de-Calais region, but it is not enough as the basis of a complete regional identity.

By the middle of the twentieth century, the regional economy was extremely advanced and prosperous, centred around the textile industries in the Lille agglomeration and the coal mining basin in the Pas-de-Calais. Beginning in the 1950s, regional leaders coined the phrase 'pilot region' and sought to create a regional identity which would solidify it in both political and economic terms, and give it a more concrete and identifiable character.[162] Early on, it was relatively easy to capitalise on the success of regional industry and to stress the general prosperity of the area, but with the economic downturn and the numerous crises which hit the region in later years, the need for a positive regional identity and character which would help to boost morale and image became all the more necessary. As the north acquired the reputation of a 'black country' which was dismal, grey and monotonous, it became all the more necessary to cultivate a positive image of the region.[163]

In the search for an identity for the north of France, diversity was a possible attribute, to counter the image of monotony, but some unifying

---

160 For a description of the physical and human diversity within the Nord–Pas-de-Calais region see André Gamblin, 'Les Régions du Nord de la France', *HTN* (1963.1), 8–23.
161 See Cobb, *French and Germans*, 38.
162 The notion of the pilot region was developed by economic planners in the 1950s who sought to transform and modernise the industrial base of the region: P. Bruyelle, 'De la Région pilote à la région déprimée, 1952–1980', in Hilaire, *Histoire du Nord/Pas de Calais*, 415–51.
163 See Wagnon, 'Transformations de l'identité régionale nordiste (1955–1985)' (Cahiers lillois d'economie et de sociologie xii, 1988), 3–4. For an example of a call for the necessity of greater coherence see Henri Deligny, *Le Nord demain*, Paris 1964.

images were still necessary.[164] Although several possible alternatives were available, it was first and foremost elements of Flemish culture and symbolism which became identifying historical and cultural characteristics of greater 'Northernness'.[165] In a similar process to that seen in earlier chapters with respect to France, the greater region also 'appropriated' Flemish characteristics and began to equate that which was Flemish with the entire region.

The first significant element to be appropriated to the greater region was the name of the smaller region itself. Where French Flanders had historically meant the Westhoek (the usage in this book), it began to be used synonymously with the 'north of France' and with 'Nord–Pas-de-Calais'. It also became more common in the latter twentieth century to describe the whole region as the French Low Countries (Les Pays-Bas français).[166] Examples of the use of French Flanders to describe the region can be found from before 1939, but it is in the post-war period that the number of examples begin to multiply.[167] History as well as travel books covering the north, in their sections about culture, dwell much more on Flemish examples than on those from other subregions (such as Picardy).[168] Many regional place names attempt to associate themselves with Flemish culture, the foremost being the city of Lille, increasingly appearing with the suffix 'Lille-en-Flandre'. Although it was historically a capital of Flanders, culturally it was more Picard than Flemish.[169] Non-political organisations and societies covering the entire region have also used the term Flanders to describe themselves.[170]

Other elements of Flemish culture, as well as the name Flanders, also began to spread throughout the larger region. The chosen emblem adorning the regional flag is the Flemish lion; much of what is described as 'northern' cuisine is in fact Flemish cuisine; and new festivals involving processions of

[164] For an example of a commentary praising the region for its diversity see Gamblin, *Le Nord–Pas-de-Calais*, 1–3.

[165] Wagnon, *Identités*, 182.

[166] For more on the debate over how to label the region, and the transition from Nord–Pas-de-Calais to the French Low Countries see Engelaere, 'Le Mouvement flamand en France de la libération', 156.

[167] For an early example see H. Ormsby, *France: a regional and economic geography*, London 1931, 174–98. See also Gamblin, *La Région du Nord*, and James Bentley, *The gateway to France: Flanders, Artois and Picardy*, London 1991.

[168] Examples of this for the Nord–Pas-de-Calais are Hilaire, *Histoire du Nord/Pas-de-Calais*; Gamblin, *Le Nord–Pas-de-Calais*, 4–7; Wayne Northcutt, *The regions of France: a reference guide to history and culture*, Westport, Conn. 1996, 169–80. For a discussion of this phenomenon see Wagnon, *Identités*, 157–8.

[169] See Olivier Engelaere, 'Le Mouvement picard en France du début des années 1970 à la fin des années 1980', *DFN/LPBF* xix (1994), 90.

[170] An example is the Bridge committee, which is very active on the coast of the Pas-de-Calais: *La Revue du Bridge dans le Nord de la France: organe du Comité des Flandres*. It is ironic to note that the later extension of the term Flanders to incorporate areas to the south and west of the Westhoek echoes claims made by some of the pan-Flemish nationalists and Nazis for the old Thiois region: that areas which had been romanised for centuries were 'really' part of Germanic Flanders.

'giants' have sprung up outside the Westhoek but within the Nord–Pas-de-Calais, linking the region together through common folklorish traditions from 'their' regional history.[171] The fact that a Flemish style of urban architecture extended beyond the Westhoek was one historical cultural element which did not have to spread, only to be identified and highlighted.

This appropriation of Flemish culture as that which represented and defined the whole of the Nord–Pas-de-Calais region was consciously initiated by regional leaders who recognised the need for a regional identity. Often forced to 'look elsewhere for what they could not find at home', the process involved the disappearance of much that had its origins in Picard culture, also native to the region.[172] The Westhoek was relieved of some of its specificity by referring to a greater region with terms which had formerly been reserved for a smaller one (leading to some possible confusion as to what is meant exactly by the term French Flanders) and many elements of French-Flemish culture, most notably language, were left out in the transition and the gradual homogenisation of the region.[173]

While they should not be exaggerated, the efforts of the regional elite to develop popular consciousness of the greater region of the north of France met with some limited success in the second half of the twentieth century. Observers have differed over the exact timing of the rise in consciousness, but all recognise its presence at the beginning of the twenty-first century.[174] The image and opinions of the inhabitants of the greater region have often been negative, and the regional elites have struggled to come up with a positive image of their region following the identity crisis which came with the decline of regional industry. With the heightened development of the European Union, the Nord–Pas-de-Calais has sought an identity as a modern cross-roads of interaction between France, Great Britain, Belgium and beyond to the east, both economically and culturally.[175] Benefiting from its

---

171 Robert Chaussois, *Géants*, Lille 1998.

172 Engelaere, 'Le Mouvement picard', 112; Wagnon, *Identités*, 132–73.

173 The Catholicism of the Flemish, which was shared by the *patronat*, was preserved in part, as the region managed to retain its images as Catholic yet at the same time socialist, attempting to ignore the obvious contradictions (both contemporary and historical). On the gradual homogenisation see Bruyelle, 'De la Région pilote à la région déprimée', 451.

174 For a discussion of the debate see Wagnon, 'Transformations', 3–9, and *Identités*, 30. Wagnon is of the opinion that the rise in Nord–Pas-de-Calais identity happened after the 1960s, and refutes the work of others who concluded that it had already begun to spread during that decade.

175 This position was outlined, for example, by the long-standing mayor of Lille and former French prime minister Pierre Mauroy in 1985 in a speech entitled 'the cultural originality of the Nord–Pas-de-Calais region', quoted in Wagnon, *Identités*, 178–80. See also Paul Drewe and Joël Hébrard, 'Le Nord de la France, région frontalière européenne: un laboratoire de l'intégration européenne', and Wim Vanhaverbeke, 'Une Stratégie d'euro-région pour le sud de la Flandre-Occidentale et le Nord–Pas-de-Calais, basée sur les points forts complémentaires des deux partenaires', both in *DFN/LPBF* xx (1995), 161–79, 282–99.

geographic position, industrial history and European institutions and opportunities, regional leaders sought (and seek) to rejuvenate the region, modernise and reassert the old traditional links across the border with Belgium.[176]

This regional identity, one more layer among the overlapping identities between the local and the national, is even more obviously a 'creation' than the French nation. Sharing little in terms of culture, history, geography or even economic activity early on in the century, the diverse elements of the region have been sufficiently integrated to bring about the existence of a genuine identity at the grass-roots level, forged out of the common historical experience of the war, and a selection of cultural characteristics drawn from Flemish culture. It cannot be claimed that northernness is the strongest element of identity of those living in the region, but neither can its existence be denied. From the outset it was never intended to be a rival to national identity, but to remain closely associated with the nation: the Nord–Pas-de-Calais or northern region was a region of France, and its very integration within France was and remains a powerful element within its identity.

Thus in the consideration of identity formation in French Flanders, a third level of identity inbetween France and the Westhoek must be considered during the second half of the twentieth century, one which made use of much of the same Flemish cultural characteristics and nomenclature as the smaller Westhoek. Before turning to general conclusions, a brief examination of the development of the Flemish movement in Belgium will contribute to an understanding of the process in France.

[176] On the economic position of the region see Georges Allaert, 'Knelpunten en perspectieven van het industrieel beleid in Noord-Frankrijk', *DFN/LPBF* xxiii (1998), 30–44. On relations across the border see Firmin Cornelus, 'Intercommunale samenwerking over de grenzen heen', and Bruno Bonduelle, 'L'Avenir économique du Nord de la France et ses relations avec la Flandre belge et les Pays-Bas', both in *DFN/LPBF* xx (1995), 133–59, 276–81.

8

The Belgian Flemish Movement

Unlike their counterparts in France, the Belgian Flemish developed a strong identity based on Flemish culture and race, rising to new heights of regional, or some would say 'national' consciousness. Not only did they avoid assimilation, but they secured rights as a community, with numerous legal safeguards to protect Flemish language and culture, in all respects equal to French within the Belgian state. The purpose of this chapter is to analyse the Belgian Flemish movement and compare it with the situation in France and the Westhoek, with a view to identifying the reasons why different weights were given to race and to culture in the identity of the two groups.

As a political entity, Belgium did not come into being until 1830. For numerous centuries previously it had been severed into parts, some independent, such as the bishopric of Liège, and others attached to various European crowns: Spanish, Austrian, French, Dutch. Under Napoléon I, all of what is now Belgium became a part of the French empire, and was divided into departments, which became modern Belgium's provinces. With the defeats of Napoléon in 1815, Belgium was awarded by the allied powers to the United Kingdom of the Netherlands of King William I. In 1830 the Belgians revolted against the Dutch state. The revolution can be seen in religious terms, Catholic Belgium wishing to be separated from the Protestant Netherlands, or it can be seen in linguistic terms, the French-speaking bourgeoisie and upper class of Belgium revolting against the Dutch-speaking elite of the Netherlands.

The linguistic aspect of the revolution ironically included Flanders, a region in which the elite was largely French-speaking in the early nineteenth century. Some, indeed most, of the Flemish bourgeoisie may have been able to speak the local Flemish dialects, but very few of those educated under the French empire or earlier knew literary or 'high' Dutch. It was only a few of the younger members of the educated classes who had been raised during the fifteen-year Dutch period who were familiar with it, could read and write it. King William had attempted to encourage the spread of Dutch throughout the Belgian provinces, and made it the official language for all dealings with the government, as well as the principal language for schools. The older members of Belgian society resented the imposition of the Dutch language which they considered inferior to French, and which placed them at a disadvantage. The linguistic policy of the Dutch government between 1815 and

1830, 'which ultimately aimed at introducing Dutch throughout Belgium, was to lead to an anti-Dutch reaction during the Belgian revolution'.[1]

With Belgian independence, a series of decrees made French the official language of the military and all legal texts (the law reporter published translations, but they were not legally binding),[2] and abolished Dutch language and literature courses in state universities. The Belgian constitution of 1831 declared that language was free and everyone had the right to use the language which he or she chose. In practice this meant that French was guaranteed domination in all official government and administrative circles, since freedom of language meant that any French-speaking official living in or transferred to a Flemish- or German-speaking area was not required to learn the language of the locality, but could remain unilingual.[3] Thus the central and provincial governments, and those of all large or even medium-sized towns conducted all their affairs, and communicated with one another in French only. Governmental dealings and communications with the public were generally in both languages, unless it was assumed that those concerned were only of the educated classes.[4] Translations were done at various levels of government and, on the whole, 'the system did not give rise to massive protest'.[5]

It was through the French language that the French-speaking bourgeoisie hoped to impose its values and maintain its control as both the political and cultural elite of the newly founded state. Even before the nineteenth century, and during the period of union with the French empire, large parts of the Belgian elite had grown attached to the French language, culture and its international prestige. A part of the rectification after the Dutch period saw the introduction of 'an eloquent Frenchification policy' by means of which 'The exclusively Francophone liberal elite was eager to establish its power by taking over the culture and language of the aristocracy.'[6]

The Dutch period was not without its impact upon the Belgian elite however. During fifteen years of Dutch rule, a number of intellectuals were trained in Dutch, and 'the union of the low countries had lasted just long enough to stir an interest in the Dutch language and an admiration for the

1 Lode Wils, 'Belgium on the path to equal language rights up to 1939', in Sergiy Vilfan (ed.), *Ethnic groups and language rights: comparative studies on governments and non-dominant ethnic groups in Europe, 1850–1940*, Aldershot–NY 1973, iii. 19.
2 See, for example, the decree of 16 November 1830, in Theo Hermans, Louis Vos and Lode Wils (eds), *The Flemish movement: a documentary history, 1780–1990*, London 1992, 71–2.
3 See H. Pirenne, *Histoire de Belgique*, VII: *De la Révolution de 1830 à la guerre de 1914*, Bruxelles 1932, 273.
4 Wils, 'The path to equal language rights', 23.
5 Ibid. 23.
6 Machteld De Metsenaere, 'Socio-professional aspects of the Flemings in Brussels during the 19th century', in Eric Aerts and Francis M. L. Thompson (eds), *Ethnic minority groups in town and countryside and their effects on economic development (1850–1940)*, Leuven 1990, 88–9.

Netherlandish culture in the minds of at least a few intellectuals'.[7] It was among these Dutch-trained intellectuals, 'swept up by the romantic revival and concerned about the growing dominance of French in Belgium', that the Flemish movement had its origins in the 1830s.[8] It is important to stress the fact that the members of this group were as much a part of the elite as the French-speakers were. Where the francophones had been disadvantaged under the Dutch, this new, young elite suffered the same fate in the essentially francophone Belgian state. Thus the Flemish movement 'developed essentially along class lines in the North, but not in the traditional Marxist sense'.[9] The leaders of the Flemish movement were drawn from the lower bourgeoisie, seeking to gain power in a state where they felt blocked by the fact that the French language was the key to social and political advancement.

The linguistic differences provoked by the Frenchification policy characterised two strata within the intelligentsia: those bourgeois of French culture on the one hand, and those who tried to attach themselves to Dutch culture, and who remained stereotypically 'petit-bourgeois', on the other.[10] This latter group fought against the Frenchification of cultural life through cultural associations and publications, but the lower classes were rarely even touched by the movement at all.[11] With the second phase of the industrial revolution towards the end of the nineteenth and beginning of the twentieth century the middle-class component of the Flemish movement was reinforced, and although remaining limited in numbers, 'received the support of significant social groups such as lawyers, doctors, professors and higher civil servants who tried to fortify the Dutch cultural basis'.[12] The existence of this Dutch-speaking elite makes the situation significantly different from that in French Flanders, where all the leaders of the Flemish movement had gone through school in French and, while caring a great deal for Flemish, were also attached to French. Members of the *Comité Flamand de France* and other Flemish leaders were never dependent upon Flemish or Dutch for their social position (or lack thereof), as a small number of their Belgian counterparts were.

It was to this group of young Dutch-trained intellectuals and writers that Jan Frans Willems, 'the father of the Flemish movement' and Jan David, a prominent Catholic Flemish activist belonged. They and others such as Henri Conscience, a prominent Belgian Flemish author of *The Lion of*

---

7   Clough, *History of the Flemish movement*, 56.
8   Alexander B. Murphy, *The regional dynamics of language differentiation in Belgium: a study in cultural-political geography*. Chicago 1988, 63.
9   Ibid. 79.
10   Witte, 'Une Flandre appauvrie', 245. See also David C. Gordon, *The French language and national identity (1930–1975)*, The Hague 1978, 103–11, for a general overview of the language question in Belgium.
11   De Metsenaere, 'Socio-professional aspects', 94.
12   Ibid. 94; Witte, 'Une Flandre appauvrie', 239.

Flanders (published in 1839) and ardent supporter of the Flemish movement typified the above description of emerging from the lower bourgeoisie through their Dutch education.[13] In the early stages, the movement was not separatist, but sought merely to preserve the valued elements of Netherlandish language and culture which had been acquired during the Dutch period, and to permit those members of the elite who were Dutch-speaking to maintain their social or political positions in the new Belgian state. Nor was the early movement attached to a identifiable region, indeed, 'Flanders' as it became known in the twentieth century was not even defined until the 1890s.[14] Part of the reason for the absence of a territorial dimension to the Flemish movement in its early stages was the lack of uniformity among the working classes in what became 'the Flemish community'. Internally fragmented, with local dialects and their own accompanying local traditions, little could be said to hold Flanders together as a territorial unit. Patricia Penn Hilden writes that a binary division between Flemings and Walloons 'was not significant during most of the nineteenth century. . . . Every locale had its own customs, songs, styles – and even its own work uniforms'.[15]

Thus in its early stages the Flemish movement in Belgium was limited to a particular group of middle-class intellectuals trained during the Dutch period, who sought merely to reserve a place for the Dutch language and culture which they valued for its own sake and as a means of preserving their social position which was threatened by the predominance of French.[16] They did not succeed in arousing much interest among the masses of the diverse regions which have now come to be called Flanders, and the Flemish culture which developed in the half-century following the Belgian Revolution was not particularly nationalistic, nor was Flemish oppression a prevalent theme among Belgian Flemish writers, composers, playwrights and artists. Their work contributed to the Flemish cause by means of its quality, rather than through direct propaganda.[17]

Their links with the Netherlands remained strong, and writers and intellectuals on both sides preserved close contacts with one another. In 1849 a congress was held in Ghent with both Belgian and Dutch scholars attending,

---

13 Clough, *History of the Flemish movement*, 94.
14 See Murphy, *Regional dynamics*, 63, 70–5.
15 Hilden, *Women, work, and politics*, 101.
16 While much of the Flemish movement in Belgium was centred around literate culture, for which language was a central question, there were other dimensions, such as attachment to neo-Flemish architecture: Benoît Mihail, 'Un Mouvement culturel libéral à Bruxelles dans le dernier quart du XIXe siècle, la "néo-Renaissance flamande" ', *Revue belge de philologie et d'histoire* lxxvi (1998), 979–1020, and 'Architecture régionaliste et conscience du passé: l'exemple des anciens Pays-Bas', *Southern Netherlandish Art and Culture*, no. 2 (Dec. 1999), www.ukans.edu/~sma/snac/snac2/ snac2.htm.
17 See Clough, *History of the Flemish movement*, 90–1.

the first of a series which would see the identification of the two movements.[18] Unlike the leaders of the Flemish movement in France, many of the
Belgian Flemish were quick to adopt ABN, 'high Dutch', rather than
restricting themselves to local dialects.[19]

On a political level, the Flemish movement made extremely slow progress
through the nineteenth century, but managed to secure a few fundamental
rights which would later help to launch the Flemish movement in earnest in
the early twentieth century. In the first few decades of Belgium's existence,
various members of the Flemish community expressed their dissatisfaction
with the situation through petitions and even speeches in the Belgian parliament, but their voices were for the most part ignored, and they made little
official headway. A twelve-point manifesto was produced in 1847, which
helped to provoke the setting up of a special commission by royal decree to
investigate and report on the Flemish question in 1856.[20] The commission
included members of the Flemish community such as Jan David and Henri
Conscience, and their report, delivered in 1859, called for all sorts of reforms
to the education system, up to and including university level, translations of
all government publications and more strongly defended legal recognition
and rights for Flemish.[21] Henri Pirenne described the contents of the report as
a reform package so complete, so radical and so impossible to put into immediate application without dangerously upsetting the organisation and func-
tioning of the state, that it produced next to nothing in the way of concrete
changes in state or government policy. It did, however, reveal the abuses
occurring throughout the existing system, and meant that afterwards the
Flemish movement had a ready-made goal in the accomplishment of the
reforms proposed by the commission.[22]

In the closing decades of the nineteenth century, numerous minor reforms
were achieved, and there were a number of laws enacted which accorded a
greater place to the Dutch language. Each one with limited scope (explaining
their large number), even taken together these laws did no more than guarantee a limited place for the Dutch language within Flanders, and did not
begin to challenge the overall supremacy of French.[23] Examples include the
possibility for Dutch to be used in criminal court cases (1873), the ability to
study Flemish literature at the University of Ghent (1876), the use of Dutch

[18] Ibid. 74–83.
[19] See chapter 7 above.
[20] For the text of the manifesto, published on 6 November 1847, see L.-Th. Maes, R. van
Santbergen and others (eds), *Documents illustrating the history of Belgium*, II: *Modern
Belgium: from 1830 up to the present day*, Brussels 1978, 144–7.
[21] See Clough, *History of the Flemish movement*, 87. The text of the report, written by
F. A. Snellaert, can be found in Hermans, Vos and Wils, *The Flemish movement*, 125–34.
[22] Pirenne. *Histoire de Belgique*, vii. 277–8.
[23] See Lode Wils, 'L'Emploi des langues en matières judiciaires et administrative dans le
royaume de Belgique', *RN* lxxiii (Jan.–Mar. 1991), 59.

in some secondary schools (1883) and the translation of the law reporter into Dutch (1885).[24] Flemish was made an official language of Belgium in 1898, although this status did not immediately confer upon it any more rights in the public sphere than it had previously enjoyed. The existence of such laws, in spite of their limited scope, is another example of a significant difference from the situation in France, where no official legal recognition of regional languages was ever granted during the nineteenth and early twentieth centuries.

In addition to mere recognition, members of the Flemish movement considered it imperative to secure a place for Flemish in the education system on a par with French. As in France, certain public schools used Flemish as the need seemed to warrant more or less unofficially, although French retained an important place in primary education, and secondary and post-secondary education was exclusively in French. As of 1850, Flemish was to be taught in several new public secondary schools created in the Flemish-speaking areas, but only as a second language and not as the medium of instruction. In the 1880s several courses were added to the programme, such as other foreign languages, history, geography and natural science, which could be given in Flemish in public schools.

The private Catholic schools accorded a much smaller place to Flemish than did the public schools however, which was of far more consequence in educational terms since most students in Flemish-speaking areas attended Catholic schools. In 1883 five times the number of students receiving public education were registered in Catholic institutions.[25] Unlike in France, the clergy in Belgium by and large supported the French language, rather than Flemish. The high clergy were French in language and culture, and they directed the schools under their jurisdiction to use exclusively French for instruction, and even the limited amount of Dutch (if any) was taught through the medium of French.[26]

Throughout most of Flanders, even primary school pupils were forbidden to speak Flemish during their recreations in the school yard, and were punished if caught doing so. Some individual priests were sympathetic to the Flemish movement, but the high clergy was always opposed, and sought to neutralise any *flamingant* activity among the lower clergy. Any Catholic teachers (or their pupils) who became too heavily involved in Flemish activism were usually discharged.[27] One example is Guido Gezelle, priest and poet from the province of West Flanders who had extended contacts with the Westhoek, and who was relieved of his teaching duties because of his

---

[24] For further discussion of the laws passed during the period see Pierre De Spiegler, 'La Législation linguistique en Belgique', *Universités* xv (May 1994), 27–9, and Maes, van Santbergen and others, *Documents*, ii. 147–50. for several texts of laws.
[25] Clough, *History of the Flemish movement*, 151.
[26] Ibid. 151–2.
[27] Ibid. 152, 251–2.

flamingantism. Here again differences emerge with respect to French Flanders, where although the archbishops of Cambrai were French-speaking, they generally supported the pro-Flemish stance of the clergy in the Westhoek. The Flemish movement even had one significant voice among the high clergy itself in Mgr Monnier, the Flemish-speaking *vicaire général* of the arch-diocese of Cambrai. In Belgium, any priest who tried to make a big deal of the Flemish movement was clamped down upon by his superiors, rather than supported.

It was not until the early twentieth century that Flemish began to work its way into Belgian Catholic schools. A law of 1910 required three hours per week of instruction in a second language for any secondary school student who wished to enter university. This law was directly aimed at Catholic schools and the lawmakers hoped to provide an impetus to encourage them to increase the number and scope of programmes in Flemish.[28]

The suffrage question

One of the main reasons for the Belgian government being able to get away with paying so little heed to the Flemish question in the nineteenth century had to do with the nature of the limited suffrage in Belgian elections. The segment of the population which met the property requirements needed in order to vote was almost exclusively comprised of French-speakers. This meant that in the legislature the direct pressure for change was limited in terms of potential voting support, and the major Belgian political parties were able to avoid even confronting the issue, remaining indifferent at best in their attitude to the language question. Unlike in France, where universal male suffrage had long since allowed voters to become aware of their ability to participate and influence the political future of their country, in Belgium the lower classes had no history of voting. Awareness of the potential political benefits or of the Flemish movement in general was further retarded by the extremely harsh social and working conditions to be found in Belgium,[29] and because the spread of bourgeois culture to the masses occurred to a much lesser extent in Belgian Flanders than elsewhere in Europe, where the lowest social strata remained largely illiterate and relatively untouched by the Flemish movement.[30] Progress in the education of the masses lagged far behind other European countries, and the illiteracy rate stood at 25 per cent

---

[28] Ibid. 153–4.
[29] For a description of working conditions in Belgium and the principal concerns of the Flemish workers see Luc Denys, 'L' Enquête de 1886 en Belgique: un système capitaliste dépourvu de restrictions légales', *RN* lvi (July–Sept. 1974), 433–6; Hilden, *Women, work, and politics*; E. Lamberts, 'Belgium since 1830', in J. C. H. Blom and E. Lamberts (eds), *History of the Low Countries*, trans. James C. Kennedy, New York–Oxford 1999, 320–2.
[30] Witte, 'Une Flandre appauvrie', 245.

in Belgium in 1914, the same year in which primary school became compulsory for all Belgian children.

The two major political parties in Belgium in the nineteenth century were the Liberal and the Catholic parties. The Liberals, who held power from the Revolution until 1884, were dominated by aristocratic, French-speakers, and were effectively opposed to the Flemish movement throughout the nineteenth century. In spite of the position of the high clergy which offered resistance to Flemish, the Catholic party was seen as more responsive to *flamingant* ideas than the Liberals, although it was never an important part of their platform. From the time they came into power in 1884, where they remained until the First World War, some limited progress was made, but substantial change was never undertaken. In the 1880s two new parties came onto the scene – the Socialist and Christian Democrat parties – which began to use the Flemish movement as a means of attracting support to their fledgling organisations.[31] The Flemish movement in Belgian politics was therefore given a significant boost in 1894 when a system of universal male suffrage with plural voting was introduced. Under this law, all men of twenty-five years of age and older were given one vote, with up to two supplementary votes for those meeting special criteria, such as land-owners, university graduates and those paying a certain rent. As the rules were established, 60 per cent of the population had three votes, 23 per cent two votes and 17 per cent one vote. The fact that Flemish-speakers, previously excluded from the vote, were now participants in the electoral system, meant that they had to be considered, and the Flemish question could take on new importance in the elections.

Both the Socialists and the Christian Democrats used the Dutch language when addressing Flemish voters, which gave them a certain advantage over their rivals in the Liberal and conservative Catholic parties. Socialist and Catholic labour leaders also benefited from their use of Dutch to create large-scale political and social organisations in the Flemish areas.[32] Beyond simple use of the local language, separate 'Flemish' trade unions were formed by both these rival groups for the support of the workers, and the Flemish question often entered into dialogue alongside questions of social justice. In the case of the Christian Democrats and Catholic unions, it was an overt policy decision to court Flemish workers with a combined platform of Flemish linguistic nationalism, religious fervour and social consciousness, whereas for the socialists a discrepancy was apparent between the leadership and the grass roots of the movement. The central leadership of the socialist party tended to downplay the language question, which many thought detracted from the socialist platform of international solidarity among workers, but they were unable to prevent the local unions from emphasising a 'Flemish' angle in

31 See Clough, *History of the Flemish movement*, 100–5; Pirenne, *Histoire de Belgique*, vii. 278; Strikwerda, *A house divided*, 37.
32 Strikwerda, *A house divided*, 312–14.

their demands, nor occasional splits in the national party along linguistic lines.[33] While they did not promote association with the language question, socialist leaders were never as overtly hostile towards it as their equivalents in France. Belgian socialists did not run into the same clerical conflict with the Flemish movement as those of northern France, since in Belgium the Church, its schools and in part the ruling Catholic party were seen as supporters of French (in spite of the position of numerous parish priests). Thus Belgian socialists could pick up on Flemish language oppression while preserving their anticlericalism, and attempt to rally the Flemish workers around the language question.

Thus the period between the advent of universal male suffrage and the First World War saw the Belgian Flemish movement begin to shift away from its narrow *petit bourgeois* origins towards a mass movement. Links began to be made between the class struggle and the Flemish question, and the two opposition parties, the Christian Democrats and the Socialist began to use both the Dutch language and the Flemish question to win voters and make inroads against Belgium's two traditional ruling parties.

The First World War

The experience of the First World War, occupation and its immediate aftermath had a substantial impact upon the Flemish movement in Belgium: it was radicalised and transformed into a territorial movement.[34] Demands went beyond the principally cultural interests of the pre-war Flemish bourgeoisie, as the Flemish movement became politicised in a combined response to the upheavals of war, the efforts by Germany to divide Belgium, the extension of the franchise and sweeping post-war social and economic changes.[35] After 1918 the strength of the Flemish social and political movement forced changes in the Belgian political landscape and saw the corresponding development of a French-Walloon response.

Most of Belgium was occupied by Germany throughout the war, and the occupying authorities put in place a programme highly favourable to the Flemish movement. Decrees were issued as early as 1916 promoting education in Dutch, and the University of Ghent was converted into a Dutch-language institution, fulfilling a long-standing goal of the Flemish movement.[36] In 1917 Belgium was divided administratively along linguistic lines and Dutch was introduced throughout the civil service in an attempt to woo the Flemish segment of the Belgian population.[37] Although individuals

33 Ibid. 314–16.
34 Clough, *History of the Flemish movement*, 175.
35 Murphy, *Regional dynamics*, 122–3.
36 Lamberts, 'Belgium since 1830', 349–50.
37 See ibid. 350, and Wils, 'The path to equal language rights', 29.

accused of collaboration were repudiated after the war, and there was a return to the *status quo ante* in legal terms, the effects of the occupation were the opposite to those in France after the Second World War. Memory of the advantages for Flemish-speakers obtained during the occupation was implanted deeply enough in popular consciousness to make serious reform necessary after 1918. The war revealed Flemish grievances to be greater than prewar leaders had imagined, and the potential threat of ethnic conflict along culturo-linguistic lines to be greater than that of social or class conflict.[38]

The war itself also 'gave a strong impetus to democratic trends' and unqualified universal male suffrage was introduced in 1919, dispensing with the previous system of multiple votes for some.[39] As with the changes of 1894, the Flemish movement benefited from increased democratisation. During the war a 'Front Party' had been formed among Flemish-speaking soldiers who became conscious of, and complained about discrimination in the army and the disadvantages of Flemish-speakers.[40] At the end of the war, the Front Party united war veterans in what became a kind of Flemish nationalist party, demanding concessions from the Belgian government and advocating federalist reform, affiliating themselves with the pan-Dutch movement which spanned the border with Holland.[41] The belated rectification of grievances, rather than calming the activists, served only to renew their confidence and increase their demands to include full linguistic equality in the name of the sacred rights of peoples to use their native languages, and to claim that the privileged position of French, the language of the bourgeoisie, in the administration, education and the army 'reduced Flemish citizens to "second-rank Belgians" '.[42]

Thus after a slight decline in fortune immediately following the war due to the taint of collaboration, the primary result of the conflict was a radicalisation of the Flemish movement in Belgium such that by the late 1920s it had completely regained its momentum and initiative.[43] One particularly sensitive point which illustrates the fortunes of the Flemish movement was the language to be used at the University of Ghent. The *flamingants'* argument was that the lower classes could never better their position without access to higher education in their own language, and that without a Flemish university, the language and its people would suffer cultural degradation, and be perennially kept down by the French. The voices in favour of converting

---

38 Strikwerda, *A house divided*, 408; Lamberts, 'Belgium since 1830', 350–1.
39 Wils, 'The path to equal language rights', 29.
40 See idem, 'Introduction', in Hermans, *Flemish movement*, 22.
41 Ibid.
42 Pirenne, *Histoire de Belgique*, vii. 383.
43 Lamberts, 'Belgium since 1830', 361–3. For an example of the radicalised programme of the Flemish movement in the inter-war period see Cyriel Verschaeve, 'The Flemish nationalist's catechism (1918)', in Hermans, *Flemish movement*, 240–53.

Ghent to Flemish had already been strong before the First World War, and they grew stronger yet after its conclusion, especially given the fact that it had been temporarily made Dutch under the Germans. The level of Flemish taught was increased in 1923, and Ghent was finally made unilingual and Flemish in 1930.[44]

The inter-war period also saw the Flemish movement acquire its territorial significance, becoming truly regionalistic. 'Flanders' and 'Wallonia' as they became known in the latter half of the twentieth century had little if any meaning in the nineteenth century or before, and to project them back in history could be misleading.[45] The linguistic geography of Belgium did not coincide with any conceptual, functional or formal divisions. The language areas had no tradition of territorial integrity, lacking any historical or polit-ical basis for linguistic regionalism, and even dialectical differences worked against language, the sole common factor across the two areas, as a unifying force.[46] So little, in fact, united either the Flemings or the Walloons as groups that it greatly slowed the development of linguistic regionalism. Flemish and Walloon 'identity' was not a significant factor for most of the population, and group consciousness existed only on the level of the commune, associated with the local dialects. In the 1930s Pirenne described with surprise the terri-torial dimension of the Flemish movement, since he could find no examples of racial conflict between the Flemings and Walloons at any time in history, declaring that the two groups had been so closely linked historically in economy, religion and state institutions that it would be impossible to write the history of either of the two groups within Belgium independently of each other.[47]

In spite of the lack of an historical sense of community betweem the two language groups, by the late 1920s territoriality began to work its way into the thinking of both the Flemish activists and the central authorities in Brussels.[48] In response to frustration at lack of success at bringing about bilin-gualism across Belgium, Flemish activists begin to demand a unilingual Flemish territory, which also met with limited acceptance among national leaders as a lesser evil and necessary compromise. In the late 1920s and 1930s a series of laws introduced Flemish into various levels of the administration and legal system, reinforcing unilingualism in certain lower levels, and the notion of a precisely defined language border made its appearance in 1932.[49]

---

[44] See Vandeputte and Fermaut, *Le Néerlandais*, 30.
[45] See Murphy, *Regional dynamics*, 34.
[46] Ibid. 52–5, 91, 122.
[47] Pirenne, *Histoire de Belgique*, vii. 384–5.
[48] Lamberts, 'Belgium since 1830', 362–3.
[49] John Fitzmaurice, *The politics of Belgium: a unique federalism*, London 1996, 37.

Towards federalism

The momentum acquired by the Flemish movement during the inter-war period was not lost during the Second World War. Belgium was again occupied for most of the conflict and the Germans put in place a concerted pro-Flemish programme of legislation and actions already conceived before the invasion and designed to play one group of Belgians off against the other and facilitate their future integration into Germany.[50] While there was less collaboration and direct involvement on the part of large segments of Flemish leadership than during the previous war, the German attempts to divide along linguistic lines and create a greater Flemish region (as seen with French Flanders) did succeed in deepening feelings of discord between Flemings and Walloons after the war.[51] The pattern was also similar to that following the First World War: a short period of general decline in the Flemish movement while a number of individuals were discredited because of collaboration, followed by a resurgence of the movement, growing stronger than ever in the years that followed.

The history of post-war Belgium is of the slow and steady triumph of the principle of 'territoriality of linguistic use'.[52] A series of constitutional revisions between 1970 and 1992 saw the transformation of Belgium from a centralised to a decentralised and then to a full federal state. Unilingual linguistic 'communities' were defined for legal and administrative purposes, with bilingualism for Brussels and the remaining national institutions.[53] The installation of a fully federal regime marked the victory of the long-standing agenda of the Flemish movement.

Thus the Flemish movement had its origins in the disadvantaged position of the Dutch language in the Belgian state for a small number of bourgeois intellectuals who had a penchant for Dutch culture and who fought throughout the nineteenth century and early in the twentieth to secure language rights. Their focus was principally upon cultural issues, and language rights as they pertained to individuals. It was only after the First World War that the emphasis shifted to group rights as they pertained to the newly defined Flemish region, and corresponding Flemish 'people'. In the period that followed the war, the reforms provoked by the Flemish movement led more and more towards the legal and administrative division of Belgium into two regions, the fulfilment of their motto 'Flemish in Flanders'. They leaned away from desiring a bilingual state, and more towards a unilingual region, excluding French from Flanders altogether.

Alexander B. Murphy concludes that although linguistic differences have

---

50 Wils, 'Introduction', 25.
51 Murphy, *Regional dynamics*, 121.
52 See De Spiegler, 'La Législation linguistique', 27.
53 For a detailed description of the transition and the workings of the federalist system see Fitzmaurice, *Politics of Belgium*.

been the backdrop for much of the political debate throughout Belgian history, the problem is not first and foremost linguistic. The Flemish movement developed initially as a reaction 'to linguistic inequalities, and language has remained the central symbolic focus of the movement'.[54] Language became an issue as a consequence of the power relationship between two groups of rival bourgeois authority in Belgian Flanders. The resulting language patterns 'are the product of a complex history of social divisions that assumed territorial significance'.[55] The political division of Belgium can also be traced to economic conflict between north and south, given the particularly close relationship between political and economic issues throughout the country's history, and the way in which economic prosperity and decline have alternated between Flanders and Wallonia.[56]

The rise of the Flemish movement and the subsequent partition of the Belgian state into linguistic communities was by no means inevitable, and to claim that little sense of 'Belgian' national identity existed to rival the burgeoning sense of Flemishness would not be accurate. The success of the revolution in 1830 provided a glorious historic moment upon which to build a proud sense of the Belgian nation, which successive national governments sought to cultivate.[57] Members of the Belgian bourgeoisie were also proud of their collective economic accomplishments in the nineteenth century, as well as the (albeit limited) success of Belgian colonisation in the Congo.[58] These early achievement laid the groundwork for a nationalism which survived into the twentieth century, and which can be seen in the strength of support for the Belgian monarchs, especially in Flanders, and in the pride in Belgium's role in the construction of the European Union.[59] Belgian nationalism, however, was always characterised by calm and reserve. 'Belgians did not boast' in the British or German manner, nor did they, like the French, 'consider theirs an exportable civilisation'.[60] This meant that an association with the greater Dutch culture was seen to be less threatening in Belgium, which looked at least in part outside its borders in all areas of cultural achievement (in French and Dutch), than it was in France, which defined its nation in a large part through its association with the French language, and meant that any *rapprochement* to another was pursued vigorously.

In spite of the proximity of the Westhoek to Belgian Flanders, their similarities in geography, history, economic and social structure, and in spite of the close cultural ties between the two communities which were discussed in

---

[54] Murphy, *Regional dynamics*, 190–1.
[55] Ibid. 1.
[56] See Fitzmaurice, *Politics of Belgium*, 64.
[57] Lamberts, 'Belgium since 1830', 330–1.
[58] Ibid. 346–7.
[59] For examples of pro-Belgian nationalist sentiment see Antoine Pickels and Jacques Sojcher (eds), *Belgique: toujours grande et belle*, Brussels 1998, and Dirk Rochtus, 'La Belgique, un choix pleinment justifié?', *L'Accent* (May–June 1997), 8–14.
[60] Hilden, *Women, work, and politics*, 159.

chapter 3, several elements in the social, political and historical contexts were not identical on either side of the border. These differences helped to contribute to the success of the Flemish movement in Belgium in achieving their cultural and political goals, whereas the Flemish movement in the Westhoek floundered and had difficulty in achieving even a modest amount of success.

The fact that the first generation of bourgeois leaders of the Flemish movement in Belgium had themselves been Dutch-trained meant that they were much closer to the Dutch language than intellectuals in the Westhoek, who for all their love of Flemish scholarship had passed through an education system entirely in French. The association of the Belgian Flemish movement with high Dutch meant that the Flemish movement in Belgium was set up from the outset as an alternative high culture, which presented the lower classes with a choice of paths into the 'modern' world of literate cultures. The handful of educated Belgian Flemish were also at a real social disadvantage in the Belgian state, and that factor, combined with their love of Dutch went so deep that they fought that much harder to secure language rights for themselves, giving the Flemish movement in Belgium a greater sense of urgency then it was able to capture in France. Their early legal successes, minor as the concessions from the government were, provided some official recognition of the Belgian movement, which instead of satisfying and pacifying the Flemish, only served to keep their hopes alive for further concessions, and was a help to its cause.

These differences, while they may seem striking and obvious in hindsight, were in fact more subtle than it appears, and the advances made in the Flemish movement in the Westhoek in the inter-war period did put the French-Flemish movement onto a similar track as the Belgian movement for a time. The Flemish courses offered at the Catholic University of Lille and the possibility of Flemish in secondary schools after 1926, the renewed vigour of the Flemish-language publishing industry under the *Vlaamsch Verbond van Vrankrijk*, the conversion of parts of the French movement to high Dutch and the politicisation of the movement led Shepard B. Clough to comment that 'There seems to be plenty of evidence that the seeds of a Flemish movement have been sown in France.'[61]

The dissimilar relationship of the Catholic Church and the socialist movements to the question of language and ethnic identity in the two countries was paramount in the political positioning and the ultimate success or failure of their respective Flemish movements. In Belgium, the church hierarchy overtly supported French and was associated with the ruling bourgeoisie, with only selected priests and the Christian Democrats supporting the Flemish movement, often in opposition to their religious superiors. The socialists, in spite of the lukewarm attitude of their leadership, embraced the Flemish

---

61 Clough, *History of the Flemish movement*, 278.

movement, especially on a local level, and between their position and that of the Catholic unions, the Flemish language became implicated in the class struggle, particularly fierce due to working conditions which lagged behind those of other European countries.

In France, in contrast, in spite of the tacit support of the church hierarchy, Christian Democrats did not support the Flemish movement to the same degree as in Belgium. The Flemish movement never escaped its conservative clerical association, and was opposed wholesale by all levels of the workers' movement. It was the differing political situations and political climates which left the French-Flemish movement little room to manoeuvre, such that the effects of the wars and two German occupations had opposite results in the two countries: where they gave new ideas to those leaders not directly implicated themselves in Belgium, they tainted the Flemish movement in France, and the movement was not strong enough to survive its collaborationist associations.

Conclusion

France has often been considered one of the most efficient countries of Europe from the point of view of assimilating and integrating its population into the nation, so that in spite of diversity from region to region, a strong national culture and sentiment links all parts of the country together. The case of the French Flemish provides a good illustration of the complex process of relatively successful national integration through a combination of cultural change, cultural appropriation and the gradual emergence and strengthening of national identity as the primary defining characteristic from among numerous overlapping identities.

Where the Westhoek and Belgian West Flanders had formed a recognised single cultural unit with a great deal of social interaction and communication well into the twentieth century, by the century's end not only did the two groups define themselves in different ways, and think of each other as 'other', but their respective cultures had come to form distinct cultural units with relatively little in common. The Westhoek had been integrated not only into the French nation, but also into the Nord–Pas-de-Calais region. Although forming only a small part of the region geographically and in terms of total population, French Flanders came to be synonymous with the greater region, and elements of French-Flemish culture to define and symbolise the whole of the Nord–Pas-de-Calais. Paradoxically then, while French-Flemish identity and much of the distinctive regional culture declined significantly in the Westhoek itself, select elements of both were preserved within the context of the greater region.

The classic explanations for the successful policy of national assimilation in France place the results generally before the First World War during the Third Republic, and identify the unilingual school system, which also taught French history and encouraged patriotism, in combination with economic modernisation, the transportation infrastructure and compulsory French military service as the key factors.[1] While these do go some way towards explaining the process of national integration, a study of French Flanders has shown that they only constitute part of the answer, and that a greater time span must be considered.

The process of change in the Westhoek was not uniform, but came in identifiable phases, with a significant turning-point mid-way through the twentieth century following the end of the Second World War. During the first phase, through the nineteenth and the first half of the twentieth centu-

---

[1] See, among others, Weber, *Peasants into Frenchmen.*

ries, industrialisation and the development of economic protectionism for the region's industry, increased levels of education, the development of democracy and the establishment of the republican constitution each contributed to the gradual spread of bilingualism in French Flanders, an increasing awareness of the Franco-Belgian border, and the development of a French political identity in parallel with Flemish ethnic and cultural identity. The traditional rural way of life remained relatively unchanged however, such that Flemish culture and integration with the Belgian Flemish cultural community continued unabated, and the seeds of a movement to defend Flemish culture and strengthen Flemish identity had been sown. In the second phase, following the Second World War, the pace of modernisation accelerated to the extent that the traditional way of life all but disappeared, and much of what remained of Flemish culture and identity along with it. It was at this time, as Flemish identity was declining in the Westhoek, that elements of Flemish identity were adopted by the greater Nord–Pas-de-Calais region.

The link between regional cultures and traditional lifestyles, resulting in their simultaneous disappearance as a product of modernisation, is not a wholly satisfactory explanation, however, for it does not explain the diversity of local variations across both time and space in the patterns of assimilation or resistance as rural regions were integrated into modern nations around Europe. The disappearance of traditional society and the cultural and linguistic assimilation of minority groups was not a universal phenomenon across the continent, since some minority cultures were able to adapt to the changing conditions brought about by modernity through the development of ethnic and cultural identities strong enough to resist assimilation. Nor can assimilation simply be explained by a lack of numbers in the Westhoek to maintain the necessary level of high culture to sustain Flemish identity, given the numerous links to the greater Flemish community with its enhanced cultural development.[2]

The results of this study suggest that three significant elements explain why a powerful ethnic and cultural identity did not develop in French Flanders: the rapidity and thoroughness of the transition to modernity relative to other regions, the political structure which discouraged regionalism as a possible power base and the successful appropriation of selected elements of regional culture such that they formed a part of French national identity.

The first possible explanation is simply the sheer rapidity of the penetration of modern agriculture and industry into the depths of rural French Flanders and the thoroughness of the transformation away from traditional lifestyles. The large numbers of immigrants and subsequent mixing of the Flemish population with other linguistic minorities helped contribute to this.

---

[2] This remains true in spite of the greater difficulties in France relative to Belgium of looking beyond the border for cultural leadership, as discussed in chapter 8 above.

By the time of the Second World War, there were no Flemish villages in France that had not already been significantly altered economically and socially by the modern lifestyle. In such regions as the Basque country or Brittany, some elements of the traditional way of life linked to the raising of livestock survived past the Second World War, and helped permit a corresponding survival of the regional cultures and languages in rural areas relatively protected and unchanged by modern ways.[3]

A second explanation is the fact that Flemish identity in France remained exclusively cultural or ethnic, and did not become political. Group consciousness or a sense of identification with larger territories and cultures, be they local, regional or national, coupled with the association between these groups and political legitimacy is a prominent characteristic of modernity.[4] In some cases, where regional consciousness dominates, regional movements arise and resist central, national movements implying an inherent rivalry between two (or more) options, as with the Flemish in Belgium. This pattern was not universal, however, and in many situations identifying with, and simultaneously belonging to two or more overlapping groups associated with geographic units of differing size was not seen as contradictory. To identify strongly with a region does not therefore automatically imply a lesser identification or sense of adherence to a nation as a whole: culturally, simultaneous local, regional and national identification can be compatible.

Yet while regionalist and nationalist dimensions of identity may be compatible on a cultural or sentimental level, they are ultimately much more difficult to reconcile at the political level. One of the definitions of nationalism discussed in the introduction is the belief that political and national units should be congruent.[5] Using this interpretation, a given group can therefore only be considered as belonging to one national unit at a time. Simultaneous national-political claims for the same space result in and imply political conflict between rival 'national' and 'regional' groups. While it is possible to feel that no inherent contradiction exists between being Flemish and being French when it comes to self definition, 'national' political loyalty cannot ultimately be divided. National political units are not mutually superimposable, and cannot therefore be congruent with more than one 'national' unit at a time.

Since it is through political action that minority rights are secured and regional cultural characteristics can find protection and encouragement, absence of a political dimension can leave a cultural movement without adequate defences. Some elements of regional culture may survive or be preserved as elements of a folk culture, but they are often confined to a particular sort of elite or at least restricted circles within the region and can be distinguished from the high culture linked with a nation. The only real

3 See Ford, *Creating the nation.*
4 See introduction.
5 Gellner, *Nations and nationalism,* 1. See also introduction.

defence against this regression is to develop the regional culture in such a way as to bring about the 'birth of a new culture in the popular masses', that is, to set it up as a rival high culture,[6] and to assert its protection through the attachment of economic and political themes to cultural claims.[7] Without the political dimension, any regionalist movement will remain confined within the purely cultural and intellectual sphere, leaving it open to encroachment and regression.

The political structure in France itself was a significant contributing factor to the absence of a political dimension to the Flemish movement. If, as John Breuilly argues, the effectiveness of nationalist movements is determined by the structure of the state, the same can be said of regionalist movements.[8] In the context of certain state structures nationalism or regionalism make sense and form a coherent part of the political process, whereas in others the nature of political discourse and the form of institutions tend to downplay their effectiveness. In France, regional figures vied with one another for central legitimisation and influence, while at the same time the possibility of multiple mandates at the national and municipal level encouraged ambitious regional leaders to seek greater influence through national representation and by working in cooperation with national institutions, rather than through the cultivation of a regionalist movement designed to oppose the centre. Furthermore, the nature of Jacobin republican centralism and its ideal of national unity which implied homogeneity meant that it was difficult to be at the same time republican and regionalist, since regionalism was associated with disloyalty, and diversity with weakness and threats to the regime. The incompatibility of regional and national identities on a political level was therefore especially acute in France, where opposition to the national idea on regionalistic grounds simply did not make political sense: it was at the same time impractical and ideologically unsustainable in the French context.

The fact that regionalism was less likely to make a positive contribution to any political cause, and represented an anathema to one of the dominant branches of the political spectrum meant that none of the principal political interest groups picked up on Flemish identity as a means to increase their power base in the Westhoek. From the socialist and labour movements through to the economically conservative Right, the position varied between indifference and hostility to a culturally or ethnically-based regionalism. The exception was the long-standing association with the conservative elements within the Catholic Church and with a certain form of regional elitism. Regionalism was never the first priority for either of these groups, and the

---

6   See Antonio Gramsci, *Cahiers de prison 27: observations sur le "folklore"*, trans. Claude Perrus and Pierre Laroche, Paris 1991, 340, who argues that folk culture should be taken seriously, and developed into 'modern' culture. This was originally written in 1935.
7   Christian Gras, 'Conclusions provisoires', in Gras and Livet, *Régions et régionalisme*, 591–4.
8   Breuilly, *Nationalism and the state*, 115.

links to the Church ironically only served to impede the Flemish movement further at a popular level, given the decline of the Church's influence over political matters and the rise of anticlericalism over the nineteenth and twentieth centuries. Although politically successful in the Westhoek, the *Démocratie chrétienne*, like the anticlerical Left, tended to concentrate more on social questions, and did not openly encourage the rise of Flemish cultural identity in the local political arena. When contrasted with the situation in Brittany as it has been analysed by Caroline Ford, where the *Démocratie chrétienne* acted in such a way as to help preserve elements of traditional regional culture and identity, several differences emerge. As Ford demonstrates, the Church in Brittany became the principal agent of the region's integration into the nation, and through the internal reforms brought about by social Catholicism, was able to construct a mediated local version of national identity.[9] In Flanders, the *Démocratie chrétienne* was never the main regional political force, but merely one among many, and in the long run it downplayed the connections with the local culture much more strongly than in Brittany, leaving Flemish identity solidly in the cultural sphere.

The regionalist movements in France as a whole were also limited as political forces not only because the political structure discouraged them, but also because of their internal diversity and the fact that regionalist movements are ideologically defined primarily in a negative manner.[10] Regionalism tended to be simply reactionary, rather than progressive, opposing the centre but unable to put forward regional culture as an alternative high culture, since little could be said to unite the various regions of France beyond a desire for decentralisation. As the regionalist Charles-Brun himself recognised, the strength of regionalism was as a method, and he also laid stress on this diversity.[11] As far as creating myths go, diversity of language and culture is not the kind of force which can inspire the creation of effective sentimental opposition or a powerful sense of collective regional identity.[12] Most of the French regionalists were also conscious that theirs were regions of France, and their goals were linked either to the reorganisation of political structures within France, essentially a desire for administrative decentralisation, or to obtaining specific cultural concessions in a limited context.

The absence of a political dimension to cultural and ethnic regionalism in French Flanders contrasts sharply with the situation in Belgium, where the various Flemish provinces, which had little to unite them historically (or even dialectically), developed a solid cultural and ethnic identity and a 'national' myth of unity, and where Flemish regionalism was adopted as a part of the political platform by both the Christian Democrats and the socialists.

9 Ford, *Creating the nation*.
10 See Thiébaut Flory, *Le Mouvement régionaliste français: sources et développements*, Paris 1966, 11.
11 Jean Charles-Brun, *Le Régionalisme*, Paris 1911, 55
12 Girardet, *Mythes et mythologies politiques*, 154–63.

In Belgium, the state itself was also more precarious, lacking the historical tradition of a powerful central authority, and regionalism as a form of general resistance and political opposition was a viable option and considerably more effective as a political platform for those seeking power than in France. It was the political demands of the Flemish movement that ultimately led to Belgian federalism, solidified Belgian Flemish identity and guaranteed cultural survival (indeed embellishment).

The lack of a popular political basis for the support and protection of Flemish identity in the Westhoek meant that even the undeniable regional cultural, political, historical and linguistic characteristics which were theoretically compatible with national identity could be undermined over the long term and gradually disappear. To cultivate the kind of conscious popular will necessary to protect, preserve and assertively cultivate a group's language and certain elements of their culture during the transition from traditional society requires more than a purely cultural or antiquarian movement. While voices supporting Flemish language and culture could be heard in France, the absence of this key political dimension left the movement much more on the margins of modern society, and thus more susceptible to cultural assimilation over time.

The final significant explanation is thus the successful application of a policy of cultural appropriation, particularly in the second half of the twentieth century, combined with the phenomenon of banal nationalism. Cultural appropriation has been defined as the (re)definition of regional characteristics as national ones, thereby strengthening national identity through emphasis on the very 'Frenchness' of whatever cultural practices existed within the boundaries of the French state and could be seen as compatible with French identity.[13] Some elements of cultural regionalism were even appropriated through the toleration, indeed the encouragement of, the retention of select elements of folklore. This was especially true when local customs had grown out of links to the land, since it could be claimed that to have strong local roots and attachment to the soil was a very 'French' characteristic, in spite of the diversity of specific local traditions. As long as regional cultural claims could be channelled into a benign form of French regional identity and prevented from developing politically, they were not harmful to nation-building. The development of a Nord–Pas-de-Calais identity, with its selection of Flemish cultural characteristics, is a key example of this process of successful appropriation of regional culture. Reinforced through cultural appropriation, French national identity received a further boost in the second half of the twentieth century from 'banal nationalism', the subtle reinforcement of national affiliation through a variety of routine daily activities and subconscious reminders of the nation.[14]

13 Festivals are compatible, for example, where a regional language is not.
14 Billig, *Banal nationalism*. See also chapter 3 above.

The growth of the mass media and of a consumer society, especially in a region as developed as the Westhoek, helps to explain the primary importance of the post-Second World War period for the success of cultural appropriation and the corresponding decline of Flemish identity. The war itself, and the charges of collaboration made against French-Flemish leaders, certainly helped to accelerate the process, and to reinforce the mid-twentieth century as a turning-point, but cannot themselves be considered as a primary cause. The marginality of the VVF and the Belgian experience, where individual collaborators were discredited, but the concessions they achieved strengthened the overall Flemish movement in the longer term, belie a simple correlation between collaboration and the decline of Flemish identity.[15]

Thus notwithstanding the level of integration, elements of French-Flemish culture and identity survived to the end of the twentieth century, in good measure through their extension to the whole of the Nord–Pas-de-Calais region and their characterisation as typical of 'northernness'. Within this context French Flanders no longer refers specifically to the Westhoek, however, and Flemish culture as it has been retained, stripped of its ethnic and linguistic components, is such that one can no longer speak of a common cultural region spanning the Franco-Belgian border. During the final fifteen years of the twentieth century, given the ever-expanding power of the regions and regional assemblies within France, combined with the policies of the European Union which target significant levels of funding towards regions, regionalism as a political force has made something of a comeback within France. It may be that the twenty-first century will witness the renewal and strengthening of regional identity within the newly-defined French Flanders, in spite of the reduced level of cultural distinctiveness which can be said to characterise it.

[15] See also Marcel Gillet, 'Postface: imaginaire collectif et identité régionale', *RN* lxiv (Apr.–June 1982), 637–42, who, without neglecting the importance of the war, clearly regards its effects as secondary.

Surveys of French- and Flemish-Speaking Communes, 1806–1928

key
a – Exclusively Flemish
b – Exclusively French
c – Predominantly Flemish
d – Predominantly French
x – not given

Département du Nord – arrondissement d'Hazebrouck

Commune	1806	1856	1906	1930	Commune	1806	1856	1906	1930
Hazebrouck-Nord					Merris	a	a	a	c
					Meteren	a	a	a	d
Hazebrouck-Nord	a	c	c	d	Vieux-Berquin	a	c	d	d
Blaringhem	b	d	d	d					
Caestre	a	a	a	a	*Cassel*				
Ebblinghem	a	c	d	d	Arnèke	a	a	a	a
Hondeghem	a	a	a	a	Bavinschove	a	a	c	d
Lynde	a	c	a	a	Buyschure	a	a	a	a
Renescure	a	d	d	d	Cassel	a	c	c	d
Sercus	a	c	a	a	Hardifort	a	a	a	a
Staple	a	a	a	a	Ste-Marie-Cappel	a	a	a	a
Wallon-Cappel	a	a	a	a	Noordepeene	a	a	a	a
					Ochtezeele	a	a	a	a
Hazebrouck-Sud					Oxelaere	a	a	a	c
					Rubrouck	a	a	a	a
Hazebrouck-Sud	a	c	c	d	Wemaers-Cappel	a	a	a	a
Boseghem	b	d	d	d	Zermezeele	a	a	a	a
Borre	a	a	a	a	Zuydpeene	a	a	a	a
Morbecque	a	c	a	a					
La Motte au Bois	a	c	a	a	*Merville*				
Pradelles	a	a	a	a	Estaires	b	b	b	b
Steenbecque	a	c	a	c	Havers-kerque	b	b	b	b
Strazeele	a	a	a	a	La Gorgue	b	b	b	b
Thiennes	b	b	b	b	Merville	b	b	b	b
					Neuf-Berquin	b	b	b	b

Commune	1806	1856	1906	1930
Bailleul Nord-Est				
Bailleul Nord-Est	a	c	c	d
St-Jean-Cappel	a	a	a	c
Nieppe	b	b	b	b
Steenwerck	b	b	b	b
Bailleul Sud-Ouest				
Bailleul Sud-Ouest	a	c	c	d
Berthen	a	a	a	a
Flêtre	a	a	a	a

Commune	1806	1856	1906	1930
Steenvoorde				
Boeschepe	a	a	a	a
Eecke	a	a	a	a
Godewaersvelde	a	a	a	a
Houtkerque	a	a	a	a
Oudezeele	a	a	a	a
Steenvoorde	a	a	a	c
St-Sylvestre-Cappel	a	a	a	a
Terdeghem	a	a	a	a
Winnezeele	a	a	a	a

Département du Nord – arrondissement de Dunkerque

Commune	1806	1856	1906	1930
Bergues				
Armbouts-Cappel	a	a	a	a
Bergues	a	c	c	c
Biernea	a	a	a	
Bissezeele	a	a	a	a
Crochte	a	a	a	a
Eringhem	a	a	a	a
Hoymille	a	a	a	c
Pitgem	a	a	a	a
Quadypre	a	a	a	a
Socx	a	a	a	a
Steene	a	a	a	a
West Cappel	a	a	a	a
Wylder	a	a	a	a
Bourbourg				
Bourbourg-ville	a	d	d	d
Bourbourg-campagne	a	d	d	d
Brouckerque	a	a	a	a
Cappelle-Brouck	a	c	c	c
Drincham	a	a	a	a
Holcque	d	d	d	d

Commune	1806	1856	1906	1930
Dunkerque-Ouest				
Cappelle	a	a	c	d
Dunkerque-Ouest	d	d	d	d
Mardyck	b	d	d	d
Grand-Synthe	a	d	d	d
Fort Mardyck	a	c	b	b
Petit-Synthe	a	c	d	d
Saint-Pol-sur-Mer	d	c	d	d
Gravelines				
Craywick	a	d	d	d
Gravelines	b	b	b	b
Grand-Fort-Philippe	b	b	b	b
Loon Plage	b	d	d	d
Saint-Georges	a	b	b	b
Hondschoote				
Bambecque	a	a	a	a

Commune	1806	1856	1906	1930	Commune	1806	1856	1906	1930
Looberghe	a	c	a	a	Ghyvelde	a	a	a	a
Millam	a	a	a	a	Hondschoote	a	a	a	a
St-Momelin	d	d	d	d	Killem	a	a	a	a
St-Pierrebrcuck	a	d	d	d	Les Moëres	a	a	a	a
					Oost-Cappel	a	a	a	a
Spycker	a	a	a	a	Rexpoede	a	a	a	a
Watten	a	d	d	d	Warhem	a	a	a	a
Wulverdinghe	a	a	a	a					
					Wormhoudt				
Dunkerque-Est					Bollezeele	a	a	a	a
					Broxeele	a	a	a	a
Bray-Dunes	a	a	a	c	Ekelsbèque	a	a	a	a
Coudekerque	a	a	a	a	Herzeele	a	a	a	a
Coudekerque-Branch	a	d	d	d	Lederzeele	a	a	a	a
					Ledringham	a	a	a	a
Dunkerque-Est	d	d	d	d	Nieurlet	a	x	c	c
Leffrinck-houcke	a	a	a	c	Volkerinck-hove	a	a	a	a
Malo-les-Bains	a	d	d	d	Wormhoudt	a	a	a	a
					Zegers-Cappel	a	a	a	a
Rosendael	a	x	c	d					
Teteghem	a	a	a	a					
Uxem	a	a	a						
Zuydcoote	a	a	a	c					

Département du Nord – arrondissement de Lille

Commune	1806	1856	1906	1930
Bousbecque	x	x	d	d
Comines-France	x	x	d	d
Halluin	x	x	c	d
Neuville-en-Ferrain	x	x	d	d
Roncq	x	x	d	d
Wervicq-Sud	x	x	c	d

Département du Pas-de-Calais

Commune	1806	1856	1906	1930
St Omer				
Clairmarais	x	c	d	d
Haut-Point	x	d	d	d
Lysel	x	c	d	d
Ruminghem	x	d	x	x

Sources: Coquebert de Montbret, 'Limite de la langue'; de Coussemacker, 'Délimitation du flamand', 377–97; Dewachter, 'Le Flamand et le français', 97–114, and 'Le Recul du flamand', 89–98

Bibliography

Unpublished primary sources

Lille, archives départementales du Nord

Series M (general administration)
M 30 28 elections, 1869
M 35 1 elections, 1885–9
M 35 7 elections, 1876–1911
M 37 33 election posters
M 59 163 *conseil général* and *conseil d'arrondissement de Dunkerque et d'Hazebrouck*, 1901–2, general information
M 85 17 municipal elections, 1865
M 89 43 municipal elections, 1888
M 149 36 affairs concerning Belgium
M 153 15 clerical manifestation, 1895
M 154 56 police records: legal proceedings against Catholics, 1900–5
M 154 58 Flemish language political brochures
M 154 317–18 police reports, 1920–9
M 473 35 census 1886, *arrondissement de Dunkerque*
M 473 36 census 1886, *arrondissement d'Hazebrouck*
M 624 6 police reports, Dunkerque, 1883–6
M 653 41 inventory of industries, *arrondissement d'Hazebrouck*, 1873

Series N (finance and conseil général)
1 N 136 prefect's report to *conseil général*

Series T (education)
1 T 80 68–72 inspection reports, 1865–9
1 T 123 5 correspondence, 1900–5
1 T 217 reports on the press, 1868–88
1 T 222 press, general information, 1890–1900
2 T 767 correspondence and reports, 1856
2 T 2403 circular letters, instructions and correspondence, 1859–76

Series V (religious affairs)
2 V 56 elections, attitude of the clergy
2 V 60–1 infractions of the law of assembly for the clergy, 1906–7
2 V 76 Flemish catechism, 1806–1902
2 V 79 correspondence, 1902
2 V 115 diocesan circulars (Cambrai), 1874–80
2 V 117 correspondence

Series 1 W (office of the prefect, 1940–4)

1 W 998 Flemish language in primary schools, 1942
1 W 1094 *frontaliers belges*: crossing the border, 1939–40
1 W 1204 police reports on authorised parties and press, 1944
1 W 1216 report on the *flamingant* movement, 1941
1 W 1274 police reports on authorised parties and press, 1942–4
1 W 1464 Flemish prisoners of war
1 W 2330 seizure of Gantois documents
1 W 2545 police reports on authorised parties, 1942

Series 5 Z (subprefectorial archives of Dunkerque)

5 Z 49 elections, 1924
5 Z 50 correspondence, 1924
5 Z 53 elections, 1928
5 Z 71 elections, *conseil général*, 1925

Series 6 Z (subprefectorial archives of Hazebrouck)

6 Z 1860 elections, *conseil général*, 1925
6 Z 1861 *conseil d'arrondissement* and *conseil général*, general information, 1910–19
6 Z 1862 elections, *conseil général*, 1922
6 Z 2072 elections, 1919–24
6 Z 2108 correspondence, 1890–7
6 Z 2269 deliberations of the 'délégation cantonal de Steenvoorde', 1875
6 Z 2279 Flemish catechism, 1901–3
6 Z 2288 police reports on the clergy, 1898–1905

Private papers dealing with Louis Cordonnier

136 J 62 newspaper and journal clippings
136 J 63 pamphlets

Paris, archives nationales

Series F 17 (education)

F 17 2682 renseignements politiques
F 17 9182 laicisation
F 17 9190 laicisation
F 17 9270 correspondence and inspection reports
F 17 9374 inspection reports
F 17 9376 inspection reports
F 17 10682 statistics
F 17 10717 statistics
F 17* 3160 attendance

Series F 19 (religious affairs)

F 19 1974 correspondence and reports
F 19 5502 correspondence
F 19 5798 correspondence
F 19 6081 correspondence

Published primary sources

Allacker, Franck *La Flandre en France* (pamphlet), n.p. 1987

'Allocuticn prononcée par Mgr. Dehaisnes 20 novembre 1888 à Hazebrouck', *ACFF* xviii (1889–90), 1–8

Anthoine, E., *L'Instruction primaire dans le département du Nord, 1868–1877: rapport rédigé en vue de l'Exposition Universelle de 1878*, Lille 1878.

———— *A Travers nos écoles: souvenirs posthumes*, Paris 1887

Ardouin-Dumazet, Victor Eugène, *Voyage en France*, 18e série: *Région du Nord*, I: *Flandre et littoral du Nord*, Paris 1899

Audiganne, A., *Les Populations ouvrières et les industries de la France dans le mouvement social du dix-neuvième siècle*, Paris 1854

Blanchard, Raoul, *La Densité de population du département du Nord au XIXe siècle: étude de dix recensements de population*, thèse présenté à la faculté des lettres de l'université de Lille, Lille 1906

———— *La Flandre: étude géographique de la plaine flamande en France, Belgique et Hollande*, Lille 1906

Blanckaert, Justin, 'La Flandre française réclame le régime de l'Occitanie, du Pays Basque et de la Bretagne: l'enseignement de sa langue', *Le Lion de Flandre* viii (Mar.–Apr. 1930), 1–2

———— 'Le Bilinguisme scolaire en Flandre française', *Le Lion de Flandre* xi (Sept.–Oct. 1930)

Bonvarlet, A., 'Un Mot sur ce que la biographie des hommes remarquables de la Flandre occidentale contient au point de vue des flamands de France', *BCFF* ii (1862), 344–5

Bourgeois, N., 'Un Tour de Flandre', in Bourgeois and others, *Flandre notre mère*, 4–29

———— P. Deffontaines, C. Looten, C. De Croocq, J. Dewachter, R. Despicht, A. M. de Poncheville, F. Beaucamps, L. Détrez, J.-E. Van Den Driessche, P. Vandame and J. Delannoy, *Flandre notre mère: la Flandre française en douze tableaux*, Bailleul 1931, repr. Steenvoorde 1994

Boutroux, Emile, 'Les Récents Manuels de morale et d'instruction civique', *Revue pédagogique* n.s. ii (15 Apr. 1883), 289–342

Carlier, J. J., Nouvelle Démonstration de l'utilité de la langue flamande', *BCFF* vi (1872–5), 28–36

Carnel, D., 'Les Sociétés de rhétorique et leurs représentations dramatique chez les Flamands de France', *ACFF* v (1859–60), 29–88

———— 'Revue du mouvement flamand', *BCFF* iii (session 3 Mar. 1864), 245–6

Carte des chemins de fer de la Belgique et des pays limitrophes, prepared by A. Vuillemin, Paris 1865

Celen, V., *Het vlaamsch in Fransch-Vlaanderen*, Brussels 1925

Charles-Brun, Jean, *Le Régionalisme*, Paris 1911

Chocqueel, Jean, *Les Chambres de Rhétorique en Flandre française* (Éditions du Beffroi de Flandre, revue régionaliste, 1920)

Cochin, Henri, *Les Deux Guerres, 1870–1871, 1914–1917: images et souvenirs*, Paris 1917

Dauzat, Albert, 'Le Déplacement des frontières linguistiques du français de 1806 à nos jours', *La Nature*, 15 Dec. 1927, 529–35

De Baecker, Louis, *Les Flamands de France: études sur leur langue, leur littérature, et leurs monuments*, new edn, ed. Gérard Monfort, Brionne 1975

Debusschere, C., 'La Bataille idéologique', *Le Lion de Flandre* xx (Aug. 1942), 366–78

De Coussemacker, E., 'Instructions relatives aux dialectes flamands et à la délimitation du français et du flamand dans le Nord de la France', *ACFF* i (1854–5), 62–9

────── 'Délimitation du flamand et du français dans le Nord de la France', *ACFF* iii (1856–7), 377–97

Defeuille, Eugène, *L'Anticléricalisme avant et pendant notre république*, Paris 1911

Defoort, Eric and Els Lion (eds), *Brieven van J. M. Gantois aan V. Celen*, I: *1925–1939*, Kortrijk 1979

Deghilage, Pierre, *L'Education sociale à l'école*, Montdidier 1906

Despicht, R., 'La Littérature flamande en Flandre française', in Bourgeois and others, *Flandre notre mère*, 104–26

Desrousseaux, Alexandre, *Moeurs populaires de la Flandre française*, Lille 1889

Détrez, L. and Joseph Crombé, *Le Régionalisme religieux: la foi de nos pères: le régionalisme familial: la famille flamande*, Lille 1926

Dewachter, J., 'Le Flamand et le français dans le Nord de la France', *Congrès international pour l'extension et la culture de la langue française*, 2e session, Bruxelles 1908, 97–114

────── *Recul du français en Belgique à notre époque*, Dunkerque 1908

────── 'La Situation du français et du flamand dans le Nord de la France après la guerre mondiale', *RFB* viii (Jan. 1928), 27–33

────── 'Le Recul du flamand dans le Nord de la France depuis 1806', in 1er *Congrès international de géographie historique*, II: *Mémoires*, Bruxelles 1931, 89–98

Discours sur la réduction des heures de travail prononcé par M. Edouard Crépy, conseiller municipal dans la réunion publique tenu Salle Meurisse le 20 février 1881 (pamphlet), Lille 1881

Eeckhout, Georges, 'Les Ouvriers belges dans le Nord', *Revue sociale catholique* iv (1900), 266–73, 340–50.

Fèvre, Joseph and Henri Hauser, *Régions et pays de France*, Paris 1909

Gilliéron, J. and E. Edmont, *Atlas linguistique de la France*, Paris 1908

Hauser, Henri, *Le Problème du régionalisme* (Histoire economique & sociale de la guerre mondiale), Paris 1924

────── Jean Maurin and Pierre Benaerts, *Du Libéralisme à l'impérialisme (1860–1878)*, Paris 1939

Lavisse, Ernest, *Questions d'enseignement national*, Paris 1885

Lemire, J., 'Confréries ouvrières d'Hazebrouck ou les corporations de cette ville considérées du point de vue religieux', *ACFF* xx (1892), 14–40

Levasseur, E., *La Population française: histoire de la population avant 1789 et démographie de la France comparée à celles des autres nations au XIXe siècle*, Paris 1889

────── *Questions ouvrières et industrielles en France sous la Troisième République*, Paris 1907

────── *Histoire du commerce de la France*, II: *De 1789 à nos jours*, Paris 1912

Looten, C., 'La Langue des flamands de France', *Revue de Lille* i (1890), 278–94, 435–61

────── *Le Comité Flamand de France de 1853 à 1903*, Arras 1904

────── 'La Question du flamand', *BCFF* (1921), 266–75

────── 'La Flandre à travers les ages', in Bourgeois and others, *Flandre notre mère*, 41–61

Lorbert, A., *La France au travail: la région du Nord (Nord – Pas-de-Calais – Somme – Aisne)*, Paris 1927

Mordacq, L., 'Notes pour servir à l'histoire de l'instruction primaire dans le département du Nord', *MSD* xvii (1871–2), 36–65

Nierynck, Nick, 'Qu'est-ce l'enracinement?', in *Le Régionalisme?* (pamphlet: dossier d'étude no. 3, Cercle Michel de Swaen), Dunkerque 1976

Ormsby, H., *France: a regional and economic geography*, London 1931

Parent, Paul, 'Les Caractères régionaux de l'architecture dans le Nord de la France', *RN* xiii (Feb. 1927), 5–43

Pécault, Félix, *L'Education publique et la vie nationale*, Paris 1897

Rapport présenté au congrès catholique de Lille à la séance générale du 30 novembre 1888 par M. Bayart, industriel à Roubaix (pamphlet), Lille 1888

Régionales et cantonales 1998 (15 et 22 mars): résultats, Paris 1998

Renan, Ernest, *Qu'est-ce qu'une nation? Et autres essais politiques*, texts chosen and presented by Joël Roman, Paris 1992

Ronse, Edmond, *L'Emigration saisonnière belge*, Gand 1913

Ryngaert, H., 'Wat wil de Torrewachter', *De Torrewachter: Maanblad voor Fransch-Vlaanderen*, 15 Jan. 1929, 1

Taverne de Tersud, Charles, *Hazebrouck: depuis son origine jusqu'à nos jours: ses corporations, ses lois, ses moeurs et coutumes, se fête du comte de la mi-carême, sa kermesse, ses gueux, ses sorciers et sorcières, ses monuments*, Hazebrouck 1890, new edn, Hazebrouck 1987

Tiersot, Julien, *Histoire de la chanson populaire en France*, Paris 1889

Tisje-Tasje's almanak 1901, produced by Vlaemsch Comiteyt van Vrankryk 1901

Tisje-Tasje's almanak voor Fransch Vlaanderen 1929, Hazebrouck 1929

Tronchet, M., 'La Place des langues dans l'enseignement', *MSD* xxi (1877–80), 187–99

Vermast, M. A., *Le Mouvement flamand en Belgique* (pamphlet: communication faite à la séance du CFF le 20 décembre 1897)

Newspapers and periodicals

L'Ami des Flandres: journal de Dunkerque & de la région: organe républicain, indépendant, littéraire, commercial, agricole et d'informations

La Chronique des Flandres: organe de défence à Paris des intérêts du département du Nord

Le Cri des Flandres: journal républicain

L'Echo de Flandre: journal politique, d'intérêt local, agricole & littéraire

L'Echo du Nord

Le Fermier des Flandres et de l'Artois

L'Indicateur de l'arrondissement d'Hazebrouck

Le Journal D'Hazebrouck et de l'arrondissement

Le Lion de Flandre

Le Mercure de Flandre

Le Monde
Le Moniteur financier de la région du Nord
Le Nord fédéral: organe des Droits de la région du Nord
Le Patriote des Flandres: journal de Steenvoorde et de l'arrondissement d'Hazebrouck
Le Petit Nord
Le Petit Steenvoordois: organe d'intérêt local commercial, agricole & littéraire de Steenvoorde & du canton
Le Progrès du Nord
La Région du Nord: journal industriel, commercial & financier: assurances, mines, metallurgie, chemins de fer
La Revue du Bridge dans le Nord de la France: organe du Comité des Flandres
La Semaine religieuse du diocèse de Cambrai
De Torrewachter: Maanblad voor Fransch-Vlaanderen
Het Vlaamsch Kruis: voor de Vlamingen van Frankrijk
Het Volk
Het Volk der Franschmans: orgaan der Franschmans: en Steenbakkersgilden van Oost-Vlaanderen

Secondary sources

Aerts, Erik and Francis M. L. Thompson (eds), *Ethnic minority groups in town and countryside and their effects on economic development (1850–1940)*, Leuven 1990

Agulhon, Maurice, 'Conscience nationale et conscience régionale en France de 1815 à nos jours', in Boogman and van der Plaat, *Federalism*, 243–66

—— *Marianne au pouvoir: l'imagerie et la symbolique républicaines de 1880 à 1914*, Paris 1989

—— *La République: de Jules Ferry à François Mittérand, 1880 à nos jours*, Paris 1990

—— 'French historians and the reconstruction of the republican tradition, 1800–1848', trans. Laura Mason, in Fontana, *Modern republic*, 173–91

—— 'Réflexions sur l'image du bourgeois français à la veille de 1848', *Quarante-huit quatorze: conférences du Musée d'Orsay* vi (1994), 4–13

Alexander, Martin S. (ed.), *French history since Napoleon*, London 1999

Allaert, Georges, 'Knelpunten en perspectieven van het industrieel beleid in Noord-Frankrijk', *DFN/LPBF* xxiii (1998), 30–44

Anderson, Benedict, *Imagined communities*, 2nd edn, London 1991

Anderson, R. D., *Education in France, 1848–1870*, Oxford 1975

Armstrong, John A., *Nations before nationalism*, Chapel Hill 1982

Asselain, Jean-Charles, *Histoire économique de la France du XVIIIe siècle à nos jours*, Paris 1984

Bailleul, Francis, 'Les Instituteurs du Nord d'après le concours Rouland de 1860', *RN* lxvii (July–Sept. 1985), 703–14

Baker, Donald N. and Patrick J. Harrigan (eds), *The making of Frenchmen: current directions in the history of education in France, 1679–1979*, Waterloo, Ont. 1980.

Baker, Robert P., 'Socialism in the Nord, 1830–1914: a regional view of the French socialist movement', *International Review of Social History* xii (1967), 357–89.

Balibar, Renée and Dominique Laporte, *Le Français national: politique et pratiques de la langue nationale sous la Révolution Française*, Paris 1974

Balthazar. Herman, 'Betrekkingen tussen het socialisme in Vlaanderen en Noord-Frankrijk (1870–1914)', *DFN/LPBF* iv (1979), 10–29

Barbagli, Marjio and Marcello Dei, 'Socialisation into apathy and political subordination', in Karabel and Halsey, *Power and ideology*, 423–32

Baycroft, Timothy, 'Peasants into Frenchmen? The case of the Flemish in the north of France, 1860–1914', *European Review of History/Revue européenne d'histoire* ii (Spring 1995), 31–44

—— *Nationalism in Europe, 1789–1914*, Cambridge 1998

—— 'Changing identities in the Franco-Belgian borderland in the nineteenth and twentieth centuries', *French History* xiii (1999), 417–38

Becker, Jean-Jacques and Stéphane Audoin-Rouzeau, *La France, la nation, la guerre: 1850–1920*, Paris 1995

Beirens, Dirk, 'De geschiedenis van "Ons Oud Vlaemsch", tijdschriff van Guido Gezelle voor Frans-Vlaanderen', *DFN/LPBF* vii (1982), 130–52

Bentley, James, *The gateway to France: Flanders, Artois and Picardy*. London 1991

Bhabha, Homi K. (ed.), *Nation and narration*, London 1990

Billig, Michael, *Banal nationalism*, London 1995

Blancpain, Marc, *La Vie quotidienne dans la France du Nord sous les occupations (1814–1944)*, Paris 1983

—— *La Frontière du Nord, 843–1945: de la mer à la Meuse*, Paris 1990

Blom, J. C. H. and E. Lamberts (eds), *History of the Low Countries*, trans. James C. Kennedy, New York–Oxford 1999

Bon, Frédéric, *Les Élections en France: histoire et sociologie*, Paris 1978

Bonduelle, Bruno, 'L'Avenir économique du Nord de la France et ses relations avec la Flandre belge et les Pays-Bas', *DFN/LPBF* xx (1995), 276–81

Boogman, J. C. and G. N. van der Plaat (eds), *Federalism: history and current significance of a form of government*, The Hague 1980

Boulad-Ayoub, Josiane (ed.), *Former un nouveau peuple? Pouvoir, education, révolution*, Québec 1996

Bourgeois, Nicolas, *'Les Hexagons': de la Gaule à la France et de la France à l'hexagone*, Dunkerque 1970

Brachin, Pierre, 'Un Pionnier: Louis de Baecker (1814–1896)', *DFN/LPBF* xiii (1988), 64–77

Braudel, Fernand, *The identity of France*, I: *History and environment*, trans. Siân Reynolds, London 1988

Brel, Jacques, *Tout Brel*, ed. Olivier Todd, Paris 1986

Brenne, Jules, 'Les Candidats ouvriers dans le Nord', *RN* lvi (Apr.–June 1974), 185–93

Breuillard-Pollet, Michèle, 'Existe-t-il un espace transfrontalier franco-belge?', *Cahiers du CRAPS* iv (Feb. 1988), 59–68

—— and others, *La Frontière et les communes: le cas des communes françaises et belges frontalières de la région Nord–Pas-de-Calais*, Lille 1987

Breuilly, John, *Nationalism and the state*, Manchester 1982

Brubaker, Rogers, *Citizenship and nationhood in France and Germany*, Cambridge, Mass. 1992

Brunot, Ferdinand, *Histoire de la langue française des origines à 1900*, IX: *La Révolution et l'empire*, Paris 1927

Brustein, William, *The social origins of political regionalism: France, 1849–1981*, Berkeley 1988

Bruyelle, P., 'De La Région pilote à la région déprimée, 1952–1980', in Hilaire, *Histoire du Nord/Pas-de Calais*, 415–51

Caron, François, *An economic history of modern France*, London 1979

Carpentier-Bogaert, Catherine, *Saints guérisseurs: rites et lieux sacrés* (Documents d'ethnographie régional du Nord–Pas-de-Calais vi), Béthune 1995

Chafer, Tony (ed.), *Multicultural France*, Portsmouth 1997

Chaline, Nadine-Josette, 'Le Catholicisme social dans le Nord au début du XXe siècle', *RN* lxxiii (Apr.–Sept. 1991), 305–14

Chanet, Jean-François, *L'École républicaine et les petites patries*, Paris 1996

Charle, Christophe, 'Région et conscience régionale en France', *Actes de la recherche en sciences sociales*, XXXV: *L'Identité* (Nov. 1980), 37–43

—— *Histoire sociale de la France au XIXe siècle*, Paris 1991

Chaurand, Jacques (ed.), *Nouvelle Histoire de la langue française*, Paris 1999

Chaussois, Robert, *Géants du Nord/Pas-de-Calais*, Lille 1998

Cholvy, Gérard, 'Régionalisme et clergé catholique au XIXe siècle', in Gras and Livet, *Régions et régionalisme*

—— and Yves-Marie Hilaire, *Histoire religieuse de la France contemporaine*, Toulouse 1988

Clough, Shepard B., *A history of the Flemish movement in Belgium: a study in nationalism*, New York 1930

Cobb, Richard, *French and Germans, Germans and French: a personal interpretation of France under two occupations, 1914–1918/1940–1944*, Hanover–London 1983

Codaccioni, Felix-Paul, 'De la Prospérité impériale à la belle époque (1851–1914)', in Trénard, *Histoire des Pays-Bas français*

Codaccioni, M., 'Vers une renaissance culturelle', in Hilaire, *Histoire du Nord/Pas-de-Calais*, 480–515

Coffey, Joan L., 'Church–State conflict: bilingualism and religious education, 1890–1905', *Proceedings of the Annual Meeting of the Western Society for French History* xxii (1995), 55–66

Collingham, H. A. C. with R. S. Alexander, *The July Monarchy: a political history of France, 1830–1848*, London–New York 1988

Coornaert, Emile, *La Flandre française de langue flamande*, Paris 1970

—— 'Flamand et français dans l'enseignement en Flandre française des annexions au XXe siècle', *RN* liii (Apr.–June 1971), 217–21

Cornelus, Firmin, 'Intercommunale samenwerking over de grenzen heen', *DFN/LPBF* xx (1995), 133–59

Dansette, Jean Lambert, *Quelques Familles du patronat textile de Lille-Armentières (1789–1914)*, Lille 1954

Dassau, Pierre, *Le Nord vu par la presse, 1860/1910*, Dijon 1981

De Certeau, Michel, Dominique Julia and Jacques Revel, *Une Politique de la langue: la Révolution Française et les patois: l'enquête de Grégoire*, Paris 1975

Defoort, Eric, 'Jean-Marie Gantois in de vlaamse beweging in Frankrijk, 1919–1939', *Ons Erfdeel* v (1974), 683–95

Dejonghe, Étienne, 'Le Nord et le Pas-de-Calais pendant la première année de l'occupation (juin 1940–juin 1941)', *RN* li (Oct.–Dec. 1969), 677–708

—— 'Un Mouvement séparatiste dans le Nord et le Pas-de-Calais sous l'occupation (1940–1944): le "Vlaamsch Verbond van Frankrijk" ', *RHMC* xvii (Jan.–Mar. 1970), 50–77

————— 'Le Nord isolé: occupation et opinion', *RHMC* xxvi (Jan.–Mar. 1979), 48–97

————— Les Relations frontalières franco-belges de 1939 à 1944', *RN* no. 2 spéciale hors-série (1988), 585–604

————— 'Les Délégués de la propagande dans le Nord/Pas-de-Calais (1942–1944)', *RN* lxxiii (Jan.–Mar. 1991), 87–101

————— and Yves Le Maner, *Le Nord–Pas-de-Calais dans la main allemande, 1940–1944*, Lille 1999

Deligny, Henri, *Le Nord demain*, Paris 1964

De Metsenaere, Machteld, 'Socio-professional aspects of the Flemings in Brussels during the 19th century', in Aerts and Thompson, *Ethnic minority groups*, Leuven 1990, 85–95

Den Boer, Pim, *History as a profession: the study of history in France, 1818–1914*, trans. Arnold J. Pomerans, Princeton 1998

Deneckere, Marcel, *Histoire de la langue française dans les Flandres (1770–1823)*, Gand 1954

Denys, Luc, 'L'Enquête de 1886 en Belgique: un système capitaliste dépourvu de restrictions légales', *RN* lvi (July–Sept. 1974), 433–6

Depestel, Nele and Tanja Termote, 'Grensarbeid tussen West-Vlaanderen en Frankrijk', *DFN/LPBF* xxiv (1999), 115–26

Deprez, Ada, 'Over Gezelles briefwisseling met de Frans-Vlamingen (1884–1899)', *DFN/LPBF* x (1985), 228–45

Deprez, Kas, 'The language of the Flemings', in Deprez and Vos, *Nationalism in Belgium*, 96–109

————— and Louis Vos (eds), *Nationalism in Belgium: shifting identities, 1780–1995*, Basingstoke 1998

Dericquebourg, Régis, 'L'Identité culturelle des flamands de France: comment peut-on être flamand?', *Plat Pays* 3–4 (1986), 1–15.

Descamps, E. H., *De Vlamingen in Frankrijk*, Antwerpen n.d.

Descamps, Pierre, 'La Vie d'une paroisse au XIXe siècle: Aubers-en-Weppes', *RN* xlvi (1964), 535–73

Deschuytter, Joseph, 'Destin du parler flamand dans le département du Nord', *Plein-Nord la gazette: revue historique et culturelle du Nord de la France* xi (May–June 1985), 33–5

De Spiegler, Pierre, 'La Législation linguistique en Belgique', *Universités* xv (May 1994), 27–9

Desplanques, Henri, 'L'Évolution récente de la maison agricole en Flandre française: l'exemple de Steenbecque', *HTN* (1974.1), 34–8

Despriet, P., *Le Patrimoine historique de la Flandre française*, Courtrai 1979

Despriet, Philippe, *Geschiedenis van Frans-Vlaanderen: van de oudste tijden tot de oorlog van 1870–1871*, Kortrijk 1988

Dessert, Gabriel, 'Alphabétisation et scholarisation dans le Grand-Ouest au 19e siècle', in Baker and Harrigan, *Making of Frenchmen*, 143–95

Deveyer, Albert, *La Flandre d'autrefois*, Dunkerque 1985

Devoldere, Luc, 'Een uitgestoken hand, 50 jaar "Komitee voor Frans-Vlaanderen" ', *DFN/LPBF* xxiii (1998), 65–75

Dictionnaire biographique illustré: Nord, 2nd edn, Paris 1909

Dion, Raymond, 'L'Évolution de la "maison agricole" à la Flamengrie (Thiérache de l'Aisne)', *HTN* (1974.1), 39–47

Dion, Roger, *Les Frontières de la France*, Paris 1947

Drewe, Paul and Joël Hébrard, 'Le Nord de la France, région frontalière européenne: un laboratoire de l'intégration européenne', *DFN/LPBF* xx (1995), 161–79

Dubois, Sébastien, *Les Bornes immuables de l'état: la rationalisation du tracé des frontières au siècle des Lumières (France, Pays-Bas autrichiens et principauté de Liège)*, Heule 1999

Ducastelle, Jean-Pierre and others, *Géants et dragons: mythes et traditions à Bruxelles, en Wallonie, dans le Nord de la France et en Europe*, Tournai 1996

Duriez, Bruno, 'La Bourgeoisie répertoriée: le livre des familles du Nord', *Ethnologie français* xx (Jan.–Mar. 1990), 71–84

———— 'La Religion de la région du Nord: l'empreinte du catholicisme', *DFN/LPBF* xxiii (1998), 11–29

Durkheim, Émile, 'On education and society', in Karabel and Halsey, *Power and ideology*, 92–105

Duveau, Georges, *Les Instituteurs*, Paris 1957

Engelaere, Olivier, 'Le Mouvement flamand en France de la libération à la mort de Jean-Marie Gantois', *DFN/LPBF* xvi (1991), 83–105

———— 'Le Mouvement picard en France du début des années 1970 à la fin des années 1980', *DFN/LPBF* xix (1994), 90–115

Ferry, Luc and Alain Renaut, *Philosopher à dix-huit ans: faut-il réformer l'enseignement de la philosophie?*, Paris 1999

Fitzmaurice, John, *The politics of Belgium: a unique federalism*, London 1996

Les Flamands de France: Qui sont-ils? Que veulent-ils? Le manifest des flamands de France adopté à la IVe université populaire flamande par les associations: Cercle Michel de Swaen, Menschen Lijk Wijder, CFF, Het Reusekoor, Tegaere Toegaen, Lille-en-Flandre 1982

Flatres P., 'L'Évolution de l'agriculture dans la région du Nord', *HTN* (1964.1), 7–21

Florin, Jean-Pierre, 'Présentation des forces politiques dans le département du Nord en 1914', *RN* lvi (Apr.–June 1974), 165–76

———— 'Contribution à une histoire des chemins du pouvoir sous la IIIe République: les conseillers généraux du Nord, du début du siècle à la veille de la seconde guerre mondiale', *RN* lxxv (July–Sept. 1993), 601–33

Flory, Thiébaut, *Le Mouvement régionaliste français: sources et développement*, Paris 1966

Fontana, Biancamaria (ed.), *The invention of the modern republic*, Cambridge 1994

Ford, Caroline, *Creating the nation in provincial France: religion and political identity in Brittany*, Princeton 1993

Forde, Simon, Lesley Johnson and Alan V. Murray (eds), *Concepts of national identity in the Middle Ages*, Leeds 1995

Foutrien, Christiane, 'Evolution récente de l'habitat agricole à Winnezeele (Flandre intérieure)', *HTN* (1974.1), 27–33

———— 'L'Élevage et les constructions subventionnés en Flandre intérieure', *HTN* (1975.1), 79–90

———— 'Flandre intérieur: région en voie de spécialisation?', *HTN* (1975.2), 41–59

'En France, une presse vivante, malgré tout', *Courrier international*, 24 Feb.–1 Mar. 2000, 39

François, Michel (ed.), *La France et les français*, Paris 1972

Frazer, W. R., *Education and society in modern France*, London 1963

Furet, François, 'French historians and the reconstruction of the republican tradition, 1800–1848', in Fontana, *Modern republic*, 173–91

——— and Jacques Ozouf, 'L'Alphabétisation: trois siècles de métissage culturel', *Annales: economies sociétés civilisation* xxxii (May–June 1977), 488–502

Gamblin, André, 'Les Régions du Nord de la France', *HTN* (1963.1), 8–23

——— *La Région du Nord*, Paris 1973

——— *Le Nord–Pas-de-Calais: 20 circuits touristiques*, Colmar 1984

——— 'Le Choix: les 22 régions administratives', in Gamblin, *La France*, i. 13–40

——— (ed.), *La France dans ses régions*, 2nd edn, Paris 1998

Gauchet, Marcel, 'Les "Lettres sur l'histoire de France" d'Augustin Thierry', in Nora, *Lieux de mémoire*, i. 787–850

Gellner, Ernest, *Nations and nationalism*, Oxford 1983

——— *Encounters with nationalism*, Oxford 1994

Gerard, Emmanuel, 'The Christian workers' movement as a mass foundation of the Flemish movement', in Kas and Vos, *Nationalism in Belgium*, 127–38

Gijsseling, Maurits, 'Ontstaan en verschuiving van de taalgrens in Noord-Frankrijk', *DFN/LPBF* i (1976), 70–85

Gildea, Robert, *Education in provincial France, 1800–1914: a study of three departments*, Oxford 1983

——— *The past in French history*, New Haven–London 1994

Gille, Christelle, 'Quarante Ans d'Action Catholique ouvrière dans le diocèse de Lille (1950–1990)', *RN* lxxix (Jan.–Mar. 1997), 139–57

Gillet, Marcel, 'Postface: imaginaire collectif et identité régionale', *RN* lxiv (Apr.–June 1982), 637–42

——— (ed.), *La Qualité de vie dans la région Nord–Pas-de-Calais au 20e siècle*, Lille 1975

Giolitto, Pierre, *Histoire de l'enseignement primaire au XIXe siècle*, II: *Les Méthodes d'enseignement*, Paris 1984

Girard d'Albissin, Nelly, 'A Propos sur la frontière', *Revue d'histoire de droits français et étranger* iii (1969)

——— *Genèse de la frontière franco-belge: les variations des limites septentrionales de la France de 1659 à 1789*, Paris 1970

Girardet, Raoul, *Le Nationalisme français: anthologie, 1871–1914*, Paris 1983

——— *Mythes et mythologies politiques*, Paris 1986

——— *Nationalismes et nation*, Paris 1996

——— 'Les Trois Couleurs: ni blanc, ni rouge', in Nora, *Lieux de mémoire*, i. 49–66

Goguel, François, *La Politique des partis sous la Troisième République*, 3rd edn, Paris 1958

——— *Géographie des élections française sous la Troisième et Quatrième Républiques*, Paris 1970

——— and Alfred Grosser, *La Politique en France*, Paris 1984

Gordon, David, *The French language and national identity (1930–1975)*, The Hague 1978

————— 'Liberalism and socialism in the Nord: Eugène Motte and republican politics in Roubaix, 1898–1912', *French History* iii (1989), 312–43

Gramsci, Antonio, *Cahiers de prison*, trans. Claude Perrus and Pierre Laroche, Paris 1991

Gras, Christian, 'Conclusions provisoires', in Gras and Livet, *Régions et régionalisme*, 591–4.

————— and Georges Livet (eds), *Régions et régionalisme en France du XVIIIe siècle à nos jours*, Paris 1977

Greene, Nathanael, 'National and local: rural politics, 1932–1936', *French Historical Studies* ix (1976), 503–20

Greenfeld, Liah, *Nationalism: five roads to modernity*, Cambridge, Mass. 1992

Guerin-Gonzales, Camille, and Carl Strikwerda (eds), *The politics of immigrant workers: labour activism and migration in the world economy since 1830*, New York 1993

Gueusquin, Marie-France, *Fêtes, géants et carnavales du Nord–Pas-de-Calais: Cassel* (Documents d'ethnographie régional du Nord–Pas-de-Calais iii), Béthune 1993

————— and Monique Mestayer, *Gayant: fêtes et géants de Douai* (Documents d'ethnographie régional du Nord–Pas-de-Calais v), Béthune 1994

Guibernau, Montserrat, *Nationalisms: the nation-state and nationalism in the twentieth century*, Cambridge 1996

Guillaume, Pierre, *Histoire sociale de la France au XXe siècle*, Paris 1992

Harp, Stephen, *Learning to be loyal: primary schooling as nation building in Alsace and Lorraine, 1850–1940*, DeKalb, Illinois 1998

Harrigan, Patrick J., 'Historians and compilers joined: the historiography of the 1970s and French *enquêtes* of the nineteenth century', in Baker and Harrigan, *Making of Frenchmen*, 3–21

Hastings, Adrian, *The construction of nationhood: ethnicity, religion and nationalism*, Cambridge 1997

Hastings, Michel, *Halluin la rouge, 1919–1939: aspects d'un communisme identitaire*, Lille 1991

Hayward, Jack, *The one and indivisible French republic*, London 1973

Héméryck, Richard, 'La Congréganisation des écoles normales du département du Nord au milieu du XIXe siècle (1845–1883): l'école normale d'instituteurs de Douai', *RN* lvi (Jan.–Mar. 1974), 13–28

————— 'L'École primaire, le clergé, et le recul du flamand durant la seconde partie du XIXe siècle', *ACFF* l (1992), 101–98.

Hennart, Robert, *Flamands de France: taches d'hier, missions de demain*, Lille 1954

Hermans, Theo, Louis Vos and Lode Wils (eds), *The Flemish movement: a documentary history, 1780–1990*, London 1992

Heywood, Colin, *The development of the French economy, 1750–1914*, London 1992

Hilaire, Yves-Marie, 'Les Ouvriers du Nord devant l'église catholique (XIXe et XXe siècles)', *Le Mouvement social* lvii (Oct.–Dec. 1966), 181–201

————— André Legrand, Bernard Ménager and Robert Vandenbussche, *Atlas électoral Nord/Pas-de-Calais, 1876–1936: Troisième République*, Villeneuve d'Ascq 1977

————— (ed.), *Histoire du Nord/Pas-de Calais de 1900 à nos jours*, Toulouse 1982

————— Fernand Boulard and others (eds), *Matériaux pour l'histoire religieuse du peuple français, XIXe–XXe siècles*, II: *Bretagne, Basse Normandie, Nord–Pas-de-Calais, Picardie, Champagne, Lorraine, Alsace*, Paris 1987

Hilden, Patricia Penn, *Working women and socialist politics in France, 1880–1914: a regional study*, Oxford 1986

—— *Women, work, and politics: Belgium, 1830–1914*, Oxford 1993

Hobsbawm, E. J., *Nations and nationalism since 1780: programme, myth, reality*, Cambridge 1990

—— 'Introduction: inventing traditions', in Hobsbawm and Ranger, *Invention of tradition*, 1–14

—— 'Mass-producing traditions: Europe, 1870–1914', in Hobsbawm and Ranger, *Invention of tradition*, 263–307

—— and Terence Ranger (eds), *The invention of tradition*, Cambridge 1983

Hopkin, David, 'Identity in a divided province: the folklorists of Lorraine, 1860–1960', *French Historical Studies* xxiii (2000), 639–82

Houvenaghel, Maurice, *Boeschepe: mon village*, Steenvoorde 1990

Hroch, Miroslav, *Social preconditions of national revival in Europe*, trans. Ben Fowkes, Cambridge 1985

Jenkins, Brian, *Nationalism in France: class and nation since 1789*, London–New York 1990

—— 'The one and indivisible republic: French identity and identities', in Chafer, *Multicultural France*, 1–6

Johnson, Douglas, 'The making of the French nation', in Teich and Porter, *National question*, 35–62

Johnson, Lesley, 'Imagining communities: medieval and modern' in Forde, Johnson and Murray, *Concepts of national identity*, 1–19

Julliard, Jacques (ed.), *Les Conflits*, i, Paris 1990

Karabel, Jerome and A. H. Halsey (eds), *Power and ideology in education*, New York 1977

Kok-Escalle, Marie-Christine, *Instaurer une culture par l'enseignement de l'histoire, France, 1876–1912: contribution à une sémiotique de la culture*, Berne 1988

Kooijman, J., 'Enseigner le néerlandais dans le Nord de la France', *DFN/LPBF* xxiv (1998), 148–61

Krejčí, Jaroslav and Vítezslav Velímsky, *Ethnic and political nations in Europe*, London 1981

Kuisel, R. F., *Capitalism and the state in modern France: renovation and economic management in the twentieth century*, Cambridge 1981

Lagoueyte, Patrick, *La Vie politique en France au XIXe siècle*, Paris 1989

Lamberts, E., 'Belgium since 1830', in Blom and Lamberts, *History of the Low Countries*, 320–2

Landriu, Jacky, 'La Vie paysanne dans la région Nord–Pas-de-Calais de 1945 à nos jours', in Gillet, *La Qualité de vie*, 180–8.

Landry, Gérard and Georges de Verrewaere, *Histoire secrète de la Flandre et de l'Artois*, Paris 1982

Langrand, Michel and Christophe Masse, 'La Frontière franco-belge: mythe et réalité', *Cahiers du CRAPS* iv (Feb. 1988), 26–38

Lawrence, Paul, Timothy Baycroft and Carolyn Grohmann, ' "Degrees of foreign-ness" and the construction of identity in French border regions during the inter-war period', *Contemporary European History* x (2001), 51–71

Leblond, Maryvonne, 'La Scolarisation dans le département du Nord au XIXe siècle', *RN* lii (July–Sept. 1970), 387–98
——— *La Scolarisation dans le département du Nord au XIXe siècle*, mémoire de maîtrise, Paris 1973
Le Bras, Gabriel, *Études de sociologie religieuse*, I: *Sociologie de la pratique religieuse dans les campagnes française*, Paris 1955
Le Bras, Hervé, *Les Trois Frances*, Paris 1986
Lebrun, François (ed.), *Histoire des catholiques en France du XVe siècle à nos jours*, Paris 1980
Lefebvre, Ch., 'Socialistes belges et français de la fin de l'empire au début de la IIIe République', *RN* xxxvii (1955), 191–8
Lefranc, G., *Les Gauches en France, 1789–1972*, Paris 1973
Legrand, André, 'La "Gauche" dans le département du Nord (1945–1962)', *HTN* (1964.2), 5–34
Lehning, James R., *Peasant and French: cultural contact in rural France during the nineteenth century*, Cambridge 1995
Le Maner, Yves, 'Les Municipalités du Nord/Pas-de-Calais sous l'occupation: pouvoir local, pouvoir français, pouvoir allemand', *RN*, no. 2 spécial hors-série (1987), 219–68
Lentacker, Firmin, 'Les Frontaliers belges travaillant en France: caractères et fluctuations d'un courant de main d'oeuvre', *RN* xxxii (1950), 130–44
——— *La Frontière franco-belge: étude géographique des effets d'une frontière internationale sur la vie de relations*, Lille 1974
——— 'La Flandre de Raoul Blanchard', *DFN/LPBF* iii (1978), 10–23
——— 'En Marge d'une métropole: hier et aujourd'hui dans "la vallée de la Lys" ', *RN* lxiv (Apr.–June 1982), 283–341
Le Priol, Pierre-Yves, 'Des Revendications toujours insatisfaites', *La Croix* (2–3 Oct. 1994), 6
——— 'La Flandre se découvre franco-belge', *La Croix* (2–3 Oct. 1994), 6
Lesaffre, Odile, 'Louis-Marie Cordonnier et l'architecture du Nord de la France', *DFN/LPBF* xxiii (1998), 45–64
Lestocquoy, Jean, *Histoire de la Flandre et de l'Artois*, Paris 1966
Lévêque, Pierre, *Histoire des forces politiques en France*, II: *1880–1940*, Paris 1994
Lévy-Leboyer, M. and J.-C. Casanova (eds), *Entre l'état et le marché: l'économie française des années 1880 à nos jours*, Paris 1991
Lodge, R. Anthony, *French: from dialect to standard*, London–New York 1993
Logie, Frank, 'Grens en sociale relaties: huwelijkskringen als voorbeeld van de sociale invloed van staats grenzen', *DFN/LPBF* xi (1986), 46–58
Loosen, Michel, *Hazebrouck: en histoire & en couleur*, Steenvoorde 1992
Lottin, Alain (ed.), *Eglise, vie religieuse et révolution dans la France du Nord*, Villeneuve D'Ascq 1990
McCoy, Rebecca, 'Alsatians into Frenchmen: the construction of national identities at Sainte-Marie-aux-Mines, 1815–1851', *French History* xii (1998), 429–51
Maes, L.-Th., R. van Santbergen and others (eds), *Documents illustrating the history of Belgium*, II: *Modern Belgium: from 1830 up to the present day*, Brussels 1978
Magraw, Roger, *France, 1814–1915: the bourgeois century*, Oxford 1983
——— *A history of the French working class*, Oxford 1992

Malet, Albert and Jules Isaac, *L'Histoire*, Paris 1958–61

Marchand, Philippe, *Le Travail des enfants au XIXe siècle dans le département du Nord*, Lille 1980

—— 'Les Petits Soldats de demain: les bataillons scolaires dans le département du Nord, 1882–1892', *RN* lxvii (July–Sept. 1985), 769–803.

Marteel, Jean-Louis, *Cours de flamand: het vlaams dan men oudders klappen: méthode d'apprentissage du dialecte des flamands de France (Westhoek)*, Dunkerque 1992

Martin-Desmidt, Judith, 'Souverainetés et sociétés: la vie de la frontière du Nord au XVIIIe siècle', *DFN/LPBF* xxiv (1999), 153–63

Marty, L., *Chanter pour survivre: culture ouvrière, travail et techniques dans le textile Roubaix, 1850–1914*, Lille 1982

Mauss, Marcel, 'Nation, nationality, internationalism (1920–1)', trans. Iain Hamilton Grant, in Woolf, *Nationalism*, 85–101

Mayeur, Jean-Marie, *L'Abbé Lemire, 1853–1928: un prêtre démocrate*, thèse pour le doctorat ès lettres présentée à la faculté des lettres et sciences humaines de l'université de Paris, Paris 1968

—— *La Vie politique sous la Troisième République, 1870–1940*, Paris 1984

—— 'Les Abbés démocrates', *RN* lxxiii (Apr.–Sept. 1991), 237–49

Meadwell, Hudson, 'Republics, nations and transitions to modernity', *Nations and Nationalism* v (Jan. 1999), 19–51

Ménager, Bernard, *La Laïcisation des écoles communales dans le département du Nord (1879–1899)*, Lille 1971

—— 'La Droite dans le Nord: 1902–1914', *RN* lvi (Apr.–June 1974), 147–9

—— *La Vie politique dans le département du Nord de 1851 à 1877*, thèse présentée devant l'université de Paris IV, Lille 1983

—— Jean-François Sirinelli and Jean Vavasseur-Desperriers (eds), *Cent Ans de socialisme septentrional: actes du colloque, Lille 3–4 décembre 1993*, Lille 1995

—— and Christian-Marie Wallon-Leducq (eds), *Atlas electoral Nord/Pas-de-Calais (1973–1992)*, Lille 1993

Meyers, Willem C. M., 'Les Collaborateurs flamands de France et leurs contacts avec les milieux *flamingantes* belges: les visées territoriales sur la Flandre française pendant la seconde guerre mondiale', *RN* lx (Apr.–June 1978), 337–49

Michel, Alain-René, 'Les Catholiques sociaux du Nord et les modèles belges et allemand', *RN* lxxiii (Apr.–Sept. 1991), 321–8

Mihail, Benoît, 'Un Mouvement culturel libéral à Bruxelles dans le dernier quart du XIXe siècle, la "néo-Renaissance flamande" ', *Revue belge de philologie et d'histoire* lxxvi (1998), 979–1020

—— 'Architecture régionaliste et conscience du passé: l'exemple des anciens Pays-Bas', *Southern Netherlandish Art & Culture*, no. 2 (Dec. 1999), www.ukans.edu/~sma/snac/snac2/snac2.htm

Milis, Ludo, 'Frankrijk en zijn minderheden: politiek en cultuursbesef in Frans-Vlaanderen van de franse revolutie tot nu', *DFN/LPBF* vi (1981), 155–82

Millon, Maurice, *La Ballade des géants de la Flandre maritime française*, Dunkerque–Hazebrouck 1970

Monfrin, Jacques, 'Les Parlers en France', in François, *La France*, 745–75

Moody, Joseph N., *French education since Napoleon*, Syracuse 1978

CULTURE, IDENTITY AND NATIONALISM

Moeré, Kenneth, 'The French economy since 1930', in Alexander, *French history since Napoleon*, 364–90

Murphy, Alexander B., *The regional dynamics of language differentiation in Belgium: a study in cultural-political geography*, Chicago 1988

Nistri, Roland and Claude Prêcheur, *La Région du Nord et du Nord-Est*, Paris 1965

Noiriel, Gérard, *Workers in French society in the 19th and 20th centuries*, Oxford 1990

Nora, Pierre, 'Ernest Lavisse: son rôle dans la formation du sentiment national', *Revue historique* ccxxviii (July–Sept. 1962), 73–106

—— 'L'"Histoire de France" de Lavisse', in Nora, *Lieux de mémoire*, i. 851–902

—— 'Lavisse, instituteur national: le "Petit Lavisse", évangile de la république', in Nora, *Lieux de mémoire*, i. 239–75

—— (ed.), *Les Lieux de mémoire*, Paris 1997

Nuyttens, Michiel, 'De weerslag van de Franse onderwijswetten op de achteruitgang van de volkstaal in Noord-Frankrijk in de 19de eeuw', *DFN/LPBF* i (1976), 137–48

—— 'Priester-volksvertegenwordiger Lemire (1853–1928) en het regionalisme', *DFN/LPBF* vii (1982), 10–32

Oddone, Patrick, *Battailes autour des beffrois ou la vie politique de l'agglomération dunkerquoise de 1945 à 1978*, Dunkerque 1979

—— 'Socialistes et communistes dans l'agglomération dunkerquoise, 1945–1981, in Ménager, Sirinelli and Vavasseur-Desperriers, *Cent Ans de socialisme*, 315–29

Ory, Pascal, 'Le "Grand Dictionnaire" de Pierre Larousse: alphabet de la république', in Nora, *Lieux de mémoire*, i. 227–38

Ozouf, Jacques and Mona Ozouf, 'La Thème du patriotisme dans les manuels primaires', *Le Mouvement social* xlix (Oct.–Dec. 1964), 3–31

Ozouf, Mona, *L'Ecole, l'église et la république, 1871–1914*, Paris 1982

—— *L'Ecole de la France: essais sur la révolution, l'utopie et l'enseignement*, Paris 1984

Pee, Willem, 'La Situation linguistique en Flandre française et les fluctuations de la frontière linguistique de 1806 à 1956', *BCFF* xvi (1958), fasc. 1, 107–24

Pellissier, Pierre, *Emile de Girardin: prince de la presse*, Paris 1985

Perret, Jean-Marie, *L'Usinor-Dunkerque ou l'espoir déçu des flammands*, Dunkerque 1978

Persyn, Francis, 'Le Néerlandais dans l'enseignement primaire et secondaire en Flandre française', *DFN/LPBF* xx (1995), 12–41

Pickels, Antoine and Jacques Sojcher (eds), *Belgique: toujours grande et belle*, Brussels 1998

Pierrard, Pierre, *Les Chansons en patois de Lille sous le Second Empire*, Arras 1966

—— 'Un Grand Bourgeois de Lille: Charles Kolb-Bernard (1798–1888)', *RN* xlviii (July–Sept. 1966), 381–425

—— *Histoire du Nord*, Paris 1978

—— *Histoire de Lille*, Paris 1982

—— 'La "Petite Loi" Falloux du 11 janvier 1850 et les révocations d'instituteurs communaux en 1850', *RN* lxvii (July–Sept. 1985), 687–702

—— (ed.), *Histoire des diocèses de Cambrai et Lille*, Paris 1978

Pierreuse, Robert, 'L'Ouvrier roubaisien et la propagande politique, 1890–1900', *RN* li (Apr.–June 1969), 249–73

222

Pinchemel, Philippe, 'De la Région du Nord à la région lilleoise', *HTN* (1963.2), 118

Pirenne, H., *Histoire de Belgique*, VII: *De la Révolution de 1830 à la guerre de 1914*, Bruxelles 1932

Plessis, Alain, *The rise and fall of the Second Empire, 1852–1871*, trans. Jonathan Mandelbaum, Cambridge 1985

Pouchain, Pierre, *Les Maîtres du Nord du XIXe siècle à nos jours*, Paris 1998

Power, Daniel, 'French and Norman frontiers in the central Middle Ages', in Power and Standen, *Frontiers*, 105–27

—— and Naomi Standen (eds), *Frontiers in question: Eurasian borderlands, 700–1700*, Basingstoke 1999

Price, Glanville (ed.), *Encyclopaedia of the languages of Europe*, Oxford 1998

Price, Roger, *An economic history of modern France*, London 1981

—— *The modernisation of rural France: communications networks and agricultural market structures in nineteenth-century France*, London 1983

—— *A social history of nineteenth-century France*, London 1987

Prost, Antoine, *Histoire de l'enseignement en France, 1800–1967*, Paris 1968

—— 'Conclusion: les légitimités du socialisme septentrional', in Ménager, Sirinelli and Vavasseur-Desperriers, *Cent Ans de socialisme*, 401–5

Przybyla, Francis, 'Les Députés du Nord au début de la Troisième République (1871–1885)', *RN* lxxv (July–Sept. 1993), 561–600

Puissant, Jean, 'Relations socialistes sans frontière: Belgique et le Nord de la France', in Ménager, Sirinelli and Vavasseur-Desperriers, *Cent Ans de socialisme*, 79–87

Ravier, Joel, 'Les Premiers Inspecteurs primaires du département du Nord: de la loi Guizot (1833) à la loi Falloux (1850)', *RN* lxxx (Jan.–Feb. 1998), 91–116

Ravier, Luc, '70 jaar Nederlands aan de katholieke universiteit van Rijsel: 70 années de néerlandais à l'université catholique de Lille', *DFN/LPBF* xxii (1997), 192–213

Rearick, Charles, 'Festivals in modern France: the experience of the Third Republic', *JCH* xii (1977), 435–60

Reed-Danahay, Deborah, *Education and identity in rural France: the politics of schooling*, Cambridge 1996

Rémond, René, *Les Droites en France*, Paris 1982

—— *L'Anticlericalisme en France de 1815 à nos jours*, 2nd edn, Brussels 1985

Revel, Jacques (ed.), *L'Espace français*, Paris 1989

Robert, Jean-Louis, 'Eléments sur la scission dans la France du Nord', in Ménager, Sirinelli and Vavasseur-Desperriers, *Cent Ans de socialisme*, 91–119

Rochtus, Dirk, 'La Belgique, un choix pleinment justifié?', *L'Accent* (May–June 1997), 8–14

Rousseau, Jean-Jacques, 'Considérations sur le gouvernement de Pologne et sa réformation projetée', in *Oeuvres complètes*, III: *Du Contrat social/écrits politiques* (manuscript dated 1772), Paris 1964, 951–1041

—— *Du Contrat Social*, first publ. 1762, Paris 1966

Rousseau, Michel, 'La Répression dans le Nord de 1940 à 1944', *RN* li (Oct.–Dec. 1969), 709–33

—— *Le Nord et le Pas-de-Calais 'zone interdite' dans la guerre, 1939–1945*, Le Coteau 1985

Roza, Joe, 'The *Félibrige rouge* and pan-latinism: ethnic identity without separation', *Proceedings of the Annual Meeting of the Western Society for French History* xxii (1995), 127–34

Ryckeboer, Hugo, 'De behoefte aan een taalsociologish onderzoek in Frans-Vlaanderen', *DFN/LPBF* i (1976), 156–68

—— 'Het Vlaams van de Franse Westhoek en het geheel van het nederlandse taalgebied', *DFN/LPBF* iv (1979), 139–56

—— and F. Maeckelberghe, 'Dialect en standaardtaal aan weersijden van de rijksgrens in de Westhoek', *DFN/LPBF* xii (1987), 129–51

Sahlins, Peter, *Boundaries: the making of France and Spain in the Pyrenees*, Berkeley 1989

Sanson, Rosemonde, *Les 14 Juillets (1789–1975): fête et conscience nationale*, Paris 1976

Schepens, Luc, 'Émigration saisonnière et émigration définitive en Flandre occidentale au XIXe siècle', *RN* lvi (July–Sept. 1974), 427–31

Schnapper, Dominique, 'Beyond the opposition: "civic" nation versus "ethnic" nation', *ASEN Bulletin* xii (Autumn/Winter 1996/7), 4–8

See, Henri, *Histoire économique de la France: les temps modernes (1789–1914)*, Paris 1942

Sepieter, Jean-Paul, *La Musique du peuple flamand/De muziek van het vlaamse volk*, Dunkerque 1981

Sieyès, E. J. *Qu'est-ce que le tiers état?*, first publ. 1789, 2nd edn, Paris 1989

Singer, Barnett, 'The teacher as notable in Brittany, 1880–1914', *French Historical Studies* ix (1976), 635–59

—— *Village notables in nineteenth-century France: priests, mayors, schoolmasters*, Albany 1983

Sirinelli, Jean-François (ed.), *Histoire des Droits en France*, Paris 1992

Sluga, Glenda, 'Identity, gender, and the history of European nations and nationalisms', *Nations and Nationalism* iv (1998), 87–111

Smith, Anthony D., *National identity*, London 1991

—— 'National identities: modern and medieval?', in Forde, Johnson and Murray, *Concepts of national identity*, 21–46

—— 'Civic and ethnic nationalism revisited: analysis and ideology', *ASEN Bulletin* xii (Autumn/Winter 1996/7), 9–11

—— *Nationalism and modernism: a critical survey of recent theories of nations and nationalism*, London 1998

Sorlin, Pierre, *Waldeck-Rousseau*, Paris 1966

Stephens, Meic, *Linguistic minorities in western Europe*, Llandysul 1976

Sternhell, Zeev, *La Droite révolutionnaire, 1885–1914: les origines française du fascisme*, Paris 1978

Strikwerda, Carl, 'Regionalism and internationalism: the working-class movement in the Nord and the Belgian connection', *Proceedings of the Annual Meeting of the Western Society for French History* xii (1984), 221–30

—— 'France and the Belgian immigration of the nineteenth century', in Guerin-Gonzales and Strikwerda, *Politics of immigrant workers*, 101–31

—— *A house divided: Catholics, socialists and Flemish nationalists in nineteenth-century Belgium*, Lanham 1997

Stuart, Robert, *Marxism at work: ideology, class and French socialism during the Third Republic*, Cambridge 1992

Taccoën, Roger, *Une Certain Joie de vivre*, Sartrouville 1993

Talmy, Robert, *Le Syndicalism chrétien en France (1871–1930): difficultés et controverses*, Paris 1965

Taylor, Lynne, *Between resistance and collaboration: popular protest in northern France, 1940–45*, Basingstoke, 2000

Tchou, Claude (ed.), *La Cuisine du Nord par ses chefs*, Paris 1996

Teich, Mikulás and Roy Porter (eds), *The national question in Europe in historical context*, Cambridge 1993

Teneur Van Daële, Monique, *Découvrez le Nord: guide pratique des promenades et des loisirs*, Lille 1975

Theys, J., 'De evolutie van de grensarbeid tussen West Vlaanderen en Noord-Frankrijk in de 20ste eeuw', *DFN/LPBF* xiii (1988), 89–104

Thiesse, Anne-Marie, *Ils Apprenaient la France: l'exaltation des régions dans le discours patriotique*, Paris 1997

Thom, Martin, 'Tribes within nations: the ancient Germans and the history of modern France', in Bhabha, *Nation and narration*, 23–43

Thumerelle, Pierre-Jean, 'La Population rurale de la région du Nord d'après le recensement de 1968', *HTN* (1973.2), 5–19

——— *La Population de la région Nord–Pas-de-Calais: étude géographique*, thèse présentée devant l'université de Rennes II, 30 mars 1979, Lille 1982

Todorov, Tzvetan, *On human diversity: nationalism, racism and exoticism in French thought*, trans. Catherine Porter, Cambridge, Mass. 1993

Tombs, Robert, *France, 1814–1914*, London 1996

——— (ed.), *Nationhood and nationalism in France from Boulangism to the Great War, 1889–1918*, London 1991

Touchard, Jean, *La Gauche en France depuis 1900*, 2nd edn, Paris 1981

Toulemonde, Bernard and André Legrand, 'Les Élections législatives des 4 et 11 mars 1973 dans la région du Nord', *RN* lvi (Apr.–June 1974), no. spéciale sur la vie politique dans le Nord et le Pas-de-Calais au XXe siècle, 263–80

Tozzi, Michel, *Apprendre et vivre sa langue*, Paris 1984

Trénard, Louis (ed.), *Histoire des Pays-Bas français: Flandre, Artois, Hainaut, Boulonnais, Cambrésis*, Toulouse 1972

——— (ed.), *Histoire des Pays-Bas français: documents: Flandre, Artois, Hainaut, Boulonnais, Cambrésis*, Toulouse 1974

Vandecuveye, Hendrick, 'Het proletarierslied: één sociaal-kulturele verschijningsvoorm van de socialistische arbeidersbeweging', *Belgische tijdschrift voor nieuwste geschiedenis/Revue belge d'histoire contemporaine* xi (1980), 171–204

Vandenbroeke, Chris, *Sociale geschiedenis van het vlaamse volk*, Leuven 1984

Vandenbussche, Robert, 'Une Élection de combat dans le Nord: 27 avril et 11 mai 1902', *RN* lvi (Apr.–June 1974), 131–9

——— 'La Région dans la guerre (1914–1918)', in Hilaire, *Histoire du Nord/Pas-de-Calais*, 193–226

——— 'La Fonction municipale sous la Troisième République: l'exemple du département du Nord', *RN* lxxvi (Apr.–June 1994), 319–37

Vandeputte, O. and J. Fermaut, *Le Néerlandais: langue de vingt millions de néerlandais et de flamands*, Rekkem 1990

Vanhaverbeke, Wim, 'Une Stratégie d'euro-région pour le sud de la Flandre-Occidentale et le Nord–Pas-de-Calais, basée sur les points forts complémentaires des deux partenaires', *DFN/LPBF* xx (1995), 282–99

Vanhyfte, Damien and Alain Wagret, *Un Village flamand . . . Sainte-Marie-Cappel*, Sainte-Marie-Cappel 1979

Vanneufville, Eric, *Apprenons notre histoire de Flandre*, 2nd edn, Steenvoorde 1989

Verbeke, Dirk, 'Nieuwport: twintig jaar Fraans-Vlaamse veertiendaagse', *DFN/LPBF* xx (1995), 181–201

—————— and others (eds), *Een halve eeuw werking voor en in Frans-Vlaanderen: Komitee voor Frans-Vlaanderen jubileumboek, 1947–1997*, Waregem 1997

Verbeke, Luc, *Vlaanderen in Frankrijk: taalstrijd en vlaamse beweging in Frans- of Zuid-Vlaanderen*, Leuven 1970

—————— *De Nederlanden in Frankrijk en het Komitee voor Frans-Vlaanderen*, Wareghem 1978

Verhasselt, Yola, Frank Logie and Bernadette Mergaerts, 'Espace géographique et formes de sociabilité: quatre exemples de régions frontalières', *RN* lxiv (Apr.–June 1982), 581–602

Verschaeve, Cyriel, 'The Flemish nationalist's catechism (1918)', in Hermans, *Flemish movement*, 240–53

Verscheure, Jacques, Gérard Deprost and Clausde Traullé, *Aspects sociologique de la pratique dominicale, diocèse de Lille*, Lille 1961

Vilfan, Sergij (ed.), *Ethnic groups and language rights: comparative studies on governments and non-dominant ethnic groups in Europe, 1850–1940*, iii, Aldershot–NY 1993

Wagnon, Claude, *Identités du Nord–Pas-de-Calais*, Lille 1988

—————— 'Transformations de l'identité régionale nordiste (1955–1985)' (Cahiers lillois d'economie et de sociologie xii, 1988), 3–9

Wardhaugh, Ronald, *Languages in competition: dominance, diversity and decline*, Oxford 1987

Watkins, Susan Cotts, *From provinces into nations: demographic integration in western Europe, 1870–1960*, Princeton 1991

Weber, Eugen, *Peasants into Frenchmen: the modernisation of rural France, 1870–1914*, first publ. Stanford 1976, London 1979; trans. by Antoine Berman and Bernard Géniès as *La Fin des terroirs: la modernisation de la France rurale (1870–1914)*, Paris 1983

—————— 'Comment la politique vint aux paysans: a second look at peasant politicisation', *American Historical Review* lxxxvii (Apr. 1982), 357–89

Willard, Claude, *Les Guesdistes: le mouvement socialiste en France (1893–1905)*, Paris 1965

—————— (ed.), *La France ouvrière: histoire de la classe ouvrière française*, Paris 1995

Willemyns, Roland, 'Language shift through erosion: the case of the French-Flemish "Westhoek" ', *Journal of Multilingual and Multicultural Development* xviii (1997), 54–66

Wils, Lode, 'L'Emploi des langues en matières judiciaires et administrative dans le royaume de Belgique', *RN* lxxiii (Jan.–Mar. 1991), 51–71.

—————— 'Introduction', in Hermans, *Flemish movement*, 1–39

—————— 'Belgium on the path to equal language rights up to 1939', in Vilfan, *Ethnic groups and language rights*, iii. 17–35

Winock, Michel, *Nationalisme, antisémitisme et fascisme in France*, Paris 1990

Withoeck, A., 'Proeve tot typologie van de Belgische leden van het Comité Flamand de France, 1853–1914', *DFN/LPBF* xix (1994), 116–39

Witte, Els, 'Une Flandre appauvrie', in Witte, Doehaerd, Blockmans, Soly and Craeybeckx, *Histoire de Flandres*, 181–245

———— Renée Doehaerd, Wim Blockmans, Hugo Soly and Jan Craeybeckx, *Histoire de Flandre des origines à nos jours*, Bruxelles 1983

Woestenborghs, Bert, 'Vlaamse seizoenarbeiders in Nord-Frankrijk, 1880–1970', *DFN/LPBF* xxiv (1999), 97–114

Woolf, Stuart (ed.), *Nationalism in Europe 1815 to the present: a reader*, London–New York 1996

Yourcenar, Marguerite, *Le Labyrinthe du monde: souvenirs pieux, archives du Nord, quoi? l'éternité*, Paris 1990

Zeldin, Theodore (ed.), *Conflicts in French society: anticlericalism, education and morals in the nineteenth century*, London 1970

———— *France, 1848–1945*, II: *Intellect, taste and anxiety*, Oxford 1977

Unpublished theses etc.

Bonnaud, Pierre, 'Terres et langages: peuples et régions', thèse de doctorat ès lettres, Clermont-Ferrand 1980

Chanet, Jean-François, 'Les Instituteurs et le régionalisme dans l'entre-deux-guerres (1918–1940): premiers résultats d'une enquête par questionnaire', Mémoire *ad hoc*, DEA de sciences sociales EHESS-ENS 1991

Engelaere, Olivier, 'Le Mouvement flamand en France de la libération au "renouveau" du début des années 70', maîtrise d'histoire contemporaine, université de Lille III 1989

Lauwers, Anne, 'Étude socio-culturelle du Westhoek francais: l'étiolement du dialecte flamand', Hoger Rijksinstituut voor Vertalers en Tolken, Brussels 1970

Libert, Louis, 'Les Élections législatives de 1871 à 1875 dans le département du Nord', mémoire principal, DES, faculté de lettres, université de Lille 1959

Lottin, Alain, 'Les Élections législatives de 1831 à 1839 dans le département du Nord', Mémoire principal, DES, faculté de lettres, université de Lille 1958

Minney, James, 'The Flemish movement of French Flanders and the maintenance of *Vlaemsch*', PhD diss. Southampton 1999

Néré, Jacques, 'Les Elections Boulanger dans le département du Nord', thèse complémentaire pour le doctorat-ès-lettres de l'université de Paris n.d.

Talmy, Robert, 'Les Tendances anti-cléricales des socialistes dans le département du Nord (1860–1900)', mémoire de licence, université catholique de Lille 1952

Triquet, G. M., Réflexion sur l'évolution historique des Flandres' (pamphlet)

Websites

'Flemish in France', Euromosaic Website, http://www.uoc.es/euromosaic/web/document/ neerlandes/an/i1/i1.html, consulted 14 Mar. 2000

'France' Ethnologue no. 16 (1996), http://www.sil.org/ethnologue/countries/ Fran.html, consulted 14 Mar. 2000

Index